Woman, Nature, and Psyche

Woman, Nature, and Psyche

Patricia Jagentowicz Mills

Yale University Press
New Haven and London

Designed by James J. Johnson
and set in Sabon types by Rainsford Type.
Printed in the United States of America by
Halliday Lithographic, West Hanover, Mass.

Library of Congress Cataloging-in-Publication Data

Mills, Patricia Jagentowicz, 1944–
Woman, nature, and psyche.

Revision of Thesis (Ph.D.)—York University.
Bibliography: p.
Includes index.
1. Women. 2. Frankfurt school of sociology.
3. Feminism. I. Title.
HA1206.M53 1987   305'.4'2   87–10408
ISBN 0–300–03537–3 (alk. paper)

1 2 3 4 5 6 7 8 9 10

Engels' Mistress

In the City of Long Chimneys he met you.
Manchester: 1843.
Beneath the constant clouds he plucked you
from the mill while he was still a stranger.

                    You were no Penelope,
dreaming at the loom. You were one of the stunted,
pale girls, thick palms and sweat-matted hair.

He was a man with clean fingernails.
He'd given pennies to the poor. Now
he could do more.

                    You were the hinge on the door
he opened. You were the wheel on the cart he rode.
Illiterate Irish factory girl, the city
was the only book you read. He studied
all the passages you marked.

        You stayed together twenty years unwed,
but not, I think, unmindful of the ironies.
Even the wife of the man he supported, champion
of the working class, refused to shake your calloused hand
because it bore no ring. She wouldn't let you
step inside her door.

    ("I am nothing and I should be everything.")

I'm not requesting miracles.
You know it's not the dying that I mind,
from illness or the things that can't be helped.
It's the long death after: the candle eaten by the flame.

I'm only asking why no one remembers your name, Mary Burns.

JANE SCHWARTZ

Contents

Acknowledgments

The impetus for this work came from the sisterhood and goals of the women's liberation movement, and through the years many women have provided the encouragement and support necessary for its completion. In particular I would like to thank Jane Schwartz, Nan Peacocke, Gretchen Salisbury, Frieda Forman, Somer Brodribb, Nancy Wood, Anny Derdeyn, and Joan Ringelheim.

I also want to thank Steve Levine, Lorenne Clark, Millie Bakan, Ioan Davies, Alkis Kontos, Ato Sekyi-Otu, Rusty Shteir, Kathryn Morgan, and Mary Grayhurst for guiding both me and my work through our institutional travels. I am indebted to the Graduate Program in Social and Political Thought at York University for encouraging a project of this kind as a Ph.D. thesis; and to the Social Sciences and Humanities Research Council of Canada for the postdoctoral fellowship that facilitated the transformation of the thesis into a book.

Special thanks are here offered to the anonymous reviewer who provided an invaluable critique of my article on "Hegel's *Antigone*" for *The Owl of Minerva*; to R. Sullivan in the history department of Simon Fraser University for his expert translations from the Greek; and to Frank Cunningham for his continued support during my tenure in the department of philosophy at the University of Toronto.

Judy Gibbs typed and retyped the first version of this manuscript with care, attention to detail, and a never-failing sense of good cheer; Linda Gilbert worked on the final draft with a patience and an adaptability to my schedule for which I am grateful.

Finally, I wish to thank Ian H. Angus and Christopher Holland Mills—Ian for his insight, intellectual support, and collaboration over the many years it took to complete this work, and Holland, my son, for his enduring sense of humor and love as we grew up together through unconventional times.

Introduction

This book is a critical analysis of the relation between the domination of nature and the domination of woman. It is a feminist work rooted in the critical theory of the first generation of the Frankfurt school—specifically in the analyses of Horkheimer, Marcuse, and Adorno, which I consider the most developed philosophical thought of our times. Some of the most important feminist thinkers in the past provided a model for this project: Mary Wollstonecraft's *Vindication of the Rights of Woman* is a critical appropriation of the Enlightenment philosophy of Jean-Jacques Rousseau; Alexandra Kollontai's feminist critique begins from the Marxism of her day; and Simone de Beauvoir's *Second Sex* is a feminist appropriation of the existentialism of Jean-Paul Sartre. All these women based their theoretical formulations on the most advanced philosophy of liberation available and, in so doing, deepened our understanding of the domination of woman.

It is important to realize that the domain of philosophy need not be ceded to the male. Philosophy, as a critical project, attempts to understand the universalizing process of civilization. Thus, philosophy is contingently, rather than necessarily, male: it asks universal questions but gives only partial answers, answers rooted in the male experience. On this basis, what is required is not an abandonment of philosophy but an immanent critique of it from the perspective of woman's experience.

The tradition of critical theory, beginning with Hegel and Marx, involves both an epistemological and sociopolitical inquiry. It attempts to extend universal freedom by criticizing the partial, limited forms of human autonomy. With the theorists of the Frankfurt school, the domination of nature emerges as the fundamental problem for this critique of society. The newly articulated claims of women for liberation require an extension of that critique to include the domination of woman in relation to the development of patriarchal-capitalist society. Throughout Western thought, woman has been identified with nature, denied intersubjective recognition and an autonomous ego; relations between women and woman's self-experience of desire have been ignored. Woman has not been seen as a historical actor or a self-conscious individual. She has been dominated both by *recognizing* her "natural" difference and confining it to the family and by *denying* this difference in civil society. By formulating the intersection of intersubjective recognition and the relation between humanity and nature, as a reformulation of the dialectic of desire and recognition within a critique of the civilizing process, critical theory offers a framework that can be appropriated for an analysis of the domination of woman.

The procedure of this book will be an analysis of central theoretical formulations in the work of Horkheimer, Marcuse, and Adorno to establish the limitations of these formulations due to the partial treatment of woman. Having identified the human experiences upon which critical theory as theory and as emancipatory project rests, it is possible to render the tradition self-reflective by incorporating woman's historical and psychological self-experience into the critique.

Feminism and critical theory are seen in this work as mutually clarifying. Critical theory offers a framework for understanding patriarchal domination but obscures this understanding through silence and the distortion of woman's experience. The necessity to overcome woman's voicelessness by naming her experience is central to the feminist project of liberation. However, the naming of woman's experience has its own dangers. It too can lead to a reification of the name in a new mythology. It requires therefore a completion in the project of critical theory: a critique of the false universalization of the name and situation of the genuinely named experience within an analysis of the civilizing process. To recapture the liberatory potential in the theory of the Frankfurt school, to free it from its implication in the domination of woman, and to create a theory of woman's liberation, we must focus on woman's experience and authenticate it within a critique of the domination of nature.

To establish the foundation for my analysis of the Frankfurt school, I examine Hegel, Marx, and Freud, three thinkers who are crucial to the development of critical theory. I begin with Hegel because he introduces a new relation between nature and history with his concept of the human agent. Prior to Hegel, traditional philosophy viewed nature as eternal and ahistorical. For Hegel the domination of nature is the condition for the emergence of intersubjectivity and a self-conscious ego. He describes a dialectical relation between nature and history in which a distinction is made between first and second nature. This distinction is important for woman because she is confined to the family, the sphere of first nature, while man moves into the realm of second nature or self-conscious political life. Since, according to Hegel, to be human is to have direct access to the sphere of second nature, and since woman does not have this direct access, one can only conclude that woman is not truly human in the Hegelian system. Hegel himself does not acknowledge this contradiction.

Nature is eventually "overreached" by history, as woman is "overreached" by man, so that, in the last instance, Hegel's dialectical formulations are inadequate. Thus, the main thesis of my analysis of Hegel is that his partial treatment of woman not only limits woman but limits his philosophy so that he cannot claim for his system of knowledge the universality that he seeks. For Hegel, the family is a "preserve," a refuge or "haven in a heartless world," but he fails to point out that this refuge is maintained at the cost of woman's self-conscious development: she never achieves self-consciousness, never becomes an "I." However, even though Hegel has an inadequate concept of the family he does recognize it as an autonomous sphere of life, a domain which has its own specific and unique logic.

Marx shows that in Hegel the dialectical relation between nature and history is ultimately resolved by collapsing matter into spirit. Marx therefore attempts to appropriate Hegel's analysis of the dialectical relation between nature and history by "turning it on its feet" to avoid falling into the idealist "solution." Marx shows that the social relations of civil society preclude the reconciliation of first and second nature that Hegel proposes in his tripartite structure of family, civil society, and state. Marx focuses on the male-female relation in his early works and claims that this relation, because it is both natural and social, reveals the extent to which our "natural" behavior has become truly "human." Later, Marx concentrates on the critique of political economy as the science of civil society so that the concern with the male-female relation changes from an analysis of the relation between nature and history to an analysis of the relation between the working class and the bourgeois family in terms of property and ideology.

Marx's critique of Hegel is based on an analysis of civil society, whereas my critique of Hegel is based on an analysis of the family. This is an important difference because in his move away from Hegel's tripartite structure to concentrate on civil society, Marx fails to acknowledge the critical autonomy of the sphere of the family and the fact that an analysis of the family requires its own specific logic. This is not to suggest that the family is entirely independent of the workings of civil society but rather that there is not a simple one-to-one correspondence between the relations of civil society and the relations of the family. Given the fact that his analysis does not acknowledge the relative autonomy of the family, Marx cannot grasp the specific nature of woman's oppression within the family.

Another important problem in Marx's work regarding "the woman question" as a question of domination concerns the process of ego development. Marx shifts the concern away from the Hegelian emphasis on "recognition of the Other" to a concern with the labor process, and he exposes competitive or possessive individualism as historically specific to capitalism; however, Marx has no fully developed model of ego development distinct from the Hegelian one. The position of the working class as "in but not of" civil society means that its members have the potential to realize themselves as individuals: they are in the sphere where individuality is possible. Because of his Hegelian bias with regard to ego development Marx initially believes that it is necessary for woman to move into civil society to gain a self-conscious identity. This move can be seen as temporary in that ultimately, Marx believes, civil society must be abolished as a separate sphere in the move toward communism; nevertheless, Marx does not see the possibility of ego development occurring within the family.

Most important, in the shift from the dialectical relation described by the male-female relation to that of the dialectical relation mediated through the labor process, "nature" becomes for Marx a sociohistoric category, and as such it becomes merely the material for manipulation by humans in civil society. In his early work, the initial schism between nature and human society, which was the riddle of history, was to be resolved in communism by a mutual interpenetration of nature and society that would reconcile "man" and nature. However, in Marx's mature work, there is no reconciliation of the schism between nature and human society but rather a resolution through the domination of nature and, consequently, a loss of nature as an independent "moment" of the dialectic. This transformation of the dialectic affects Marx's analysis of woman's situation in that he moves away from an examination of the direct male-female relation to an emphasis on an abstract equality between men and women in the sphere of productive relations. That is, the primary concern becomes the establishment of sexual equality in civil society without regard for the unique experiences of woman *outside* that sphere. The equality proposed for woman in the productive sphere ignores both her personal patriarchal domination within the family and the abstract domination of patriarchy that permeates all spheres of society.

In the critical theory of Horkheimer, Marcuse, and Adorno, Marx's project is renewed and extended in a critique of the domination of nature that attempts to uncover the psychic and social basis of the solidification of repressive society and tries to theorize and generate new possibilities of critical consciousness. This reconceives the dialectic of nature and history and focuses attention on the specific logic of the family as the social institution in which individuals develop the capacity for self-conscious critique and action. For these three thinkers, the domination of nature entails social domination and self-domination within the ego.

Critical theory, thus, changes the focus from the objective movement of civil society to subjectivity. This shift in emphasis is due to the fact that Marx's analysis of the contradictions of capitalism does not explain the way in which, in a patriarchal-capitalist society, we are not only dominated by others but suffer from self-domination (what Kate Millett in *Sexual Politics* calls "interior colonization"); that is, Marx's analysis cannot explain how domination is reproduced in self-consciousness. The conceptualization of self-consciousness in critical theory entails a redefinition of "second nature," which is widened to include the psyche and no longer confined to self-conscious political life as in Hegel or self-conscious activity in labor as in Marx. In this context, the Frankfurt school's consideration of the relation between nature and authority is important. That is, the relation between nature and authority is not completely separated from the context of the social relations of production but is shown to profoundly affect the development of the psyche within the family.

Given the concern with subjectivity, Horkheimer, Marcuse, and Adorno turn to an examination of the dynamics of ego development in Freud's work to find a basis for the development of an autonomous ego and for social relations free from domination. Freud's sensitivity to the importance of childhood for personality development and his understanding of the conflict between psyche and society lay the foundation for an analysis of unconsciously motivated behavior. Freud shows that ego development occurs within the family rather than among strangers in the public realm. But the critical theorists accept the historical character of the family and thereby attempt to maintain both an objective and subjective approach to a critique of society: the family is seen within a network of economic, social, and psychological processes. Thus, the Frankfurt school sees the development of the psyche as a process that occurs within the family, and the family is seen as a sphere of first *and* second nature.

However, in the turn to Freud, Horkheimer, Marcuse, and Adorno fail to clarify the relation between the Hegelian and Freudian models of ego development and fail to note Freud's own distinction between the male and female processes of ego development. While they denounce the possessive character of the individual in our society, they are also wary of the development of the "mass individual." They want to retain a notion of individuality as a precondition for a free society. Thus, while the atomic character of the individual ego is seen as the result of an "abstract negation," it is nevertheless seen as a necessary, if insufficient, step toward the development of the social individual. But the autonomous ego discussed in critical theory is grounded in the Freudian account of *male* ego development and ignores the specificity of the female's situation. The focus is on the relation between father and son, and the mass individual is seen partially as a result of the transformation of society into a "society without the father." These thinkers do address the specificity of woman's condition when they acknowledge her maintenance role in the family. Yet as they resuscitate nature as an independent moment of the dialectic they resuscitate the concept of the family as a preserve or refuge without recognizing the full import of the oppression of woman in this Hegelian notion of the family.

The three major thinkers of the Frankfurt school do not represent a single position. Especially concerning "the woman question," they differentiate themselves in terms of basic assumptions about "the feminine," the family, nature, and the dialectical process. However, given the common reference points of Hegel, Marx, and Freud and the common focus on the domination of nature, it is not necessary to present each position in its entirety. I chose Marcuse as the central representative of critical theory since his thought directly addresses the concerns of the recent woman's movement for liberation within a critique of the domination of nature. His theoretical trajectory is thus most aligned with the concerns of this work. Within a careful study of Marcuse's position the relevant positions of Horkheimer and Adorno will be presented in order to clarify the theoretical basis of their divergence.

In Marcuse, the concept of the "return of the repressed" implies that there is no distortion in what has been repressed. Marcuse attempts to present an alternative to patriarchal-capitalist society in a new "reality principle" based originally on maternal Eros and later on the traditionally "feminine" qualities that have become "second nature" to woman. Since he sees the creation of "surplus repression" as necessary for the maintenance of the established mode of production, the essential prerequisite for liberation becomes the redefinition of human needs through a transformation of all facets of our second nature. The "feminine principle" is held to be the antithesis, the "definite negation," of the surplus aggressive and repressive needs and values of capitalism as a form of male-dominated culture. Horkheimer and Adorno, on the other hand, emphasize the distortion of first nature due to the fact that this nature has been repressed. The return of the repressed is, in Horkheimer, a "revolt of nature" that has a regressive element and offers no *necessary* claim to being kind, gentle, maternal, or liberatory. Horkheimer ends up in a lament in which he opposes the rationalization of family life and the move of woman out of the home and idealizes the traditional mother role.

By rejecting the identity of nature and history Adorno offers a unique conceptual framework for a dialectical analysis of the woman question. Woman, as she represents first nature, can be seen as representing something that can never be fully mastered by the concept: the concept cannot fully master experience, and woman as Other has come to symbolize that which the concept cannot grasp. This recognition of the non-identity of nature and history, psyche and society, is important for an analysis of the domination of woman. But Adorno sees the "feminine" as the negative imprint of domination and the scar tissue of social mutilation. Thus, in contradistinction to Marcuse's analysis, the "feminine principle" in nature's revolt can be seen as potentially reactive-repressive when viewed from Adorno's perspective.

In his critique of the domination of nature Marcuse retains a notion of "identity" or reconciliation with nature that ends by swallowing woman into an identitarian male framework. While the recognition of non-identity seems more secure in Horkheimer and Adorno, they fail to achieve a logic of non-identity that recognizes woman as a historical actor. Critical theory attempts to offer the conceptual and analytic understanding through which we may avoid the Scylla of biological determinism and the Charybdis of economic determinism, but at each step a view *of* the female substitutes for a view *by* the female. Both versions of critical theory speak primarily about what woman *represents*, not about her experience. Because of this, and because of its partial treatment of woman's condition, this tradition, against its own intentions, often reflects and reinforces woman's domination.

My analysis will show that the relations between women and woman's self-experience of desire have been left out of the account of ego development in critical theory. These issues must be addressed if the account of the development of self-consciousness is to be genuinely universal. In critical theory the dialectic of desire and recognition is rooted in two incompatible theories: the theories of Freud and Hegel, as theories of the family and civil society, respectively. Following this, there are two myths—the myth of the primal horde and the myth of Odysseus—that inform critical theory's diagnosis of civilization. Within contemporary feminist theory this unresolved duality reappears as an uncertainty about the central mode of ego development (motherhood or sisterhood), which is reduplicated as an uncertainty about the key arena for social change (family or civil society).

The elements of woman's experience that have been validly named by feminism fall short of their task unless they are brought into an analysis of the civilizing process per se. Thus, the diagnosis of civilization in critical theory, through the theme of the domination of nature, completes the feminist project of naming woman's experience and analyzes the formation of this experience through the dialectic of desire and recognition.

By inserting a concern for woman into the tradition of critical theory we make it self-reflective: through such self-reflection we may exorcise the distortions of male domination that obliterate woman's experience by making her the representation of domination or liberation. Thus, we get a self-critical theory from naming woman's experience. But this experience is not just the social history of what happened and continues to happen to women in their everyday lives and in their struggles for liberation: it is also the experience that is revealed by using a psychoanalytically informed analysis to examine the process of female ego development within the family. The articulation of woman's experience is called for by the theory itself: a new reflection on woman's experience is not inserted arbitrarily but as a consequence of the theoretical lacunae in critical theory's project of human liberation.

PART I

Dialectical Beginnings: Woman and the Dialectic in Hegel and Marx

CHAPTER ONE

Hegel:
Recognition, Intersubjectivity, and Desire

HEGEL CLAIMS THAT HIS DIALECTIC OF MUTUAL RECOGNITION grounds intersubjectivity. That is, the reciprocity of the self's desire for recognition from an Other offers a philosophical perspective on human existence necessarily based on intersubjectivity. However, I argue that this necessity is not met in the relation between man and woman as it is characterized by Hegel, so that his system does not permit woman to be viewed as fully human. Hegel contradicts himself by claiming a universality for his system that his partial treatment of woman prohibits him from achieving.

Central to an understanding of woman's place in Hegel's system is his interpretation of Sophocles' *Antigone*. This play fascinates Hegel; he uses it in both the *Phenomenology of Spirit* and the *Philosophy of Right* to demonstrate that familial ethical life is woman's unique responsibility. Antigone is revealed as the paradigmatic figure of womanhood and family life in both the pagan and modern worlds, although Hegel sees fundamental differences between these two worlds.[1]

> One must begin with Hegel's *Phenomenology,*
> the true point of origin and the secret of
> the Hegelian philosophy.
>
> KARL MARX, *Economic and Philosophic*
> *Manuscripts of 1844*

THE PHENOMENOLOGY OF SPIRIT

Hegel's *Phenomenology of Spirit,* published in 1807, analyzes human consciousness from its initial stages to the highest categories of reason. It begins with the most elementary stages of consciousness, ordinary "natural" consciousness, and advances dialectically upward until it reaches the stage of consciousness in which the human mind achieves absolute knowledge. The *Phenomenology* describes the successive stages of consciousness as the unfolding of Spirit or *Geist,* defined as self-thinking thought or the self-knowledge of the universe. For Hegel philosophy must present the truth in its entirety as a system of thought whose concepts reveal the life of Spirit: Spirit comes to know itself in and through the activity of the human mind. Beginning from an epistemological orientation the study advances from sensation to perception and understanding (*Verstand*) and culminates in reason (*Vernunft*); it explains how the lower stages of consciousness are overcome by the higher until consciousness reaches the point of view of Spirit as the self-conscious subject.

This philosophy of experience describes the relation between subject and object: each stage reveals consciousness in an essential relation to an object, which may be either external or internal. Consciousness attempts to know its object directly and immediately, and the ways in which the object appears to consciousness are, at the same time, the processes by which consciousness discovers the significance of the object. According to Hegel, there are three main stages of consciousness. The first is sense-certainty or consciousness in a limited sense (*Bewusstsein*). Here, the subject apprehends the sensible object as something external and other than itself—the world of objects is experienced as completely alien. The second stage is self-consciousness (*Selbstbewusstsein*). Here consciousness turns back on itself in its encounter with the Other and discovers a finite self. At the third stage, reason (*Vernunft*), consciousness is revealed as the objective expression of the unity of consciousness and infinite Spirit: "Reason is Spirit when its certainty of being all reality has been raised to truth, and it is conscious of itself as its own world, and of the world as itself."[2] At this final stage reason is realized as the unity or identity-in-difference of subject and object.

In each stage of consciousness the same dialectical logic of becoming is at work, as Spirit moves through what it is immediately to become its opposite. That is, Spirit undergoes a forcible separation, a process of diremption in which it alienates or externalizes itself and struggles with what appears to be Other. Spirit then returns what has been alienated or externalized back to itself, but in the process it is transformed. As Spirit moves dialectically through its progressive stages it finds itself increasingly engaged in conflict with externalized reality. These conflicts transform Spirit from existing *in itself* to existing *for itself*. That is, through contradiction Spirit comes to know itself. Thus, Spirit externalizes or alienates itself, overcomes this alienation or externalization (*Entausserung*), returns to itself, and is, finally, complete self-knowledge.

Each of the initial stages of the dialectical process is "abstract" or "partial" because it leaves out its essential opposite. In each stage a contradictory "moment" or negation emerges through Spirit's self-alienation or externalization; a profound struggle between the two moments then takes place, from which emerges a moment that simultaneously maintains, negates, and transcends the earlier moments. This is the negation of the negation. Hegel uses a single term to describe this complex process: the original "moments" are *aufgehoben*. (*Aufgehoben* is the past participle of the verb *aufheben*; *Aufhebung* is the noun. The German includes all three elements—preservation or maintenance, negation, and transcendence—of a process that may occur instantaneously or over time; there is no simple translation.) Each stage is preserved and transcended in the next, such that whatever comes first is understood in terms of what comes later. In the final "concrete" understanding of the totality, where opposites are reconciled, the truth is to be found.

In his formulation of the dialectical process Hegel endeavors to reconcile "the life of thought and the thought of life."[3] Through dialectical logic, thought thinks the relation between two concepts in such a way that both concepts are maintained—one is not dissolved into the other—while at the same time a true unity is achieved. Thus, dialectical logic reveals the movement of life as a process that overcomes the conceptual dualism or mutual exclusivity of the concepts of the understanding (*Verstand*). At the stage of reason or *Vernunft* a higher unity of concepts emerges, fusing concepts without canceling out their differences: reason can apprehend the concepts as an identity-in-difference. The *Phenomenology* thus challenges the dualisms of mind and matter, nature and history, self and Other, man and woman.

Hegel assumes a necessary connection between his system of philosophy, its dialectical movement, and the historical evolution of humanity. Consciousness or Spirit does not transcend historical experience. Rather, rationality is nourished by history such that there are correlations between stages of the dialectic of consciousness and historical transformation. While Hegel's project is not simply one of abstract knowledge, the *Phenomenology* does not set out to give a complete, objective account of history. Hegel focuses on what he believes to be the turning points or crises in human history, which are also critical moments in the development of human consciousness: the ancient world of Greece and Rome and its dissolution; the emergence of Christianity; the rise of civil society; the unfolding of the Enlightenment and the crisis of the French Revolution; Germany under Napoleon. He describes the development of individual human consciousness within an abbreviated analysis of the historical stages through which the consciousness of humanity has passed. In this way the development of Spirit is told in both subjective and objective terms; the historical stages of development that the human race goes through are recapitulated in the psychological development of the "universal individual."[4]

The most significant turning point in the *Phenomenology* for my analysis is Hegel's account of the Other in the development of self-consciousness. Here Hegel depicts self-consciousness (being-for-itself) as rooted in desire. Self-consciousness is mediation and as such it reveals the relation between desire and the object of desire. In the initial stages of the development of self-consciousness consciousness encounters reality as a whole, as an immediate totality that is abstract and not comprehended. Here the object of desire is organic or animal life envisioned as totality. The desire for life appears as something alien, something external to and other than the self yet simultaneously identical with the self. As we become aware of our life as alien to us, we estrange or dirempt ourselves from it and thereby negate it. The life of the self becomes an object for the self, and self-consciousness emerges through an exchange with the world.[5]

The "pure ego" or naive self-consciousness attempts to achieve its goal of self-certainty in the immediate *aufgehoben* of the object as nothing more than an object for consciousness. But here desire experiences the resistance of the object: as a moment of nature the object activates and sustains the opposition of each consciousness to that which is other than itself. The resistance and independence of the object as Other, as a moment of nature, cannot be satisfactorily overcome. Self-consciousness, as human existence, is possible only when it is recognized by another self-consciousness in the conflict between being-for-itself and being-for-other.[6]

The Hegelian self, as desire, needs the Other in such a way that the Other becomes an ontological condition for the existence of the self. The desire that constitutes the self exists only if it is an object of another desire. Human desire becomes the desire for the desire of the Other. Since each self-consciousness must be recognized by another, recognition grounds the universality of self-consciousness. Our self-consciousness is mirrored in the Other such that it not only achieves a being-for-itself but also sees itself as external and determined, as a being-for-others. And the same process takes place for the Other. By virtue of the Hegelian dialectic of mutual recognition, each self is conscious of itself as a self; the reciprocity of the self's desire for recognition from an Other offers a philosophical perspective of human existence necessarily based on intersubjectivity.[7] As we shall see, this necessity is not met in the relation between man and woman as characterized by Hegel. I shall argue, therefore, that Hegel's system does not permit woman to be viewed as fully human.

If primary desire is desire for organic life, then, according to Hegel, for us to become aware of ourselves as human, as creatures of Spirit distinct from organic life, there must be opposition to the natural order. In human consciousness this opposition occurs through the risk of life. As each self-consciousness demands from the Other the recognition without which it could not exist, there occurs a life and death struggle. Each self-consciousness intends the death of the Other in this struggle for recognition because each one not only desires to be recognized as pure being-for-itself but wants to suppress its limited or determined representation as a being-for-the-Other.[8] Hegel describes this fundamental struggle of life: "it is only through staking one's life that freedom is won; only thus is it proved that for self-consciousness, its essential being is not [just] being, not the *immediate* form in which it appears, not its submergence in the expanse of life, but rather that there is nothing present in it which could not be regarded as a vanishing moment, that it is only pure *being-for-self.*"[9] To be truly human one must be willing to risk one's life and aim at the death of the Other in a struggle for recognition. Thus, the necessary intersubjectivity is a hostile one—a kind of Hobbesian "each against each."

Hegel first puts forth the historical perspective of the onto-logical encounter in his section "Lordship and Bondage." Here domination grounds not only intersubjectivity but also objectification. If, in the life and death struggle for recognition, one self-consciousness destroys the Other, the project does not succeed because the death of the Other creates an abstract negation rather than the negation that preserves and maintains what is superseded. If, however, the struggle ends in such a way that both survive, then a relationship of negation is established, one of dominance or subjugation. One self-consciousness is "independent consciousness whose essential nature is to be for itself"; the other is the "dependent consciousness whose essential nature is simply to live or to be for another. The former is the lord, the other is bondsman."[10]

But in a dialectical turn Hegel points out that the master's *need* for a slave or bondsman and the objects he produces defeats the master's search for independence. In the attempt to become an independent self-consciousness, the lord or master has enslaved himself. "The *truth* of the independent consciousness is accordingly the servile consciousness of the bondsman." While the master's relation to the slave is mediated by the objects the slave produces and his relation to the objects is mediated by the slave, the essential nature of the slave is expressed in the things he produces. In the process of work as objectification, the slave's consciousness is "bound up with an existence that is independent, or thinghood in general."[11] Through his work the slave masters nature and thereby achieves a freedom from nature and a sense of self that the master lacks. The domination of nature through work transforms the "natural" world to create history. Thus, the slave who prefers life to death and saves himself by surrendering his claim for recognition nevertheless creates an independent self through the process of labor as objectification. Hegel's idea of freedom here is a purely interior reality that the slave experiences while remaining enslaved.

What emerges from the analysis of the master-slave dialectic is an account in which the consciousness of death inaugurates a truly human existence. Hegel says that the slave's "consciousness has been fearful, not of this or that particular thing or just at odd moments, but its whole being has been seized with dread; for it has experienced the fear of death, the absolute Lord."[12] This fear of death is the negativity that haunts our self-consciousness and transforms our limited or determined being into free being. It moves humanity out of the merely natural world into the world of Spirit. The slave internalizes this negativity and transforms existence through the process of objectification so that the world is no longer a merely natural "given." The slave creates a human world, and the negativity of his own self-consciousness achieves consistency and stability through work. Thus labor and the struggle to the death for unilateral recognition are the conditions of self-consciousness: they ground history as they make it possible.[13]

The master-slave dialectic reverberates in the writings of many philosophers and political theorists who see in it the quintessence of Hegel's thought. Karl Marx picks up Hegel's category of objectification as it is first developed in this paradigm and shows the effects of objectification grounded in domination: work or labor that is rooted in the domination of others is a central point of his critique of capitalism. Marx praises Hegel for having understood that we develop through our own activity, and he, like Hegel, challenges the ontological division between the person or subject and the thing or object that person creates. For both Hegel and Marx the product or object is neither merely external nor indifferent to the nature of the person who has produced it. In *The Second Sex* Simone de Beauvoir claims that passages in Hegel's analysis of the master-slave dialectic are germane to the relationship between man and woman, for woman, if not man's slave, has always been dependent on him: woman has always suffered from male domination and is the most perfect example of the dependent consciousness. Both Marx and de Beauvoir elide critical parts of Hegel's paradigm to make their points.

In the *Economic and Philosophic Manuscripts of 1844* Marx claims this dialectic describes the situation of the worker under capitalism while he simultaneously claims that the process of capitalist commodity production offers the workers a relation *to each other* through which they may achieve independence from the capitalists. Marx begins not with a process of consciousness based on recognition but with human exploitation, and he ties an intersubjective orientation to the relations between workers in the capitalist form of production. Thus in the historical development from slavery (personal domination) to capitalism (abstract domination) there is a qualitative shift. The development of capitalism has freed the slave from personal dependence on a master by offering the worker the formal "freedom" of waged labor; more important, capitalism presents the possibility of workers uniting as active laborers. Labor becomes not only an individual response to necessity but cooperative creation. For Hegel, however, the slave is involved in independent creation and there is no necessary intersubjective relation developed between slaves: true intersubjectivity only develops between those who are already free.

In *The Politics of Reproduction* Mary O'Brien shows clearly and concisely how de Beauvoir's analysis of woman as the dependent slave consciousness described in Hegel's dialectic is incomplete and inadequate. De Beauvoir argues that because woman has not participated in productive labor and has not made history, she can only aspire to transcendence—a transcendence defined in terms of male values. But transcendence in de Beauvoir's existentialist philosophy is not the acceptance of values secondhand but rather the affirmation and realization of a project. De Beauvoir never considers the implication for woman that within his dependence the slave recreates the world to create history. While the slave labors and creates, woman, in de Beauvoir's view, simply adopts the possibility of freedom she has been *shown* by man, and does not, like Hegel's slave, *create* that possibility. Freedom for woman is reduced from a confrontation with Otherness to an act of mimesis: woman does not confront man as the Other but merely mimics his attempt to realize his freedom. De Beauvoir misses the crucial point that woman neither is nor can be master or slave in Hegel's schema precisely because for Hegel (as for Aristotle) woman does not experience a contradiction between herself and nature that she must negate.[14]

If we want to critically appropriate the master-slave dialectic to illuminate the relations between the sexes as well as to illuminate the relations between the classes, we must bear in mind that "Lordship and Bondage" is only one brief moment in the Hegelian movement of Spirit toward universal self-knowledge. For Hegel neither work (as objectification) nor the dialectic of dependent-independent consciousness is most significant; rather, self-consciousness finding itself in an Other, equal self yields the reconciliation that leads to universal self-consciousness:

> Universal self-consciousness is the affirmative awareness of self in an other self: each self as a free individuality has his own "absolute" independence, yet in virtue of the negation of its immediacy or appetite without distinguishing itself from that other. Each is thus universal self-consciousness and objective; each has "real" univer-

sality in the shape of reciprocity, so far as each knows itself recognized in the other freeman, and is aware of this in so far as it recognizes the other and knows him to be free.[15]

As groups or individuals struggle for mutual recognition they achieve an objective common interest. In fact, the universality of self-consciousness exists and is grounded in the interweaving of desires that are expressed by the mediating action of a recognition of equals. We enter into the world in full consciousness that it is our own world and we are certain of finding ourselves there. The truth of self-consciousness is the " 'I' that is 'We' and 'We' that is 'I.' "[16]

The process of mutual recognition in the Hegelian schema necessarily excludes woman. Hegel believes nature has assigned woman to the family, the sphere of first nature, and he keeps her imprisoned there on nature's behalf. Whereas man finds a self-conscious reality or second nature in the community, woman remains in the sphere of immediate biological life. Since Hegel does not feel impelled to look beyond first nature in his discussion of woman in the *Phenomenology*, the historical " 'I' that is 'We' " grounded in recognition and labor is an all-male one. Hegel's philosophy is a quintessential example of what Robert Graves has called "the philosopher's escape...into intellectual homosexuality."[17]

The Hegelian problem of recognition emerges implicitly and explicitly in the work of feminist theorists concerned with analyzing reproductive consciousness. Jessica Benjamin points to the process of recognition, as Horkheimer appropriates it from Hegel and Freud, and argues that mothering, as an intersubjective relation of nurturance and recognition, is a unique relationship with liberatory potential. In a similar vein Caroline Whitbeck finds a model of a nondominating relation between self and Other(s) in the relation between mother and child. She takes Hegel to task for describing the self-Other relation as primordially oppositional and for failing to examine the mother-child relation. Whitbeck considers the intersubjectivity of mother and child to be a unique relation of recognition in which the child differentiates itself from the mother-self through a process very different from the hostile opposition of the Hegelian paradigm of self and Other. Mary O'Brien implies that the risk of death in childbirth is equivalent to the risk of death Hegel sees in the process of recognition between master and slave and that motherhood can therefore be seen as a paradigm of intersubjectivity.

What these theorists miss is the crucial fact that for Hegel the process of mutual recognition requires *in the first place* that both subjects have the ability to recognize the Other as equal. And, who is master and who is slave is not predetermined but is the result of the struggle for recognition. In her extrapolation of Hegel's argument O'Brien omits consideration of the fact that the child cannot recognize the risk of death involved in childbirth as the mother does and, of course, who is mother and who child is predetermined. The child is therefore not an equal Other but a dependent Other upon whom the mother confers recognition. Even though mothering is a unique and significant human experience, the mother-child relation cannot offer mutual or equal recognition.[18]

As we have seen, for Hegel the goal of philosophy is to present systematically the structure and teleological movement of Spirit, which culminates in the universe's knowledge of itself. Nature is conceived as Spirit's opposite, but it is an opposite that is the necessary precondition for the realization of the dialectical movement of Spirit's self-development. Nature itself, as contingent and immediate, is seen as other than Spirit and as sleeping consciousness/Spirit. Emil Fackenheim describes how, for Hegel, philosophical thought attempts to recognize and conquer the actual world as nature gradually supersedes all natural determinations and passes over into Spirit as its higher truth. However, within Hegel's analysis first nature is "overreached" by Spirit in Spirit's movement toward universal self-knowledge. Thus, Hegel's attempt to include dialectically all oppositional moments presents us with an abstract negation: nature itself, as immediate and contingent, cannot be raised in itself to an essence above contingency, and the concept or logical Idea can never completely master experience. In an effort to preserve contingency in his system Hegel ultimately denies it.[19] I will argue that, in the same way that first nature is overreached by Spirit in Hegel's system of philosophy, woman is overreached by man: man's desire overreaches woman's desire and the spheres of man's second nature overreach the sphere of first nature to which woman is confined.

In Hegel's analysis of the master-slave dialectic, there is no mention of woman: master and slave are both seen as males even though historically many slaves were women. When we look for woman in the *Phenomenology* we must proceed to the section on the pagan ethical world and, more specifically, to the analysis of the family embedded in the interpretation of Sophocles' *Antigone*. Here we learn that history can be understood as a dialectic of particular and universal: man seeks recognition of his particular self from all men; he seeks universal recognition of his particularity. And universality, as the *Aufhebung* of the opposition between particular and universal, is "concrete" or universal individuality. Thus Spirit moves from immediate, undifferentiated unity (bare abstract universality) through difference and particularization to the concrete unity of universal and particular.[20]

The ethical pagan world of ancient Greece is seen as a specific historical moment in the movement of Spirit toward self-realization. In this world Spirit exists in its truth as ethical substance but without self-consciousness; the dialectical opposition between the particular and the universal cannot be overcome in the life of the pagan world. The polis or city-state only recognizes or realizes the universal aspect of human action and risk while the particular remains embedded in the family. Spirit attains self-consciousness through the historical diremption of itself that leads to the demise of the pagan world and the emergence of a higher stage.

Man is necessarily a member of a family and the family is the sphere of the particularity of the pagan male's existence. Within the family, man is *this* particular father, *this* husband, *this* son, and not simply *a* father, *a* husband, *a* son. But the family is the sphere of "merely natural existence," "mere particularity," and as such its supreme value is essentially inactive biological existence or animal life. While man has particularity inside the family circle, it is an unconscious particularity because, within this circle, there is no negating action—no risk of life for recognition. Within the family man cannot achieve self-consciousness or truly human satisfaction because, according to Hegel, in the pagan world the truly human demands the conscious risk of life.[21]

While neither male nor female can achieve self-consciousness within the family, the pagan male moves out to become a citizen. He does so "because it is only as a citizen that he is actual and substantial; the individual, so far as he is not a citizen but belongs to the Family, is only an unreal insubstantial shadow."[22] Hegel writes that within the polis "the community is that substance conscious of what it actually does," as opposed to the family, whose form is that of "immediate substance or substance that simply is."[23] The community draws man away from the family: by subduing his "merely natural existence" and his "mere particularity," it induces him to live "in and for the universal." While the family remains the sphere of womanhood, what is achieved in the polis through action and risk is "the manhood of the community." However, while the universal aspect of a man's existence is recognized in the polis, this existence is not truly *his*: it is not he as a particular that is recognized by the polis. Acting on behalf of the polis man achieves universality at the expense of his particularity. The Aufhebung of the familial particular and the political universal that results in concrete or universal individuality is possible only in death in the pagan world.[24]

The transcendence of death in the pagan world is achieved through the historical memory of the family. The ethical familial relation is not based on love or sentiment but duty in connection with burying and remembering the dead as well as avenging them if need be. By burying and remembering its members the family, represented by woman, maintains the continuity of the human community through time. Whereas man's life is dedicated to courting death on behalf of the universal, woman's life is dedicated to giving birth and raising the dead back to life. Prior to man's death his unconscious particularity is embedded in the family in such a way that it is completely separate from his action in the polis on behalf of the universal. This division between the familial particular and the political universal means that true individuality cannot be realized. Only through woman's obligation to the dead is man raised from mere isolated individuality to universal individuality or the individuality that achieves an identity-in-difference of particular and universal.

In life, the family and the polis—the particular and universal spheres of man's existence—are mutually exclusive: the family represents life, the polis the risk of life. In the pagan world the conflict between these two spheres is inescapable and unalterable. Man cannot renounce the family since he cannot renounce the particularity of his existence nor can he renounce the universality of his action in and for the polis. Since the particular is not included in the polis, the polis is not truly universal and pagan man is as little satisfied by his existence as a citizen as he is by his family life. The conflict between the familial and the political determines the tragic character of pagan life and creates a fundamental antinomy between family life as the natural ground of ethical life and ethical life itself in its social universality in the polis.[25] (It should be noted that this entire discussion refers to the "masters" of the pagan world, not to the "slaves.")

For Hegel the conflict between family and polis, particular and universal, is also a conflict between divine law and human law as represented in the conflict between woman and man in the pagan world. Nature, according to Hegel, assigns woman to the divine law and man to the human law. Any open conflict in the polarized pagan world sets woman against human law, which she sees as "only the violence of human caprice." In his turn, man sees obedience to the divine as merely "the self-will and disobedience of the individual."[26] The full impact of these conflicts in the pagan world is revealed, according to Hegel, in Sophocles' play *Antigone*.

> The *Antigone* [is] one of the
> most sublime and in every respect
> most excellent works of art of
> all time.
>
> G. W. F. HEGEL, *Aesthetics*

HEGEL'S ANTIGONE

In the section on the pagan or Greek ethical world in the *Phenomenology of Spirit* where the interpretation of *Antigone* appears, and where we find the only discussion of woman, Hegel searches for the ideal relationship between a man and a woman as a relation of identity-in-difference. He begins with heterosexual marriage and says that there is reciprocal recognition between husband and wife in the pagan world, but this recognition is "natural self-knowledge," not realized ethical life. That is, it is recognition rooted in the immediacy of desire or affective understanding, not in conscious ethical intention.

Hegel claims that the wife's desire for the husband always has a universal significance whereas for the husband desire and universality are separate. Here Hegel accepts the traditional view that there is a separation of morality and desire in man's relation to woman, but that morality and desire are united in woman's relation to man, and, therefore, woman is ethically "purer" in her love relations. Thus, a wife's ethical relation to her husband is not one of sentiment or love but is, rather, a relation to the universal:

> In the ethical household, it is not a question of *this* particular husband, *this* particular child, but simply of husband and children generally; the relationships of the woman are based, not on feeling, but on the universal.... Since, then, in this relationship of the wife there is an admixture of particularity, her ethical life is not pure; but in so far as it *is* ethical, the particularity is a matter of indifference, and the wife is without the moment of knowing herself as *this* particular self in the other partner.[27]

While woman remains confined to, and defined by, the family, man lives within the polis as well. In this way Hegel distinguishes the family for itself from the family in itself. That is, woman represents the family as immediately universal for itself while, from the perspective of the man, she represents the family in itself as the sphere of particularity. What creates the separation of morality or universality and desire or particularity in man is the bifurcation of his life into the public and private spheres. For Hegel, the husband acquires the rights of desire over his wife precisely because he has the rights of a citizen. The husband's authority and position in the polis allow him to have sexual domination over the wife in the family and simultaneously keep him "detached" from his desire for her: man rules woman in the private sphere because he rules in the public world. And as he rules in the public world and in the family he rules himself.

What is most significant in Hegel's analysis of desire in marriage is that it is *male* desire that taints the purity of the male-female relationship: the husband's desire for the wife is expressed as merely particular desire, so that a moment of indifference and ethical contingency is introduced into the relationship. However, insofar as this relationship *is* ethical the wife lacks the moment of knowing herself as *this* particular self in and through an Other. Thus, in the ethical family of the pagan world the husband gains an unconscious particularity, as *this* husband, through the wife's exercise of universal recognition of him as *a* husband, while his recognition of her is such that she never achieves particularity. Man, says Hegel, achieves particularity in the pagan family, through the wife's recognition of him, precisely because he leaves this sphere to attain universal recognition in the political sphere. But woman never enters the political sphere; she is caught and bound within the immediacy of the family circle.

For Hegel, the relationship between husband and wife in the pagan world is a mixed and transitive one in which male desire infects the process of recognition between a man and a woman so that each maintains a knowledge of dissimilarity or "independent being-for-self." Husband and wife are separated as male and female. Thus, the husband and the wife retain an independence—a being-for-self—such that the "return-into-self" of the relationship cannot take place. Instead, the relationship is nec-

essarily externalized through the child. The husband-wife relation needs the child to complete it, and the child changes the
relationship.[28] Given this, marriage is not the ideal relationship
of identity-in-difference between man and woman.

However, this ideal relationship obtains between a brother
and a sister because, Hegel believes, this relationship is without
desire and therefore without the separation and ethical uncertainty that male desire entails:

> The relationship [between man and woman] in its unmixed form is
> found, however, in that between brother and sister. They are the
> same blood which has, however, in them reached a state of rest and
> equilibrium. Therefore, they do not desire one another, nor have
> they given to, or received from, one another this independent being-
> for-self; on the contrary, they are free individualities in regard to
> each other.[29]

Brother and sister are not independent of one another because
they are united through the blood tie. Thus, the brother-sister
relationship is a unity of male and female that is not recognition
as separation, distinctiveness, or dissimilarity: it is a relationship
of identity-in-difference. Their recognition is that of "free individualities in regard to each other," which transcends the indifference or ethical contingency characteristic of marriage.
Whereas mere particularity is implicated in the husband-wife
relationship through male desire, "the brother . . . is for the sister
a passive, similar being" and the recognition of the sister in the
brother "is pure and unmixed with any natural desire." The
brother's nature is ethically like the sister's—that is, directly
universal, which allows for the realization of self in and through
an Other. The sister's recognition of herself in the brother is
therefore pure and complete, as is his recognition of himself in
her, and "the moment of the individual self, recognizing and
being recognized, can here assert its right."[30] Thus, Hegel distinguishes between, on the one hand, recognition between man
and woman based on an immediate unity (an immediate universality grounded in blood), which is transcended through the
process of recognition into a unity or identity-in-difference

(brother-sister), and, on the other hand, recognition grounded in desire, with the mere particularity of male desire, which necessarily retains separation and dissimilarity in such a way that a unity of male and female cannot be fully realized (husband-wife). In his *Philosophy of History* Hegel describes Apollo as "pure" precisely because "he has no wife, but only a sister"—Artemis, the virgin-goddess of the hunt.[31]

George Steiner sets Hegel's idealism concerning the brother-sister relation within an account of the development of nineteenth-century thought as "active meditations on Athens."[32] He claims that the love between brother and sister was rooted in a romanticism that went beyond the dark impulses of the id. According to Steiner, this relation should not be seen only in terms of pathology, of incest. Nineteenth-century man searched for the psychic/spiritual twin or "soulmate," and the sister came to represent the perfected Other as self.[33] We find an echo of this longing for the psychic twin in a twentieth-century poem by the feminist Adrienne Rich but she exposes the dark side of this quest from woman's perspective:

> The phantom of the man-who-would-understand,
> the lost brother, the twin—
>
> for him did we leave our mothers,
> deny our sisters, over and over?
>
> did we invent him, conjure him
> over the charring log,
>
> nights, late, in the snowbound cabin
> did we dream or scry his face
>
> in the liquid embers,
> the man-who-would-dare-to-know-us?
>
> It was never the rapist:
> it was the brother, lost,
>
> the comrade/twin whose palm
> would bear a lifeline like our own:
>
> decisive, arrowy,
> forked-lightning of insatiate desire

> It was never the crude pestle, the blind
> ramrod we were after:
>
> merely a fellow-creature
> with natural resources equal to our own
>
> Meanwhile, another kind of being
> was constructing itself, blindly
>
> —a mutant, some have said:
> the blood-compelled exemplar
>
> of a "botched civilization"
> as one of them called it
>
> children picking up guns
> for that is what it means to be a man...
>
> And that kind of being has other forms:
> a passivity we mistake
>
> —in the desperation of our search—
> for gentleness...[34]

Notwithstanding Steiner's analysis of the brother-sister bond, Freud's theories and anthropological studies of incest taboos would seem to make Hegel's assertion that "brother and sister ...do not desire one another" at least dubious if not altogether untenable. However, it is significant that Hegel believes that this lack of desire offers woman, as sister, the possibility of truly mutual recognition. The death of a brother thus becomes an irreparable loss for the sister, since with his death she loses the ideal relationship with a man.

Woman as sister in the pagan world is the paradigmatic fore-shadowing of ethical life precisely because she represents familial duty to man which is "purely" spiritual. The nature of the brother-sister relationship is such that the sister's obligation to the brother is the highest in terms of honoring and remembering him after his death. But the duties owed a brother do not reflect a *conscious* ethical life; rather, the law of the family is the sister's immediate, unconscious nature. The sister cannot realize or ac-tualize this life completely because the dualism of the pagan world resists the possibility of transcendence or the realization in consciousness of ethical life.

> The feminine, in the form of the sister, has the highest *intuitive* awareness of what is ethical. She does not attain to *consciousness* of it, or to the objective existence of it, because the law of the Family is an implicit, inner essence which is not exposed to the daylight of consciousness, but remains an inner feeling and the divine element that is exempt from an existence in the real world. The woman is associated with these household gods [Penates] and beholds in them both her universal substance and her particular individuality, yet in such a way that this relation of her individuality to them is at the same time not the natural one of desire.[35]

The unity of the brother-sister relationship necessarily "passes beyond itself" when the brother "leaves this immediate, elemental, and therefore, strictly speaking, negative ethical life of the Family, in order to acquire and produce the ethical life that is conscious of itself and actual."[36] The sister merely moves into another family situation by marrying: she moves from the family of origin to the family of procreation. Thus, the brother passes from divine to human law while the sister continues to maintain divine law as wife. In this way, according to Hegel, natural sexual difference comes to have an ethical determination.

At this point it is important to note several problems in the brother-sister relationship that Hegel does not address. First, this relationship takes place *within* the family of origin before the brother has entered the sphere of the polis and accepted its claims on him. Woman is said to realize herself within the family, but insofar as the brother is still only part of the family, he is an adolescent, not part of the manhood of the community and therefore not an adult male in Hegelian terms. The fact that the brother is at this time only a potential man, not a realized one, undermines Hegel's claim that brother and sister represent the ideal relationship between man and woman. Second, the brother-sister relationship does not entail equal responsibility. Since the brother's vocation is to accept the bifurcation of life, and with it the separation of desire and morality, he leaves the family of origin and does not look back. The sister assumes the familial obligations of divine law, which require that she bury and remember her brother when he dies, but there is no mention of any responsibility the brother has to his sister in terms of human or political law. Thus woman, as sister, assumes a responsibility for the brother that the brother does not reciprocate. This unequal responsibility mitigates the sense in which the brother-sister relationship can be seen as ideal. And third, Hegel seeks the self-complete relationship between man and woman that is an identity-in-difference: it must be a "natural" relationship that is dialectically transcended through consciousness (recognition/history). But there is no guarantee that a woman will have a brother. Insofar as Hegel attempts to institutionalize forms of consciousness this means that a woman without a brother can never achieve even a glimmer of an unconscious self that might be the equal of man's.

Setting aside these objections for the moment we find that in Sophocles' *Antigone* Hegel finds the superiority of the sister-brother relationship demonstrated in a way that reveals the profound ethical conflict inherent in the pagan world between family and polis, woman and man, particular and universal, divine law and human law. Thus, while the central *conflict* occurs between Antigone and Creon, the central *relationship* is, for Hegel, that between Antigone and Polyneices: Antigone's enduring sense of duty to her dead brother is explained in terms of the ideal male-female relationship of mutual recognition.

Both Hegel and Sophocles see the loss of Antigone's brother as irreparable, but they differ in their understanding of what makes it so. Because Antigone's parents are "hidden away" in death the replacement of a brother has become a physical impossibility. Antigone says:

> Not for my children, if I had been a mother, nor for my husband, if his dead body were rotting before me, would I have chosen to suffer like this in violent defiance of the citizens. For the sake of what law do I say this? If my husband had died, there would have been another man for me; I could have had a child from another husband if I had lost my first child. But with my mother and father both hidden away in Hades, no other brother could ever have come into being for me.[37]

Sophocles shows that the uterine relationship exerts the primary claim on Antigone: "If I had suffered him who was born of my mother to lie in death an unburied corpse, in that case I would have sorrowed....It is nothing shameful to revere those... from the same womb." Here the ancient womb/tomb imagery, the association of woman with life and death, is revealed as an integral part of the play. Creon shifts the discussion away from the uterine relationship to the more general concept of blood ties, a shift which changes the issue from matrilineal descent to patriarchal privilege.[38]

From Hegel's perspective not only the "merely natural" death of her brother and parents makes Antigone's loss irreparable. Hegel believes a woman's ideal relationship of mutual recognition takes place with her brother: only this relationship between a man and a woman is unambiguously free from desire. I have argued that within the family of origin Polyneices was only a *potential* man; he becomes fully a man only when he severs his relation to his sister to join the polis—a point that works against Hegel's view of this relationship as the ideal one between woman and man. However, Antigone "premonizes and foreshadows" most completely the nature of familial ethical life in Hegel's schema precisely because she represents the relation between man and woman not as wife but as sister. She is the paradigm of the law of the family as she carries out her highest duty toward her brother in attempting to bury and honor him.

While it is true that Antigone's burial of Polyneices represents familial duty (and in particular that between sister and brother), Hegel does not consider the play in its entirety. His references to the *Antigone* are scattered throughout the *Phenomenology*'s discussion of the ethical world and ethical action to support his claims regarding the relationship between male/human law and female/divine law in the pagan world. But Hegel's interpretation oversimplifies the play, particularly the conflict between Creon and Antigone, to fit his view of the tragic character of pagan life as a conflict between equal and contrary values.

Hegel begins with the situation that precedes the action in the *Antigone*—the struggle between the two brothers, Eteocles and Polyneices, for control of the city of Thebes. "Nature" has provided two potential rulers where only one can rule. In the pagan world the ruler is the community as individual soul: two cannot share power. Hegel claims that each brother has an equal right to rule; rejecting the right of primogeniture, Hegel asserts that the inequality of the natural order of birth can have no importance when Eteocles and Polyneices enter the ethical community of the polis. However, the equal right of the brothers to rule destroys them both, since, in their conflict over power, they are both wrong.

In human law or political terms, the right of possession takes precedence. Thus, because Eteocles was in power when Polyneices attacked the city, Eteocles is given a formal burial by Creon, who has become the ruler of the war-torn city-state. But Creon's edict, which forbids anyone to bury Polyneices on pain of death, denies sacred claims: without burial Polyneices' soul cannot safely enter Hades. By honoring one brother and dishonoring the other, human and divine law are set in opposition. And the "right" of human law is revealed as "wrong" through the vengeance of war waged on Thebes by Argos.[39]

Hegel explains how the tragic conflict between the universalistic polis and the particularistic family ends in the destruction of the pagan world, as it becomes one "soulless and dead" bare universal community. Not only external forces threaten the community, for within the community lie the seeds of its own destruction in the family. The family is "the rebellious principle of pure individuality," which, in its universality, is inner divine law; and this law, as Hegel claims again and again, is the law of woman.[40] Thus, woman, as the representative of the family principle, the principle of particularity that the polis represses, is the agent of destruction of the pagan world. Since particularity is not *included* in the polis, it destroys the polis.

> Since the community only gets an existence through its interference with the happiness of the Family, and by dissolving [individual] self-consciousness into the universal, it creates for itself in what it suppresses and what is at the same time essential to it an internal enemy—womankind in general. Womankind—the everlasting irony

[in the life] of the community—changes by intrigue the universal
end of the government into a private end, transforms its universal
activity into a work of some particular individual, and perverts the
universal property of the state into a possession and ornament for
the Family.[41]

Woman, acting from the immediacy of family life, represents the
subversive spirit of individualism. She persuades the young man
who has not yet completely detached himself from his family
and therefore not yet subordinated his particular existence to the
universality of the polis to exercise his power for the family
dynasty rather than for public welfare. She does this by asserting
the power of youthful male authority: as son, as brother, or as
husband.[42]

Hegel's analysis of the pagan world relies on an interpretation
of that world as suffering from a dualism in which first nature,
represented by woman in the family, conflicts with second nature,
represented by man in the polis, such that the pagan world is
doomed: there can be no reconciliation or Aufhebung of this
conflict. Reason, as political life in the ancient world, is not truly
universal in that it does not include particularity. Hegel claims
that woman acts on behalf of particularity; however, as I see it,
she is never a particular—what prompts her to this intrigue is
her confinement to the family, the sphere of first nature, and the
limitation to the immediate. As Hegel says, "immediacy has the
contradictory meaning of being the unconscious tranquillity of
Nature, and also the self-conscious restless tranquillity of
Spirit."[43]

Hegel scholars generally slide over "the woman question" in
the *Phenomenology*. Alexandre Kojève, for example, finds it
"curious" that woman is the agent of destruction in the pagan
world, and Charles Taylor writes off woman's role by saying
that the ethical spirit goes under, "in any case, by whatever exact
steps."[44] Both miss the critical significance of woman's role,
which not only limits woman but limits Hegel's philosophy.

Exactly how woman can represent the sphere of particularity
while never knowing herself as a particular self is a question
never addressed by Hegel. Adorno challenges Hegel on precisely

this transformation of the particular into particularity. For Adorno, "The particular would not be definable without the universal that identifies it, according to current logic; but neither is it identical with the universal."[45] Thus, the particular is a concept of the dialectics of nonidentity, whereas particularity eliminates the particular *as* particular in order to absorb it into a philosophy of identity dominated by the universal. For Adorno, Hegel "shrinks...from the dialectics of the particular, which destroyed the primacy of identity" when he substitutes the concept of particularity for that of the particular.[46] The transformation of the analysis from the particular to particularity in relation to woman illustrates Adorno's point. That is, Adorno shows that Hegel's identity philosophy necessarily excludes forms of human experience; I contend that it is primarily forms of *female* experience, which Antigone symbolizes, that are excluded.

Antigone, as the paradigm of the ethical family, does not, in the *Phenomenology*, represent woman as the principle of particularity destroying the polis through intrigue and perversion; nevertheless, Hegel misses what is most significant: Antigone must enter the political realm, the realm of second nature, in order to defy it on behalf of the family, the realm of first nature. In doing this, as we shall see, Antigone transcends Hegel's analysis of "the law of woman" as "natural ethical life" and becomes a particular self.

Antigone must reconcile her obligations to the family and its gods with the demands of the political sphere represented by Creon. Her tragedy is that no matter which course of action she chooses she cannot be saved. If she defies the law of the polis and buries Polyneices, she will die; if she fails in her familial duty to her brother she will suffer divine retribution and loss of honor. She defies Creon and in so doing brings divine law into the human community in opposition to the authority of the polis.

According to Hegel, in the pagan world the two forms of law, human and divine, as represented by man and woman, exclude and oppose each other; their separation means the loss of certainty of immediate truth and creates the possibility of

crime and guilt. Crime is defined here as the adherence to one
of the two laws over and against the other. Thus, there is no
Aufhebung of the two laws, but only opposition. For Hegel,
"essential reality" is the unity or identity-in-difference of both
human and divine law; that is, there can be no justice without
revelation.[47] But such an Aufhebung is only possible in the modern world, after the advent of Christianity. It is the revelation
of God in Christ that allows man to acquire the knowledge
necessary to make the transition to an ethical life that is self-
conscious and therefore truly universal. In the pagan world conflict is always "resolved" on one side or the other, but the two
laws are inextricably bound up with each other such that the
fulfillment of one calls forth the other's revenge. The purer ethical
consciousness acknowledges the other law but interprets it as
wrong and acts as it deems necessary because what is *ethical*
must be *actual*.[48] In this sense Antigone wittingly commits the
"crime." However, the higher ethical consciousness, having acknowledged the other law, concedes that it has committed a
crime against this law—it must admit guilt.

Here, in the analysis of the relation between crime and guilt,
we begin to see the inadequacy of Hegel's interpretation of the
Antigone. Sophocles does not create Antigone and Creon as ethical equals. Antigone alone is the ultimate defender of the good,
as one sees from the fate meted out to Creon. In order to fit the
Antigone into his view of the tragic character of pagan life in
terms of crime and guilt, Hegel takes liberties with Antigone's
final words; he makes it seem as if Antigone acknowledges
guilt for the "crime" of burying her brother. What she actually
says is

> I have done no wrong,
> I have not sinned before the gods. Or if I have,
> I shall know the truth in death. But if the guilt
> Lies upon Creon who judged me, then, I pray,
> May his punishment equal my own.[49]

With her death, Antigone believes, she will enter the world of
the gods, who will determine whether her act was right or wrong.

In a dialectical turn, Creon ends up living the fate he has tried to inflict on Antigone by entombing her alive: he must endure the solitude of a "living death," for his actions lead to the suicides of his son and his wife. In the end he declares: "I alone am guilty."[50]

Antigone chooses to obey divine law; nevertheless, she does not admit to a transgression of human law.[51] From Hegel's point of view Antigone must admit guilt for her ethical consciousness to equal that of Creon and for the play to represent the tragic conflict of pagan life. When we adhere to what actually happens in the play and put it within Hegel's interpretative framework we find that Creon's admission of guilt makes him the hero of the play, since it shows that Creon has attained the higher ethical consciousness that enables one not only to acknowledge the opposing law but to realize one's guilt before it. Thus, there are not two equal and contrary values opposed in the conflict between Antigone and Creon, as Hegel claims, but rather a higher political consciousness of the male and a lower familial consciousness of the female. From this perspective only Creon has the self-recognition made possible through the admission of guilt. While the action of the play transforms Creon from a criminal to a tragic figure for both Sophocles and Hegel, within Hegel's framework Antigone remains "criminal" in that she upholds only the law of the family and does not recognize the law of the polis as legitimate. Thus, Hegel wants Antigone to be a tragic character but he cannot show her as such without misrepresenting what she says.

In his interpretation of the *Antigone*, with its emphasis on crime and guilt, Hegel misses several critical components of the play that are central to an understanding of female experience. To begin with, Antigone retains a steadfast devotion to what is noble and just, a commitment which goes far beyond the mere intuition of natural ethical life. Antigone has the moral courage to choose a course of action even though it condemns her to death. Whereas Hegel claims that the sister's intuition of ethical life is not open to the daylight of consciousness, the chorus in Sophocles' play cries out to Antigone: "Your death is the doing

of your conscious hand."[52] Sophocles shows Antigone choosing
to carry out her duty to her brother and choosing to disobey
Creon's edict. Her decision does not spring from an unconscious
intuition of her ethical duty, as Hegel would have us believe.
Rather, it is a noble stance, consciously taken.[53]

According to Hegel, the woman who remained in her place
never felt the tragic character of pagan life, never felt the conflict
between particular and universal because she never entered the
polis, the sphere of universality. Thus, it is Ismene, Antigone's
sister, rather than Antigone herself, who maintains the traditional
place of woman. Curiously, Hegel fails even to mention Ismene
in his discussion of the play, probably because Ismene's "instinc-
tive" reaction is contrary to her supposed "natural ethical orientation": she explicitly sides with the political authority of the
polis against the divine law. And in siding with the law of the
polis Ismene bows to male domination. When Antigone asks
Ismene if she wishes to help bury their brother Ismene cries out:

> Think how much more terrible than these
> Our own death would be if we should go against Creon
> And do what he has forbidden! We are only women,
> We cannot fight with men, Antigone!
> The law is strong, we must give in to the law
> In this thing, and in worse.[54]

However, Ismene, motivated by feelings of sisterhood, overcomes
her initial fears and attempts to share the responsibility for burying Polyneices. Antigone protests that they both need not die for
something she alone has done. Ismene replies, "What do I care
for life when you are dead?"[55] We see here a second, more
traditional woman, a woman representing conventional womanhood, created in human rather than heroic proportions, choosing an honorable death over the continuation of an ignoble life.[56]
Although Ismene wavers in her commitment to the good her final
decision to do what is right is rooted in the familial devotion
between sisters, not the sister-brother relationship. Hegel completely disregards this aspect of the play.

Unlike Ismene, Antigone *acts* on behalf of the family, the

sphere of inaction. She moves outside the family and consequently becomes different *within* the family. Her brother is dead,
but, as we saw earlier, the brother-sister relationship of mutual
recognition, in which the sister is said to realize herself, necessarily ends when the brother leaves the family of origin. If Antigone were to proceed as a "normal" woman, she would marry
her betrothed, Creon's son. Hegel claims that there is reciprocal
recognition between husband and wife, but when we examine
this claim carefully we find that it contradicts his claim concerning what one is to gain from the process of recognition within
the family of procreation, that is, particularity. Man gains an
unconscious particularity through woman's relation to the universal, but man's relation to the universal is separate from his
relation to woman so that she is never a particular self. While
the husband cannot renounce the particularity of his being in
the pagan world, the wife never achieves it. She cannot achieve
an unconscious particularity as *this* wife within the immediacy
of the family, and she is not allowed into any other sphere of
life. In the Hegelian schema woman cannot even attain the self-
consciousness of the slave because she does not *do* anything—
she is not involved in the process of work as objectification or
world creation. Seen not as someone who *acts* but as someone
who merely *is*, she has no universal recognition of her action or
humanity in the polis. Since woman remains confined inside the
family she can never know herself as a particular self: she remains
one of the walking dead, an "unreal insubstantial shadow."[57]
But Antigone, like the male, leaves the family to risk her life in
the polis. Granted, she enters the polis on behalf of the family,
the sphere of first nature; nevertheless, she experiences the duality
of pagan life and has the potential to become a particular self.
Through the conscious risk of life in the sphere of the polis
Antigone transcends the limitations of womanhood set down by
Hegel.

    If we accept Hegel's interpretation of pagan life as a tragic
conflict between the familial particular and the political universal, then Antigone's decision to commit suicide, which Hegel
does not discuss, is of paramount importance. That is, unlike

the male, Antigone cannot live out the contradiction of pagan life. Man is able to endure the duality of pagan life through his relation to woman, who maintains the family as the sphere of his particularity while he acts in the polis, the sphere of universality. But woman's relation to man does not offer her a way to make this duality tolerable. His desire for her is such that she is never a particular self in relation to him, nor does she experience the universality of the polis through him. When Antigone leaves the family, her relation to man cannot sustain her. Thus, man *lives* the tragic conflict of pagan life but woman *dies* from it. By violating the norms of womanhood, Antigone comes to embody the tragic conflict inherent in Greek life. Her suicide expresses the inability to be both particular and universal in the pagan world. There can be no reconciliation, no Aufhebung, of particular and universal in that world.

In addition, we can see Antigone's suicide as defiance of male domination. If we extrapolate from Hegel's theory of desire we can see Antigone's suicide as maintaining her purity since she never marries and therefore never has a husband whose desire can overreach her ability to become a particular self. More important, by choosing to kill herself Antigone does not allow Creon to have the ultimate power over her fate: she takes her own life to refute the power of the male, the power of the universal, over her. In Greek society death was seen as preferable to slavery; it was more noble to kill oneself than to have one's fate controlled by another. Hegel himself writes of the liberatory aspects of suicide, although not in regard to Antigone's tragedy. In his essay on natural law (*Naturrecht*) Hegel claims that voluntary death is a manifestation of freedom because it reveals one's independence from the life situation. He qualifies this by saying that suicide is not a realization of freedom, since it ends in nothingness rather than free existence.[58] However, in Antigone's situation a manifestation of freedom is all that is possible since her choices are only death or submission to the male principle as the principle of universality. Antigone's suicide shows that she prefers honor to male domination.[59]

J. B. Baillie says that in the *Phenomenology* "action is the principle by which distinction in unity is carried out in social life. The consideration of its significance is thus an essential problem of social mind."[60] Yet Hegel chooses to emphasize only Antigone's burial of Polyneices and misrepresents her "confession." When one considers all of Antigone's actions we see, first, that her burial of Polyneices was a moral imperative surpassing the mere intuition of ethical life and that she confesses no guilt in terms of the human law; second, that her action in the sphere of the polis allows her to transcend the Hegelian framework (which confines her to the family) so that she becomes a particular self; and third, that her suicide can be seen as the ultimate expression of the tragic character of pagan life as well as a refutation of male domination. Thus, through her actions Antigone goes far beyond what Hegel attributes to her.

For Sophocles Antigone and Creon are transformed from criminal to tragic figures because they come upon the limits of their respective spheres. Hegel concurs with this, but his interpretation misrepresents both Antigone and Creon. That is, just as Hegel does not consider the consequences of the fact that Antigone must leave the family in order to protect it, he also does not consider that Creon's behavior must necessarily be unjust since it denies the claims of divine law. Hegel's interpretation of Creon as the just representative of the law of the polis is as radical a departure from Sophocles' tragedy as is his portrayal of Antigone. The conflict between the just moral law and the unjust political law that is central to Sophocles' *Antigone* is muted in Hegel's interpretation. For Sophocles, Creon's rule is *not* that of reasoned arguments and the rational order of the city-state; nor is Creon the community as an individual soul. Rather, Sophocles' Creon is a misogynist and a tyrant who requires unquestioned obedience.

Creon is forever fearful that man shall be "done in" by woman, yet he expects a man to bury Polyneices; he finds it unthinkable that a woman, even as the necessary defender of the divine law, would act in the public realm to transgress human laws. When he finds out that Antigone has committed the "crime" he exclaims: "If we must lose, / Let's lose to a man, at

least! Is a woman stronger than we?" And when his son challenges Creon's decision condemning Antigone to death, Creon
rebukes him: "Fool, adolescent fool! Taken in by a woman!"[61]
Although the polis sides with Antigone Creon declares:

> Whoever is chosen to govern should be obeyed—
> Must be obeyed, in all things, great and small,
> Just and unjust!
> . . . .
> My voice is the one voice giving orders in this City!
> ... The State is the King![62]

Confronted with the inexorable force of Antigone acting on behalf of the family, Creon becomes irrational precisely because
he cannot incorporate the claims of the family within the political
sphere that he rules. In a world divided between family and polis,
particular and universal, Antigone becomes tragic when she must
leave the family to protect it, and Creon becomes tragic when,
to protect the polis, he must become an irrational and unjust
ruler.

In summary, what we find are four aspects of Sophocles'
Antigone that Hegel overlooks in his attempt to reveal the pagan
world as a world defined by tragic conflict between particular
and universal, family and polis, divine law and human law,
woman and man. First, Hegel completely disregards the sister-
sister relationship in his search for the ideal relationship as a
male-female relationship of identity-in-difference. He describes
the family as the sphere of womankind without showing any
curiosity about the relations *between* women. This is like describing the sphere of pagan political life as "the manhood of
the community" without ever discussing the relations between
men! Although Antigone rejects Ismene's show of solidarity, it
is nevertheless important to note the attempt at sisterhood and
to recognize that Ismene does not display the "natural ethical
orientation" required of her sex: she instinctively sides with male
political authority rather than the divine law of the family.

Second, Hegel disregards the conscious choice involved in
Antigone's actions. Sophocles creates a conflict in which Anti-

gone represents not only eternal familial values but individual moral choice, in opposition to Creon who represents not only temporal legal authority but dictatorial rule.[63] Hegel fails to see Antigone's action as anything more than the result of her intuition of the natural ethical law of the family, just as Creon fails to see it as anything more than the result of female rebellion against his absolute, patriarchal authority. But Antigone's tragedy is the result of strength and moral courage—the so-called masculine virtues—not an emotional "feminine" intuition. (One wonders if Hegel would have "reduced" Socrates' *daimon*—a private intuition unrecognized and persecuted by the polis— to the level of "feminine intuition" if Socrates had been a woman.)[64]

Third, Antigone transcends woman's place in Hegel's framework because she breaks out of the confines of her assigned sphere. She represents the ethical family and as such must relate to the universal as immediate, but, according to Hegel, she is not to know herself as a particular self. Woman is bound to immediacy as wife within the family through male desire, which overreaches her ability to become a particular self in and through her relationship with her brother. The brother-sister relationship of mutual recognition is transitory, ending when he enters the polis. The sister merely moves into another family to become wife, the object of male desire. The husband's life in the pagan city-state overreaches the wife's familial life. Woman has no contradiction to negate between herself and first nature—she lacks negativity because she is confined within the sphere of "mere animal life" and thus remains an "unreal insubstantial shadow." But Antigone becomes, like man, a participant in both spheres. She does not represent the principle of particularity that changes the community through intrigue but openly insists on the rights of the family, the rights of first nature, within the polis. While subordinating herself to the universal, Antigone, unlike other women, comes to know herself as a particular self and thus to epitomize the tragic conflict between particular and universal that, for Hegel, characterizes the ancient Greek world.

And, finally, Hegel fails to discuss Antigone's suicide. The chorus recognizes Antigone as unique, as the exception to female behavior ("What woman has ever found your way to death?"), and therefore not the paradigm of divine law as represented by woman.[65] By acting in the public sphere on behalf of the private sphere, the sphere of inaction, Antigone becomes the precursor of the women who, in the recent past, proclaimed the personal as political.[66] Antigone rebels against Creon's claim to the right of the universal over the particular and in so doing she refuses to fit neatly into the Hegelian enterprise in which universality ultimately dominates. In criticizing Hegel's interpretation of the *Antigone* in the *Phenomenology* we begin to see another story in Western philosophy besides Hegelian reconciliation: the revolt of the particular against subsumption under a universal schema.

Given the inadequacy of the account of *Antigone* in the *Phenomenology of Spirit*, it is not surprising to find that Hegel's use of the play in the *Philosophy of Right* is also partial and therefore "false." Hegel's own philosophy of the modern world cannot reconcile the opposition between particular and universal in the context of sexual difference any more than the ancient world could. The Hegelian schema of the modern world, with its tripartite structure and dialectical movement, is still made at woman's expense.

THE PHILOSOPHY OF RIGHT

In the *Philosophy of Right*, published in 1821, Hegel develops his concept of ethical life as man's second nature through an explicit analysis of how Spirit objectifies itself as law, social and political activity, and the state. The aim of this work is to resolve the relationship between desire, morality, and ethical life; the analysis begins with a discussion of sexual desire within marriage, shifts to a focus on the generalized desire of civil society and the abstract morality of that sphere, and ends with a consideration of the concrete ethical life, or *Sittlichkeit*, of the state. The bifurcation of reason in the pagan world is shown to be *aufgehoben* in Spirit's movement toward universal self-knowledge with the development of the modern world into a triad consisting of family, civil society, and state. The economic activity that had been limited to the family and therefore to first nature in the pagan world becomes a separate sphere of man's second nature in the modern world, the sphere of civil society. Thus, the bourgeois family is the sphere of the universal as undifferentiated unity or immediacy; civil society is the sphere of particularity; and the state is the sphere of universality in which the universal and particular are reconciled. Along with this development Christianity, as the religion of freedom, emerges, making possible the true reconciliation of first and second nature, particular and universal.

Hegel begins the section on ethical life in the *Philosophy of Right* with the family because the family is, logically, the first form of society insofar as it represents the universal in its first moment of immediacy. The family is the sphere of undifferentiated unity in that there is an immediate identification of interests among family members. According to Hegel the family is completed in three phases: (1) marriage, (2) family property and capital, and (3) the education of children, followed by the dissolution of the family. The family's bond of union is love, an immature or immediate form of reason. But an ethical marriage changes "the natural sexual union . . . into a union on the level of . . . self-conscious love."[67] However, the moment of knowledge in the modern world, as in the pagan world, is the moment of mediation and withdrawal. Therefore one must leave the immediacy of the family to "know" oneself; the family unity is thus negated when the men leave to participate in civil society.

Civil society, not the family, is now the sphere of the particular.[68] Civil society comprises a plurality of male individuals each of whom pursues his own commercial and economic interests while endeavoring to satisfy his own particular needs and provide for his family. Individual interests and divergent needs are coordinated through the laws of political economy.

The state must mediate the conflicting interests of the possessive individualism of civil society in order to realize the goals of art, religion, and philosophy, the ultimate expressions of humanity.[69] Thus, "the state is the actuality of the ethical Idea," and the reconciliation of particular and universal occurs through the establishment of the state as a constitutional monarchy.[70] Even though the universality of the state transcends family and civil society Hegel believes both moments are preserved in this form of government. The monarch preserves the moment of the family since he inherits the right to rule through kinship or blood ties; and the estate structure of the government, by representing the different classes or estates of civil society, preserves the moment of particularity.[71]

For Hegel, particularity must necessarily be incorporated into political life in order for that life to be truly rather than abstractly universal. But this does not mean that woman qua woman needs incorporation into the political sphere. Rather, Hegel develops a philosophical system in the *Philosophy of Right* in which he conceives of particularity without the impediment of immediacy. Whereas in the pagan world woman is confined to the family as the representative of particularity, in the modern world she is restricted to the family as the representative of immediacy; particularity and immediacy are separated, and particularity is taken up into the male realm of civil society. Thus, the *Philosophy of Right* details man's progressive movement into a world that reconciles particular and universal, but woman is forced to take a step backward: she now represents immediacy, a moment *preceding* particularity and therefore a less developed form of reason.

Hegel wants to claim that freedom is realized in the modern world, yet at the same time he excludes woman from civil society and the state, the spheres in which man manifests his freedom. Woman's exclusion is made necessary by the dialectical structure, which requires that the sphere of the family be maintained or preserved as well as negated in the process of the development toward the universality of the state. Modern man leaves the family to move into the realm of civil society, where he emerges as a particular, but the sphere of undifferentiated universality or immediacy must be maintained. Therefore, modern woman is forced to do the family "maintenance" work required by the

Hegelian dialectic: woman is kept at home in the name of love to create and preserve the family.

When we analyze woman's situation in the *Philosophy of Right* in terms of Hegel's exposition on love we find a critical inconsistency. Hegel says that the family is characterized by love and that for two people in love with each other the meaning of each one's existence is revealed in the Other who is loved: the Other is the self externalized.[72] But while love is a desire for recognition the dialectic of love is not grounded in the hostility of a life and death struggle. And where the recognition in universal self-consciousness has transcended this initial struggle, recognition in a universal sense is only possible between equals who know themselves to be free. In Hegel's philosophy I am myself only in distinguishing myself from the Other. Since woman is never consciously confronted as a particular, she never becomes an "I." Modern woman, like her pagan sister, lacks the negativity resulting from the initial sundering from nature and therefore never achieves an independent self-consciousness. She is never an equal Other and never knows herself to be free. Only man dirempts himself; only he struggles for recognition in the universal sense. Woman can achieve only an abstract or undifferentiated identity.

In the *Philosophy of Right*, as in the *Phenomenology*, one finds that man can truly love only after he has created himself as a human being in the world outside the family. Woman, imprisoned in the dialectic of love, cannot truly love because she never creates herself as human in the spheres of second nature. Thus, a man and a woman cannot recognize one another as equals, as Other. This presents us with a contradiction in that the modern woman is defined in terms of love and yet cannot truly love. Since only man can achieve a truly human existence one would have to conclude that a truly human love is only possible between men.

The confinement of woman to the family entails the ethical imperative of female chastity: "It must be noticed in connexion with sex-relations that a girl in surrendering her body loses her honour. With a man, however, the case is otherwise, because he has a field for ethical activity outside the family. A girl is destined in essence for the marriage tie and for that only; it is therefore demanded of her that her love shall take the form of marriage and that the different moments in love shall attain their true rational relation to each other."[73] Since woman has only one realm in which to play out her entire existence she must not make any mistakes. If, however, the man should err within this sphere he can always leave home and be ethical in public.

Hegel describes the married state as an "identification of personalities, whereby the family becomes one person and its members become its accidents."[74] This he claims is the ethical mind/Spirit at work. What it means for woman is the total loss of self because the one person that the family becomes is necessarily the husband: "The family as a legal entity in relation to others must be represented by the husband as its head. Further, it is his prerogative to go out and work for its living, to attend to its needs, and to control and administer its capital."[75] But this is circular reasoning. The argument that the man *must be* the legal head of the family rests on the fact that he has the "prerogative" to participate in public life and the woman does not. Woman is assigned to the family in the name of love and then told that she cannot have any authority there but must remain dependent on her husband, precisely because she is not a public person. Woman does not and cannot meet man on the terrain of mutual recognition that love requires. The assumption of male domination precludes the kind of mutuality that Hegel conceives as the essence of marriage.

To keep us from worrying too much about the problem of love Hegel informs us that love is to be subordinated to the claims of marriage and reproduction, which in turn are to be subordinated to the claims of property: "the family, as person [read husband/father], has its real external existence in property; and it is only when this property takes the form of capital that it becomes the embodiment of the substantial personality of the family"; "the introduction of permanent property is linked with the introduction of marriage."[76] For Hegel property is the manifestation of ethical self-consciousness in the material and public world. Man expresses his freedom and gains historical continuity by effectively appropriating and transmitting property.

However, in order to realize the universality required by the sociopolitical spheres, property relations cannot be tied arbitrarily to the individual but must be established as a relation between the general community and the individual. Hegel believes that the right of inheritance of property through the family accomplishes the necessary connection between the general community and the individual, as well as establishing the ethicality of owning property, because the subject of property is the family as a unit. Therefore, when one inherits family property one inherits property that, in principle, is communal.[77] The universality of this property is safeguarded in Hegel's system by limiting the freedom to pass it on to others.

Within Hegel's framework it seems that the bourgeois woman can own property during her lifetime but cannot bequeath it to others. For all the talk of equality between husband and wife, it is the husband who distributes the family property. While a wife may divorce her husband and claim an equal share of the family property, she cannot effectively use the property, by transferring it to others, to express her humanity. Thus she cannot experience the freedom and historical continuity that man gains through the right not only to own property but to bequeath it to others.[78]

In the *Philosophy of Right* the issue is not really man and woman coming together in love but rather the inheritance of family property. Hegel claims that the husband and wife need the child as an externalization of the unity of their love.[79] However, the underlying concern is that the bourgeois woman reproduce heirs for the transmission of property. Clearly woman is not a free and equal Other (as lover) within the family. She is there to bear children. Hegel's attempt to base the male-female relationship on love and to give woman as person equal rights to the family property is overreached by his concern with the entailment of family property. In the end woman remains confined to the realm of immediacy as mother.[80]

The bourgeois woman does not enter second nature on her

own, and ultimately she, like first nature, remains tied to the immediate. Her tie to the immediate is necessary for the schema, because Hegel tries to maintain or preserve first nature as well as to transcend it: man is to gain access to first nature through woman just as woman is to gain access to second nature through man. But woman's bondage to nature as immediate and contingent confirms her bondage to her husband. Without passing through negativity via a contradiction between herself and first nature and without direct access to the spheres of second nature, woman cannot be truly human in the Hegelian schema.

The relationship of woman to first nature in Hegel's complex system is significant because man's relation to first nature is one of domination: domination grounds objectification in the Hegelian schema and means the domination of some men by other men. What is not acknowledged is that this domination of some men over other men includes the domination of all women.

While Hegel often masks his misogynist tendencies with a mystification that comes from his conception of woman as necessarily tied to first nature, it is not difficult to find his prejudices revealed by his own words. In the *Philosophy of Nature* he writes that "the male is the active principle, and the female is the receptive, because she remains in her undeveloped unity."[81] In the *Philosophy of Right* he expands on this:

> The difference in the physical characteristics of the two sexes has a rational basis and consequently acquires an intellectual and ethical significance.... Thus one sex is mind in its self-diremption into explicit personal self-subsistence and the knowledge and volition of free universality.... The other sex is mind maintaining itself in unity as knowledge and volition of the substantive.... It follows that man has his actual substantive life in the state, in learning, and so forth, as well as in labour and struggle with the external world.... Woman, on the other hand, has her substantive destiny in the family.[82]

Fortunately, the man can come home after a hard day of "self-diremption" to the woman who offers him "a tranquil intuition of ... unity"; in this way man achieves a wholeness, a connection to first nature, through woman.[83] Given this account, one wonders what woman receives in return. However, lest we wonder *why* she must remain at home Hegel details her limitations:

> Women are capable of education, but they are not made for activities which demand a universal faculty such as the more advanced sciences, philosophy, and certain forms of artistic production. Women may have happy ideas, taste, and elegance, but they cannot attain to the ideal. The difference between men and women is like that between animals and plants. Men correspond to animals, while women correspond to plants because their development is more placid and the principle that underlies it is the rather vague unity of feeling. When women hold the helm of government, the state is at once in jeopardy, because women regulate their actions not by the demands of universality but by arbitrary inclinations and opinions. Women are educated—who knows how?—as it were by breathing in ideas, by living rather than by acquiring knowledge. The status of manhood, on the other hand, is attained only by the stress of thought and much technical exertion.[84]

The logic of Hegel's system requires the tripartite structure of family, civil society, and state: the family must be maintained as well as negated in the dialectical process of development toward the universality of the state. Therefore, Hegel takes the socially conditioned given of the bourgeois woman locked into family life and raises it to the level of "essential nature." Woman does the family maintenance work required by the Hegelian dialectic. The spheres of man's second nature can be realized only if woman stays home to maintain the sphere of first nature while man moves into civil society and the state. In preserving the family through the bearing and rearing of children, modern woman, like woman in the ancient world, is forced to sacrifice her claim to self-consciousness. Thus, modern man's realization of himself and the dialectical structure are at modern woman's expense.

Given a schema that relegates woman to the family, Hegel must systematically misrepresent Antigone, especially her movement into the polis. His failure in the *Phenomenology* to analyze comprehensively Antigone's actions means that he cannot bring an analysis of these actions into the discussion of Antigone in the *Philosophy of Right*. Rather, he misuses her as a transhistorical ideal of woman as wife and mother confined to the family as the sphere of animal life, the sphere of inaction.

> You've come a long way Antigone
> but you haven't gotten very far...

HEGEL'S ANTIGONE IN THE MODERN WORLD

The reference to the *Antigone* and the only discussion of woman in the *Philosophy of Right*, as in the *Phenomenology*, appears within a discussion of the ethical life of the family. And, as in the *Phenomenology*, the *Antigone* is used as a paradigm to justify woman's confinement to the family. But, significantly, here the play does not represent the relationship between brother and sister as a bond untainted by male desire; nor does it represent the relationship between crime and guilt. Hegel uses the play's depiction of the relationship between man and woman to analyze the relationship between husband and wife.

In the *Philosophy of Right* Hegel does not attempt to find the relationship between man and woman that is free from desire, as he did in the *Phenomenology*, but to show how the relationship of desire can be transcended. Hegel claims that the husband-wife union is the ideal ethical relationship between man and woman in the modern world because the secret moment of desire, the moment of physical passion, is transformed into self-conscious love through marriage. Physical desire vanishes when satisfied, while the spiritual bond of Christian marriage rises above the contingency of desire.

The marriage ceremony, as a public proclamation of the ethical intention to take responsibility for family life, puts sensual desire into the background. The marriage contract transcends the standpoint of contract.[85] That is, a contract is a relation of civil society between atomic individuals, while the ethical family is a unity bound together by love in such a way that one exists in it not as an atomic individual but as a member of the group. Through a relation of civil society the family transcends the familial problem of desire: the marriage contract eliminates the capricious subjectivism of love as sentiment, an immediate form of reason, and makes love the ethical or self-conscious moment in marriage.

This is quite a different situation from the one we encountered in the *Phenomenology*, where love in the pagan world was not self-conscious and where male desire infected the relationship between husband and wife so that it could not be the ideal relationship between man and woman. The bifurcation of man's life in the pagan world into public and private spheres caused a split between desire and morality that introduced a moment of ethical contingency into the marriage. Only the brother-sister relationship, which was supposedly free from desire and which took place before the brother entered the polis and experienced the bifurcation of his life, could be seen as ideal. According to Hegel, the modern Christian world has radically transformed the situation so that male desire is no longer a problem. The tripartite structure of family, civil society, and state overcomes the dualism of the pagan world and allows the reconciliation of desire and morality through the marriage ceremony, which is both a contractual relation (a relation of civil society) and a religious (familial) one.

Thus, in the *Philosophy of Right* the ideal form of recognition between man and woman shifts from the relationship between brother and sister, who are *free* from desire, to that between husband and wife, who *transcend* desire. This shift is characteristic of the Hegelian philosophy's claim to overcome the externality of Greek philosophy and society with the realization of philosophy in historical life. Significantly, the shift changes the site of the paradigm of male-female relations from the family of origin to the family of procreation. Here Hegel wants to distinguish the "natural" feeling of love, which binds family members through an original blood tie, from a later, deeper, self-conscious tie of love in marriage.[86] He defends the nuclear family against the rights of the extended family of origin. In the modern world any conflict of claims regarding duties and obligations between the family of origin and the family of procreation is always resolved in favor of the higher ethical family, the family of procreation: that which comes later is a more mature form of reason. The focus on the family of procreation also replaces the contingency noted earlier in the discussion of Hegel's use of the *Antigone* in the *Phenomenology*—that is, while only some women may have brothers in the family of origin all women may potentially have husbands.

According to Hegel, the wife and mother in the modern world, like her sister in the pagan world, is a passive and subjective being who has knowledge only as feeling or intuition. "Her substantive destiny [is] in the family, and to be imbued with family piety is her ethical frame of mind." Once again Antigone is held up as the representative of true womanhood: "Family piety is expounded in Sophocles' *Antigone*—one of the most sublime presentations of this virtue—as principally the law of woman, and as the law of a substantiality at once subjective and on the plane of feeling, the law of the inward life, a life which has not yet attained its full actualization."[87] However, the reference to the *Antigone* in the *Philosophy of Right* occurs within a context that puts the claims of the family of procreation over and above the claims of the family of origin, whereas Hegel's interpretation of the *Antigone* in the *Phenomenology* concerns the highest claim of duty and obligation within the family of origin, that is, the duty of the sister to bury and honor her brother. Given Hegel's original interpretation of Antigone as the paradigm of ethical family life precisely because she represents the relationship between man and woman not as wife but as *sister*, this new appropriation of the play within the context of a discussion of marriage in the modern world seems quite untenable. Since Antigone represents "holy sisterly love" and never marries, it is hard to see how she can serve as a model for wifely piety in the modern world. Hegel's attempt to use the play to reinforce his assumption that modern woman must stay within the family lacks the historical and conceptual analysis that would justify such a use. Most significantly, Hegel posits Antigone as a transhistorical paradigm of ethical family life and the role of woman: the play has lost its historical apposition in the *Philosophy of Right* in order to justify the circumscription of woman within the modern family. While Hegel's system is meant to be a historical account of the development of humanity, woman is presented as outside history.

Examining Hegel's work in the *Philosophy of Right* via his discussion of Antigone raises two crucial issues: the problem of female desire and the question of whether or not the sphere to which woman has been assigned *can be* taken up and dialectically *aufgehoben* in Hegel's sense if woman is allowed her freedom.

In the *Philosophy of Right*, as in the *Phenomenology*, Hegel tries to solve the problem of the division of man's life by drawing on woman's undivided familial existence. Marriage to woman is said to resolve the bifurcation of modern man's life between family and civil society by mediating two forms of desire: desire as familial, heterosexual union and desire as general and differentiated in civil society. Woman affords man an intuition of unity; if she lived in two spheres she could not offer man access to the wholeness he seeks. However, Hegel does not address the fact that *because* she lives in only one sphere woman has no internal motive for seeking marriage as mediation. That is, there is no necessity for the institutional mediation of two forms of desire in woman's life since she does not experience two forms. Therefore, woman does not need marriage as ceremony and contract. From her perspective, marriage is the result of external coercion: man's need for marriage forces her to accept it. Given this conceptual framework, what emerges is that woman's confinement to the family as the sphere of immediacy indicates that she can represent desire only as capricious and contingent. Just as woman has no internal motive for marriage, she also has no internal motive for desiring one man over another. Female desire itself, if it is to focus on a stable object (one husband rather than many lovers), must be coerced. Thus, we find that Hegel's schema of the modern world solves the problem of male desire only by creating a problem of female desire.

Antigone, who represents woman as actor, refuses to fit neatly

into Hegel's dialectical system. Her move out of the family transforms her so that she has the potential to be a particular self.
However, when woman in the modern world follows in Antigone's footsteps by participating in civil society and the state,
the spheres of particularity and universality, then the family is
not preserved or maintained as well as transcended in the Hegelian sense. If woman is given truly human status and not confined to immediacy and the family, she cannot offer man
intersubjective recognition as the intuition of unity, and therefore
the dialectical structure breaks down. The denial of woman's
humanity required by the dialectical process means that Hegel's
system cannot provide a true Aufhebung of the opposition between familial and nonfamilial, first and second nature, woman
and man.[88]

With the limitation of woman there is a limitation of the
Hegelian system. Hegel's universal is necessarily male and male
is *not* universal. Humanity is both male and female; the claim
to encompass the universality of human experience must allow
for woman's experience and participation outside the family. It
must allow for a more comprehensive account of the *Antigone*
than Hegel can provide.

Hegel's philosophic formulation of the relation between
woman and man in the modern world is important because it
reveals the problem of how to achieve unity in a world in which
each one seeks satisfaction of particular needs and desires. But
Hegel does not adequately formulate the required mediation.
The progressive movement of Spirit toward universal self-
consciousness is never recapitulated in woman's development.
Woman can never aspire to "concrete" universality or individuality since she cannot attain particularity much less universality.

Hegel shows that the family is a unique sphere of life with
its own specific logic; nevertheless, his patriarchal prejudice ultimately falsifies and obscures familial relations. The Aufhebung
in which the family is maintained by woman on the level of
feeling comes not only at the expense of woman becoming an
equal Other but also at the expense of the ontogenetic principle.
Woman, like man, has the ability to reason and the capacity to

act—to partake of second nature—yet she is limited to animal life in the Hegelian system.

The fundamental problem of woman and first nature, vis-à-vis man and second nature, is as unresolved in Hegel's philosophy as he shows it to be in the ancient pagan world. The reciprocal recognition between some men in the polis of the ancient world relied upon the domination of nature, the domination of some men by other men, and the domination of all women. The modern world described by Hegel still rests on this domination.

CHAPTER TWO

Marx: The Double Dialectic

MARX'S ANALYSIS, LIKE HEGEL'S, FAILS TO PROVIDE A COMPRE-
hensive framework for the woman question because of the inadequacies of his dialectical formulations. In his early writings
the initial schism between nature and human society, which is
"the riddle of history," is to be resolved in communism by the
mutual interpenetration of nature and society that will "resur-
rect" nature and reconcile it with "man." In the context of this
dialectical understanding, Marx focuses on the heterosexual love
relation as the paradigmatic form of intersubjectivity. With the
development of his critique of political economy, Marx concentrates on the relation between nature and history as a historical
dialectic in which labor is central to the formation of consciousness. Within this understanding of the dialectic the paradigmatic
form of the intersubjective relation occurs within civil society
between workers; it is a relation mediated by the process of
objectification (object-creating). "Nature" becomes a sociohistoric category, merely the material for manipulation by humans
in civil society for human purposes. There is no longer any "resurrection" of nature, no "reconciliation" of the schism between
nature and human society, but rather the domination of nature
and, consequently, a loss of nature as an independent "moment"
of the dialectic.

This transformation of the dialectic affects Marx's analysis of woman's situation in that he shifts from the personal man-woman relationship and the specific logic of the family to a mediated relationship of abstract equality between man and woman in the sphere of productive relations. However, the equality proposed for woman in the sphere of production ignores both the direct domination of patriarchy in the family and the abstract domination of patriarchy, which permeates all spheres of society. The unique character of the two dialectical formulations and the point of transformation are critical moments for a rethinking of the relation of Marx to woman's liberation.[1]

MARX'S PROJECT

As we have seen, Hegel attempts to develop a philosophical system in the *Phenomenology* that demonstrates how Spirit becomes the universe's knowledge of itself. Within this system the ontogenetic principle assures that the historical development of humanity is recapitulated in the psyche of the universal individual. And in the *Philosophy of Right* Hegel attempts to show how Spirit objectifies itself in the social sphere. While my critique of Hegel centers on the family, Marx, in his *Contribution to the Critique of Hegel's Philosophy of Right* (1843), lays bare the ideological content of Hegel's philosophy through an immanent critique that argues that civil society dominates both the political and familial spheres. The social relations of civil society preclude the reconciliation of particular and universal that Hegel claims for his system. Civil society as depicted by Hegel only develops with the rise of capitalism, and Marx reveals the objective organization of the state under this system as the various particular interests of civil society *masquerading* as the universal. The state is not universal and free from the rule of the particular as Hegel would have us believe; rather it reflects in a distorted way the class differences and property relations of the dominant mode of production in civil society.[2]

Marx exposes the ideological content of Hegel's argument concerning the aristocracy's unique suitability for positions of authority. For Hegel the fact that this class receives and maintains its property through the family guarantees that its members will conduct themselves according to the highest ethical standards. However, since only the first-born son inherits everything there is only the semblance of family solidarity. The antagonisms of particularity, which Hegel wants to confine to civil society, infect the aristocratic family through the very property that is supposed to guarantee its freedom from such antagonisms.[3]

Hegel argues that the "actual Idea" divides into family and civil society in order to return into itself, to be conscious of itself, in the state. Marx argues that this is an inversion of the fact that the family and civil society are the foundation of the state. Since the Hegelian state presupposes and divides into family and civil society what we have is a philosophy derived not from the particular nature of the family, civil society, and the state "but from the *general* relationship of *necessity* to *freedom*," of mind/Spirit acting "on a specific principle with specific intent."[4] Marx's critique reveals that it is *logic* rather than the philosophy of right that is the central concern in Hegel's work.

The argument in the *Critique* centers around Feuerbach's transformative method. Claiming that Hegel made thought the subject of philosophy and relegated human existence to the predicate, Feuerbach set out to develop a philosophy that made human existence the subject, the beginning point of philosophic deliberation, and thought the predicate.[5] Using Feuerbach's method Marx focuses on social class divisions and property and shows how there has been an inversion of property and persons in bourgeois society—a person is not a subject but a predicate of property. Marx sees private property as the negation of an original communal ownership of land and calls for a revolutionary inversion in which the abolition of private property achieves the "negation of the negation" or Aufhebung of capitalism. Human beings will emerge as the subjects of existence in the process of making property the predicate. Thus Hegelian logic, when the transformative method is applied to it, becomes a way to change the world. Marx writes: "It may be generally pointed out that the turning of the subject into a predicate, and the predicate into a subject, the inversion of the determining and determined, always signifies the next revolution."[6]

Hegel attempted to show how the political sphere must necessarily determine the sphere of civil society and how the estate structure was the means by which particular interests were to achieve the legitimacy of political universality. But Hegel failed to comprehend the relation between the institutions of everyday life and commodity production; he provides an ideological defense of capitalism by rationalizing the private economic interests of civil society. The mutual recognition realized in civil society is the recognition of the atomic or possessive individual. Thus Marx shows that Hegel falsifies and obscures the relationship of civil society to the family and the state.

Having disclosed the class-character of the political structure, Marx concentrates on the significance of the social class that has only marginal status in civil society but whose existence is the necessary condition for the functioning of that sphere. In the introduction to the *Critique of Hegel's Philosophy of Right* (written in 1843–44 after the *Critique* had been completed) Marx portrays the German proletariat as a revolutionary class endowed with the final realization of universality. It is the "class of concrete labour" that has revolutionary potential precisely because it does not share in civil society—it is "in but not of civil society." Marx declares:

> A class must be formed which has *radical chains*, ... a class which has a universal character because its sufferings are universal, and which does not claim a *particular redress* because the wrong which is done to it is not a *particular wrong* but *wrong in general*. There must be formed a sphere of society which claims no *traditional* status but only a *human* status ... a sphere, finally, which cannot emancipate itself without emancipating itself from all the other spheres of society, without, therefore, emancipating all these other spheres, which is, in short, a *total loss* of humanity and which can only redeem itself by a *total redemption of humanity*. This dissolution of society, as a particular class, is the proletariat.[7]

The focus on the proletariat reverses the Hegelian understanding of universality as recognition between free and equal participants in civil and political life and recalls Goethe's words:

> ... Men do not know each other—
> Only galley slaves do that. They sit

Chained on a single narrow bench together
And grasp for breath.Where no-one makes demands,
And none has anything to lose, they know
Each other.[8]

In the *Economic and Philosophic Manuscripts of* 1844 Marx
points out that bourgeois political economy "conceals the es-
trangement inherent in the nature of labour by not considering
the *direct* relationship between the *worker* (labour) and production" and makes the economic development of civil society
appear to be controlled by immutable laws.[9] Marx develops a
critique of political economy to show that the economic "laws"
of civil society are not immutable. Such a critique is meant to
show the possibility of the freedom to act to change our lives.

In these early works Marx concerns himself with Hegel's
Phenomenology of Spirit and his *Logic*. He praises Hegel for
having recognized the "dialectical process of negativity as the
moving and generating principle" of reality.[10] Since capitalist
production moves in contradictions that are constantly overcome
but just as constantly posited, the dialectical mode of thought is
necessary to an understanding of capitalism. However, in Hegel's
philosophy the same dialectical logic of becoming is at work in
an ontological system that is supposed to be identical with the
rational movement of history. For Hegel, Spirit is an *absolute
subject*, a single totalizing principle that experiences diremption
and self-opposition in order finally to return to itself. All knowledge is self-knowledge of the absolute subject. Marx denies an
absolute subject and rejects the notion of a single logic of everything at work; instead, he argues, dialectical logic is the specific
logic of capitalism: "Comprehending does not consist, as Hegel
imagines, in recognising the features of the logical concept every-
where, but in grasping *the specific logic of the specific subject*."[11]
According to Marx his dialectical analysis arises from the subject
matter under consideration, the social relations of capitalist production, not from the movement of Spirit.

Seeing the profound effect that the sphere of civil society has
on society as a whole, Marx abandons the Hegelian tripartite
schema; the political and familial spheres (as well as all "super-

structural" spheres) are seen to depend on the economic sub-structure. Consequently, he considers political economy the science of civil society and believes that only through emancipation of the working class will universality be realized. In the preface to the *Critique of Political Economy* (1859) Marx says:

> The mode of production of material life conditions the social, political and intellectual life process in general. It is not the consciousness of [human beings] that determines their being, but, on the contrary, their social being that determines their consciousness... With the change of the economic foundation the entire immense superstructure is more or less rapidly transformed.[12]

The thesis that productive activity conditions and/or determines, directly or indirectly, the political, familial, and all other super-structural spheres implies that *all* forms of human interaction will change when the relations of production change. This formulation lends itself to an economic determinism and contradicts Marx's own insight that each specific subject requires its own logic. That is, it denies the specificity of both familial and political relations.

Marx picks up Hegel's category of objectification as it is first developed in the master-slave dialectic and makes it a central point of his critique of capitalism. He praises Hegel for having understood that we develop through our own activity. The master-slave dialectic presents the creation of the individual in which the individual posits and produces a self through objectification, a process characterized by alienation and its Aufhebung. Human history comes about and completes itself through our work as a relation to nature: through labor, as the creation of an object- world, we constitute human reality: "In creating a *world of objects* by his practical activity, in his *work upon* inorganic nature, man proves himself a conscious species being."[13] Here labor is understood as that specifically human activity through which existence is confirmed and realized. Marx sees labor as something that has more than economic significance— it is our "life-activity" and our genuine realization as human beings: we *are* as we have realized ourselves in the objects of our labor.[14] Both Hegel and Marx challenge the ontological division between a person or subject and the thing or object that person creates. The object is not a merely external thing, indifferent to the constitution of human subjectivity.

For Marx, objectification is an activity that reveals human beings as social beings. The sphere of objectification, the sphere in which we labor, is the sphere of shared life activity: in and through the objects we create we show ourselves to each other as we are. Our relation to the object is a social relation in that it is a relation to those with whom we share the object and it is a relation to the self as a social being. Although Marx believes Hegel spiritualizes or idealizes human history, he retains the Hegelian thesis that human history is to be understood through transforming activity. The inherent meaning of objectification and its Aufhebung is praxis: "free self-realization, always taking up, superseding and revolutionizing pre-established 'immediate facticity.' "[15]

Marx concentrates on the fact that domination and servitude as presented in the master-slave dialectic give a general description of the social situation of humanity as it labors under capitalism. He transforms the problem of the origin of private property into the problem of the relation of alienated labor to the process of historical development. Objectification results in alienation when we produce in such a way (conditioned by the political economy of the society in which we find ourselves) that our products are simultaneously a manifestation of our labor-power and a negation of our potentialities or "species-being." Our products become hostile to us and dehumanize us. Just as for Hegel the slave both is and is not his product, for Marx a product is and is not an expression of the producer. A product *is* the producer in that it is a congealed form of the producer's activity, but it *is not* the producer when it dehumanizes the producer by assuming an independent, hostile dimension.[16] For Marx capitalism is characterized not merely by political or economic crises but by a crisis affecting the human creative potential. We are alienated from a self-conscious knowledge of that potential as we are alienated from the product of labor and from each other. Although all classes are affected the forms of alienation differ and the working class suffers most profoundly.

The contrast to an alienated society is eloquently expressed by Marx in his *Comments on James Mill, Élemens d'économie politique*, written in 1844:

> Let us suppose that we had carried out production as human beings. Each of us would have *in two ways affirmed* himself and the other person. 1) In my production, I would have objectified my *individuality*, its specific character, and therefore enjoyed not only an individual *manifestation of my life* during the activity but also when looking at the object I would have the individual pleasure of knowing my personality to be *objective, visible to the senses* and hence a power *beyond all doubt.* 2) In your enjoyment or use of my product I would have the *direct* enjoyment both of being conscious of having satisfied a *human* need by my work, that is, of having objectified *man's* essential nature, and of having thus created an object corresponding to the need of another *man's* essential nature. 3) I would have been for you the mediator between you and the species, and therefore would become recognized and felt by you yourself as a completion of your own essential nature and as a necessary part of yourself, and consequently would know myself to be confirmed both in your thought and your love. 4) In the individual expression of my life I would have directly created your expression of your life, and therefore in my individual activity I would have directly *confirmed* and *realised* my true nature, my *human* nature, my *communal* nature.[17]

And in "Private Property and Communism" he writes: "We have seen that man does not lose himself in his object only when the object becomes for him a *human* object or objective man. This is possible only when the object becomes for him a *social* object, he himself for himself a social being, just as society becomes a being for him in this object."[18] For Marx the individual can enter into a meaningful relation with another only in a society where we consciously recognize our intersubjectivity. Echoing Hegel's theme of the need for the Other, Marx claims that only in a communist or socialist society can our basic need for another human being become self-conscious; only in such a society can we recognize that our needs go beyond those of mere physical existence.[19]

In his analysis of society as it develops under capitalism Marx distinguishes different classes defined by their relationship to the production process. The two primary classes are the capitalist or bourgeoisie and the waged workers or proletariat, that is, those who own the means of production and those who actually labor to produce.[20] These two groups have essentially antagonistic interests. Marx explains how the necessity that leads the laborer to work for his survival facilitates the production and reproduction of capitalism as a social relation. That is, capitalism maintains itself by the production and reproduction of a relation where the capitalist is on one side and the waged laborer on the other. It is also in the nature of the capitalist mode of production to transform all production, or as much as possible, into commodity production. Historically this process creates the increasing separation of the means of production from the workers as the use-value production of earlier epochs is continuously transformed into commodity production. This entails an ever-increasing division of labor, the most pernicious form of which is the separation of physical and mental labor.

The development of commodity production obscures the relation of the worker to production so that the subject (the worker) looks like the predicate (a factor of production). Under capitalism the fundamental nature of human relations is concealed or mystified as the system strives toward a situation in which all traditional intersubjective ties will be replaced by the principle of exchange. As Georg Lukács points out, the commodity form of society and the relations of exchange become universal; alienation is universalized so that "the fate of the worker becomes the fate of society as a whole."[21] While other classes of society may harbor illusions about their lives the members of the working class necessarily gain insight into the dehumanizing effects of capitalism, according to Marx, precisely because they are forced to live their lives *as* commodities, forced to sell their labor power or "life-activity" as a "thing." The insight required to see the human in the objective and to see through alienation and reification is available to the proletariat because of this unique role in the capitalist system.[22]

Not Antigone but Prometheus provides the mythic paradigm for Marx's analysis.[23] Prometheus stole fire from the gods and gave it to humanity. To punish him for doing this Vulcan chained him to a rock and each day an eagle came to feed on his liver. It may be that Goethe's fascination with this myth influenced Marx. In any event, Prometheus does not represent a concern with the family and kinship ties (as Antigone does in Hegel's philosophy) but instead symbolizes the worker in modern civil society. The law of capitalist accumulation binds the laborer to capital more surely than Prometheus was bound to his rock. Like Prometheus, the worker is devoured each day by the capitalist production process but lives to labor again tomorrow.

Marx distinguishes the relations of production described above from the material forces of production. These two elements constitute the economic substructure of society, and the relations of production are said to depend on the stage of development of the forces of production. The class struggle becomes momentous with the maturation of the forces of production whereby the existing social relations (particularly property relations) become an impediment or fetter. A revolutionary transformation of society cannot take place until the productive forces develop to the *full* extent possible within the existing relations of production—only then are the material conditions for the emergence of a new social epoch present within the old. Through a continuous process of quantitative change within the given society a contradiction matures and achieves the qualitative change to a new society.

While Marx's dialectical analysis may be viewed as a continuing meditation on themes first explored in the *Economic and Philosophic Manuscripts of 1844*, there are several significant changes in his later formulations. In 1844 Marx had not completely integrated his study of British political economy into his critique of Hegel, Feuerbach, and the French utopian socialists. By 1857 the works of Adam Smith and David Ricardo become extremely significant for the development of his labor theory of value. As his critique of philosophy is overshadowed by his critique of political economy, the concern with alienation is transformed into an analysis of commodity fetishism. As early as the writing of *The German Ideology* (1846–47) there is no longer any mention of human *self*-alienation although alienation is still discussed. By the time Marx wrote the first volume of *Capital* (1867) he is primarily concerned with the "peculiar character" of social labor in which a "definite social relation between men ... assumes ... the phantasmagoric form of a relation between things."[24] Commodity fetishism, not self-alienation, causes us to perceive society as a system of objects and objective laws that prevail over and against our intersubjective relations.

In *Capital* Marx identifies the inherent contradiction in the dialectical development of capitalism between the socialization of production (the increasing cooperation or interdependence of the working class) and the exploitation of the worker in production through the extraction and appropriation of surplus value by the capitalist class. This is a more comprehensive formulation of the contradiction between the means and the relations of production found in the preface to *A Contribution to the Critique of Political Economy*. Within his analysis of the labor process, Marx interweaves a discussion of capitalism and its contradictions with a description of the difference between capitalist and precapitalist societies.

Marx shows that political economy examines the process of exchange but does not attempt to analyze what exchange presupposes: the exploitation of the worker in production. He therefore transforms the analysis of wealth as commodities in the sphere of exchange into an analysis of capitalist production in the factory. In developing his labor theory of value he distinguishes between use value, which the created object embodies in all historical forms to fulfill human needs, and exchange value. The commodity created for exchange in capitalist society embodies both use value and exchange value and is "a very queer thing" whose "mystical character" originates in exchange value.[25] The twofold character of the commodity as the embodiment of use value and exchange value coincides with the twofold character of labor as concrete and abstract. Concrete, particular labor creates use value while abstract, homogeneous labor creates exchange value. Abstract labor is the quantitative, undifferentiated labor power specific to capitalism that integrates the productive power of society and provides the basis for the exchange of commodities: "Along with the useful qualities of the products themselves, we put out of sight both the useful character of the various kinds of labour embodied in them, and the concrete forms of that labour; there is nothing left but what is common to them all; all are reduced to one and the same sort of labour, human labour in the abstract."[26] Thus, the ability to equalize commodities for exchange is based on a reduction of the concrete and specific qualities of the object, and the labor necessary to produce it, to undifferentiated labor time.[27]

Marx explains the development of the abstract equalization necessary to exchange through capitalism's reversal of the simple circulation of commodities (commodity–money–commodity). Within precapitalist societies exchange is simply a way to transfer the use values of commodities: circulation ends when a commodity is consumed for its use value (C-M-C). In contrast, capitalism begins and ends with exchange value and is characterized by the fact that the exchange value with which it ends is larger than that with which it begins (M-C-M'). This self-expanding value depends upon the capitalist's appropriation of the productive power of labor. Capital must find within the exchange process a commodity whose use value is the creation of surplus value, and labor power is just such a commodity. In the consumption of labor power's use value, capital is increased.[28]

Workers in capitalist society own their capacity to labor but must sell it as a commodity in the market. And like any other commodity, labor power has both use value and exchange value. As a commodity it is equalized or homogenized through the exchange process; and it is consumed outside of exchange in the industrial production of the factory. When the capitalist buys labor power at its exchange value and realizes its use value in production, surplus value is created. The creative capacity of labor, its use value as "world-creation," is ceded to the capitalist; the worker is exploited in the process of production, not in the exchange process.

Marx shows that the rate of surplus value is the rate of capitalist exploitation and then expands his analysis by making a distinction between absolute and relative surplus value. The rate of surplus value depends on two factors: the length of the working day and the productivity of labor. The surplus value realized as a consequence of the lengthening of the working day Marx calls absolute surplus value; it has finite limits set by human endurance and the struggles of the working class to decrease mandatory work hours. Therefore, the capitalist class must focus on revolutionizing technology in order to increase surplus value. The surplus value realized from technological innovations is relative surplus value; it has no set limits and creates the working-class struggle over the intensity of production.

Technological development increases both the productivity of the working class and capitalist accumulation. The result is a tendency toward centralization or monopoly capitalism and periods of economic crises of overproduction. This in turn creates unemployment, which generates and maintains an "industrial reserve army." For Marx the regressive tendencies of capitalism are offset by the socialization of labor, which creates the preconditions for liberation. Workers cooperate in the process of production as each worker performs a concrete form of labor for the capitalist. But labor is not *directly* social in capitalist society as it is in precapitalist societies where direct domination and traditional hierarchies create and maintain the social division of labor. Rather, the enforced cooperation of labor in capitalism is established through abstract domination in which labor power as a commodity is exchanged in the market. Capitalism initiates a universalization of society through the equalization of abstract labor; it establishes an abstract equality between workers as each performs private, individual labor within the social production process. The contradiction between the ever-increasing socialization of production and the exploitation of workers motivates the workers to transform their involuntary cooperation into a free association in which "the free development of each" will be the condition for "the free development of all."[29]

For Marx, the social relations of capitalism are to be overcome but the productive powers of capitalism are to be retained. The working class is to put the productive capacity of society, as well as its accumulated wealth, at the service of the entire society. In the third volume of *Capital* Marx writes that the realization of freedom will follow from "socialized [human beings], the associated producers, rationally regulating their interchange with Nature, bringing it under their common control, instead of being ruled by it as by the blind forces of Nature."[30]

Marx's formulation of the liberatory potential of labor first occurs within the context of an examination of Hegel's philosophy. While Marx maintains the Hegelian thesis that the transformation of nature through objectification creates history, there is, as we have seen, a shift in the paradigm of labor. In Hegel's master-slave dialectic the process of objectification provides the slave not with a relation to other slaves but with a relation to nature, through which he may achieve independence from the master, if only as an interior reality. Marx's concern is not with the processes of human consciousness per se but with human exploitation. He therefore ties intersubjectivity and the relation to nature to the capitalist relations of production: the factory becomes the means to the goal of true intersubjectivity. Here the need for the Other is found in the human association of workers mediated by the process of objectification. Not consciousness as such but the laboring process as conscious activity makes us human. Labor becomes not only a response to necessity but cooperative creation through which human beings can organize their relations with nature and with each other for freedom.

While there are many difficult problems raised by Marx's project, what is central to our concern with woman's liberation is the formulations of the dialectic in Marx. We shall therefore consider his dialectical development in order to explain its significance for Marx's understanding of "the woman question."

DIALECTICAL DISCONTINUITY

Initially Marx held to a dialectical conception of the relation between nature and history that Alfred Schmidt characterizes as "the mutual interpenetration of nature and society within the natural whole."[31]

Here Marx focuses on the overcoming of alienation within communism that "humanizes" nature as it "naturalizes" humanity: "Communism as completed naturalism is humanism, as completed humanism it is naturalism. It is the *genuine* resolution of the antagonism between man and nature and between man and man"; "thus [communist] *society* is the completed, essential unity of man with nature, the true resurrection of nature, the fulfilled naturalism of man and humanism of nature."[32] Here the schism between nature and society, the "riddle of history," is to be healed in communism in such a way that nature is "resurrected." From the dialectical contradiction between the forces and relations of production there results a double resolution: a resolution of the class conflict *within* society and a resolution of the antagonism *between* society and nature. In this formulation nature is an independent moment of the dialectic that is resolved in a unity or identity-in-difference of nature and human society.

The process of objectification performed "in freedom" and "according to the laws of beauty," does not dominate nature but aids nature to realize itself: "The animal ... produces in a one-sided way while man produces universally. . . . The animal builds only according to the standard and need of the species to which it belongs while man knows how to produce according to the standard of any species and at all times knows how to apply *an intrinsic standard to the object*. Thus man creates also according to the laws of beauty."[33] In communism the new relation between society and nature and the new relation between human beings entails "the complete emancipation of all human senses and qualities."[34] Communist humanity enjoys the world it creates; it experiences the emergence and satisfaction of truly human needs. The primary human need, the need for the Other, is both a "natural" and social need whose paradigm is the relation between man and woman.

This initial formulation of the dialectic in the 1844 *Manuscripts* was developed through Marx's critique of Hegel and Feuerbach. With the development of his critique of political economy his concern with the "elemental" dialectic of nature and history within the natural whole is transformed. He comes to believe that only in precapitalist societies is the relation between nature and history embedded in nature; in capitalism this relation becomes part of "socio-historical creation."[35] History becomes the dominant moment of the dialectic as nature becomes an object of mere utility, the "stuff" or matter upon which humans labor. The transformation of nature becomes more and more an "appropriation" of nature that culminates in the hubris of domination.[36] In the *Grundrisse* Marx sees the domination of nature as part of "the great civilizing influence" of capitalism:

> Thus capital creates the bourgeois society, and the universal appropriation of nature as well as of the social bond itself by the members of society. Hence the great civilizing influence of capital; its production of a stage of society in comparison to which all earlier ones appear as mere *local developments* of humanity and as *nature-idolatry*. For the first time, *nature becomes purely an object for humankind, purely a matter of utility*; ceases to be recognized as a power for itself; and the theoretical discovery of its autonomous laws appears merely as a ruse so as to subjugate it under human needs, whether as an object of consumption or as a means of production.[37]

Production and consumption in civil society require the domination of nature and this domination entails the overcoming of all "natural" relations by social relations. Marx considers this overcoming of our embeddedness in nature a precondition for freedom. He believes, as we have seen, that the secret of capitalism is the social character of abstract labor. This is contrasted with the precapitalist division of labor in which the social character of labor is manifested in "natural" (that is, familial, patriarchal, tribal) divisions of labor. There, the individual relates to society as a functional and "naturally" determined and sub-ordinate part; relations between individuals result from their relations to the whole within a hierarchical structure in which domination occurs in a direct form. With the development of labor power as a commodity society no longer retains a "natural" division of labor, and it becomes possible for humanity to con-sciously control its destiny. The process of capitalist commodity production offers the workers a relation to each other through which they may achieve freedom not only from the capitalists but from nature as well.

Marx emphasizes that the domination of nature in industrial production will continue in socialist society and will in fact be-come an even more determining feature of the production proc-esses, because socialism is to be a society of wealth, not scarcity, and nature does not spontaneously provide this social wealth. There will be a total automation of industrial production through which the worker's role will be transformed:

> Labour no longer appears so much to be included within the pro-ductive process; rather, the human being comes to relate more as watchman and regulator to the production process itself....No longer does the worker insert a modified natural thing as middle link between the object and himself; rather, *he inserts the process of nature, transformed into an industrial process, as a means between himself and inorganic nature, mastering it.* He steps to the side of the production process instead of being its chief actor. In this trans-formation, it is neither the direct human labor he himself performs, nor the time during which he works, but rather the appropriation of his own general productive power, his understanding of nature and his mastery over it by virtue of his presence as a social body—it is, in a word, the development of the social individual which appears as the great foundation-stone of production and wealth.[38]

In this formulation there is a *qualitatively different relationship* between nature and human society than that found within Marx's earlier writings. Nature has become merely an object to be dominated through ever-increasing technological innovations and with an ever-decreasing expenditure of labor and time: na-ture is only to serve humanity as the material substance for the creation of objects for consumption. Here Marx is primarily concerned with nature as it is implicated in the productive apparatus. This apparatus distorts the processes of nature by incorporating them into the machinery of production, which is directed by scientific and technological rationality. By combining the forces of nature with the machinery of production labor becomes extraordinarily productive.[39] The quantitative increase in the domination of nature—which entails the quantitative reduction in labor time—culminates in the qualitative change from an unfree to a free society. But here Marx assumes what it is necessary to prove: that the quantitative increase in the domination of nature *necessarily* results in freedom. He does not consider problematic the qualitatively different relation *to* nature, now merely the "stuff" of domination.

Within this revised formulation of the dialectic of nature and history, history becomes a "dominant moment," and nature as an independent moment of the dialectic is lost. Even if one concedes that the moment of history is central to the dialectical process, there can be no dominant moment. In Hegelian terms this is an "abstract negation" wherein nature, as the necessary opposite of history, no longer maintains an independent identity—nature and history do not form a unity in which there is an identity-in-difference.[40] In the same way that Hegel's understanding of the dialectical process becomes a philosophy of identity in which the particular as Other is dominated by the universal, Marx's formulation of the relation between nature and history becomes a theory of identity in which nature as Other is dominated by the human subject. Adorno sums this up in *Negative Dialectics*: Marx "underwrote something as archbourgeois as the program of an absolute control of nature. What is felt here is the effort to take things unlike the subject and make them like the subject—the real model of the principle of identity, which dialectical materialism disavows as such."[41]

Marx attempts to retain a dialectic within his focus on the domination of nature by distinguishing two interrelated aspects of human labor. On the one hand, he says, we are natural beings and our capacity for labor is itself part of nature's energy; on the other hand, as we labor we ourselves are changed, new needs develop, and we transform nature in order to satisfy these needs:

> [Man] opposes himself to Nature as one of her own forces, setting in motion arms and legs, head and hands, the natural forces of his body, in order to appropriate Nature's productions in a form adapted to his own wants. By thus acting on the external world and changing it, he at the same time changes his own nature. He develops his slumbering powers and compels them to act in obedience to his sway.[42]

Here the emphasis falls on the way in which the manipulation of external nature entails the development of humanity's creative capacities, our internal nature. The domination of both external and internal nature is seen as progressive.

Earlier Marx had acknowledged that negative consequences result from our domination of nature: mastery or domination of nature is simultaneously a subjection *to* nature. In 1856 he writes: "At the same pace that mankind masters nature, man seems to become enslaved to other men or to his own infamy. ... All our invention and progress seem to result in endowing material forces with intellectual life, and in stultifying human life into a material force."[43] Marx contends, however, that the domination of nature entails social and self-domination because this domination takes place within a society characterized by class conflict. The domination of nature under capitalism does not take place in freedom. It is not a spontaneous relation to nature but one compelled by conflicting class interests. In a socialist society the domination of nature will not entail social and self-domination because this domination will serve the aims of human liberation, not class interests. But this dialectical understanding is still an abstract negation. Nature as immediately given facticity, apart from human nature, is not necessarily realized in our creation in freedom as it was in the early formulation of the dialectic. Rather, nonhuman nature is to be so completely mastered that it will simply become part of our conscious and rational control of production, and as such it will not be able to rebound in social and self-domination.

Within this attempt to retain a dialectical analysis based on labor the unresolved problem of the double dialectic, the dialectic within society and the dialectic between society and nature, emerges in Marx's conception of human freedom. That is, there are two formulations of freedom rooted in his dialectical development: a conception of freedom *in* labor and a conception of freedom *from* labor. Although in emphasis these two formulations correspond to Marx's early and later writings, both forms remain unreconciled throughout his work.[44]

The Hegelian understanding of labor as self-formation informs and pervades Marx's early work, and it leads to the vision of freedom in which humanity's relation to nature will be such that within the process of objectification the individual will become many-sided and universal. Here freedom is the realization of the creativity of labor in the "all-round development" of the individual's capacities *in* labor. Thus, in *The German Ideology* we read:

> In communist society, where nobody has one exclusive sphere of activity but each can become accomplished in any branch he wishes, society regulates the general production and thus makes it possible for me to do one thing today and another tomorrow, to hunt in the morning, fish in the afternoon, rear cattle in the evening, criticise after dinner, just as I have a mind, without ever becoming hunter, fisherman, shepherd, or critic.[45]

However, a parallel passage in *Capital* on "the fully developed individual, fit for a variety of labours, ready to face any change of production, and to whom the different social functions he performs, are but so many modes of giving free scope to his own natural and acquired powers" is only a pale reflection of *The German Ideology*'s description of communism's triumph over the division of labor.[46]

Hunting, fishing, and herding are all labors of precapitalist societies (and assumed to be male occupations). The change in Marx's understanding of the radical differences between precapitalist and capitalist societies makes these examples clearly inappropriate to a socialist society built on the technological advances of capitalism. It is difficult to reconcile the "all-round development" of the individual with the description of labor as supervising automated machinery. Performing many different, specialized, and isolated tasks within the production process as a "watchman or overseer" hardly constitutes all-round development in labor. What we find instead in the *Grundrisse* and *Capital* is an emphasis on freedom from labor.[47]

Marx describes the decrease in labor under socialism as the precondition for "the free development of individualities": "The general reduction of the necessary labour of society to a minimum ... corresponds to the artistic, scientific etc. development of the individuals in the time set free, and with the means created, for all of them."[48] In the historical advance achieved by capitalism's domination of nature socialized labor triumphs over scarcity, a conquest that enables humanity to transform society and enjoy freedom outside the realm of labor.[49] Social wealth lays the foundation for a free society in which "necessary labour time will be measured by the needs of the social individual" and "*disposable time* will grow for all."[50]

The production of wealth in capitalism and socialism requires that nature be dominated and incorporated into the production process in order to free the worker from labor. Nature is therefore no longer an independent moment of the dialectic, and with this abstract negation of nature comes a dialectical discontinuity in Marx. The concept of the domination of nature as necessary for the production of wealth conflicts with the concept of nature as an independent moment of the dialectic that culminates in the "all-round development" of individuals. Both the realization of the self in necessary labor and the realization of the self outside of necessary labor depend on the transformation of nature to overcome scarcity. But whereas freedom *in* labor is also the realization of nature in the original formulation of the dialectic, in Marx's understanding of freedom *from* labor nature is not realized but dominated.

An emancipatory theory must rescue nature as an independent moment of the dialectic. A dialectic of non-identity, the process by which we know historicized nature, must have a conception of nature as something more than the raw material for human domination or an abstract Otherness with an "eternal essence." To see nature as merely the material for domination is to move away from a dialectical analysis to an identity theory that denies difference, while to view nature as an abstract Other is to fall into romantic idealism.[51]

The relation between nature and history takes on particular significance when we recognize that woman's biological difference has been used to justify her subordination within the social structure. Thus, a consideration of the place of nature within Marx's dialectical analysis is central to an understanding of his approach to "the woman question."

> Dialectical movement is the co-existence of two contradictory sides, their conflict and fusion in a new category. Merely to formulate the problem of eliminating the bad side is to cut short the dialectical movement.
>
> KARL MARX, *The Poverty of Philosophy*

MARX AND WOMAN'S LIBERATION

An analysis of the woman question must begin with the family because it is here that woman's oppression begins. We must examine how love, sexuality, biological reproduction, domestic labor, ego development or individuality, waged labor, and property are to be understood in a patriarchal-capitalist society. Within the analysis of the family we must compare the working-class and the bourgeois family and distinguish the family of origin—the family into which we are born—from the family of procreation, the family we create through marriage or commitment. But an analysis of "the family" often obscures the *woman* question. If, as Marx says, the turning of the subject into the predicate requires a revolutionary turn through the application of the transformative method, then for any "revolution" to have meaning for woman she must emerge as the subject, making the family part of the predicate of her existence.

Since woman does not describe a class or a caste but a sex, the project of understanding her unique and specific oppression must go beyond the exploitation and socialization of labor in civil society to consider the direct man-woman relation, the formation of woman's psyche within the family of origin, and woman's reproductive and domestic labor in the family of procreation. While neither the family nor woman's domination can be understood apart from an analysis of capitalism in its present form, the categories of political economy are the categories of civil society and cannot simply or strictly be applied to the sphere of the family. The family has its own specific logic, and the unique relations of this sphere do not simply mirror the relations of production. Since woman's domination and her role within the family are fundamentally conditioned by her reproductive potential, we must investigate how this potential is mediated through the social matrix. Biological "obviousness" must be revealed as the foundation of male domination.[52] The unique role of biology in woman's oppression requires that we understand and retain a dialectical analysis of the relation between nature and history for an analysis of "the woman question" to have significant explanatory power.

In his *Economic and Philosophic Manuscripts of 1844*, as we have seen, Marx attempts to formulate nature as an independent moment of the dialectic within a natural whole to be realized in communism. In communism a new relation between human beings and between human society and nature will be established; the paradigmatic form of this new relation between humans and nature is the relation between man and woman. Marx condemns both bourgeois marriage and the "community of women" proposed by crude communism: bourgeois marriage is rooted in private property and the communal sharing of women is rooted in an atavistic form of communism. Both these forms of the man-woman relation entail the domination of woman, as the servant of man's property needs and/or the prey of his lustful desires. But in his domination of woman man reveals his own "infinite degradation."[53] In *The Holy Family* (1844) Marx quotes Fourier's assertion that "nobody is punished more for keeping woman a slave than man himself."[54] Here, however, woman's domination is more of a problem for man than it is for woman.

Marx claims that the man-woman relation reveals the extent to which our merely natural needs have become truly human:

> The immediate, natural, necessary relationship of human being to human being is the *relationship of man to woman*.... From this relationship one can thus judge the entire level of mankind's development. From the character of this relationship follows the extent to which *man* has become and comprehended himself as a *generic being*, as *man*; *the relationship of man to woman is the most natural relationship of human being to human being*. It thus indicates the extent to which man's *natural* behavior has become *human* or the extent to which his *human* essence has become a *natural* essence for him, the extent to which his *human nature* has become *nature* to him. In this relationship is also apparent the extent to which man's *need* has become *human*, thus the extent to which the *other* human being, as human being, has become a need for him, the extent to which he in his most individual existence is at the same time a social being.[55]

In the relation between man and woman our sexual needs are "immediate, natural and necessary." But if the relationship remains at the level of animal need it is not truly human, not a free expression of intersubjective mutuality. For Marx a response to mere need is an animal response, not a human one. When men prey on women to fulfill their sexual needs or marry them to acquire male heirs, when women have no choice but to sell themselves as instruments of reproduction, as sexual commodities, in exchange for financial security—these are not truly human relationships. They are relations of sexual intercourse trapped in the realm of necessity, the realm of the merely natural/animal. But Marx believes that it is possible to realize freedom through the transformation of sexual need. When men and women come together conscious of their sexual need as a need for the Other, a need for another human being, then they are confirmed as both natural and social beings. The degree to which we can create a society that grounds our sexual and procreative behavior in a free expression of mutuality is the degree to which

we have progressed from the realm of merely natural necessity
to the realm of freedom. Man and woman must recognize each
other as persons, as free individuals. Thus, the monogamous
heterosexual love relation becomes for Marx the paradigmatic
form of intersubjectivity in which nature and history are reconciled.[56] But here Marx accepts a conception of woman as
someone who does not *act* but simply *is*. Woman is seen only
in relation to man—she is not an active historical agent.

The man-woman paradigm is not carefully analyzed or developed in Marx's work. As he shifts to a concentration on the
critique of political economy as the science of civil society his
concern with woman changes. He moves away from a consideration of the direct man-woman relation to an analysis of the
bourgeois family in terms of private property and the ideology
of love and then to a comparison of the working-class and the
bourgeois family in terms of the social relations of production.

Marx identifies "three aspects of social activity": "the production of material life," "the production of new needs," and
human biological reproduction.[57] All three are social insofar as
they are cooperative, purposeful, and conscious activities. Here
biological reproduction is seen as a unique social activity as well
as a "natural" one and is initially determined by its own specific
social relations and material conditions:

> The production of life, of one's own life in labor and of another in
> procreation, now appears as a double relationship: on the one hand
> as a natural relationship, on the other as a social one. The latter is
> social in the sense that individuals co-operate, no matter under what
> conditions, in what manner, and for what purpose.[58]

But as human society moves out of its embeddedness in nature,
the family, as the sphere of reproductive relations, is subsumed
within the larger social structure: "The family, initially the only
social relationship, becomes later a subordinate relationship...
when increased needs produce new social relations and an increased population creates new needs."[59] The social relations
of reproduction are seen finally as reflecting the social relations
of production, and the specific logic of the family is explicitly denied

in the analysis of the development from a precapitalist to a capitalist society. Marx's discussion of the family reflects the change in his thinking on nature—whereas he once posited nature as an independent moment of the dialectic, Marx comes finally to an abstract negation of nature.

In *The German Ideology* we are told that one cannot analyze the family according to "the concept of the family"; such a treatment obscures historical development in general and the reality of class differences in particular. As we have seen, Marx shows the Hegelian concept of the family as an abstraction that perpetuates and generalizes a particular form of the family: Hegel assumes the bourgeois patriarchal family as the universal family. Marx makes a distinction between the ideological appearance of the bourgeois family and its material reality; the bourgeois family is not "immediate" as Hegel claims but is, in fact, mediated by the concerns of civil society. The reality of the bourgeois family is conditioned, like all facets of life in a capitalist economy, by the sphere of commodity production. Economic concerns regulate the choice of a marriage partner (usually made by the father), the creation and socialization of children, and the "spiritual" values that govern the everyday life of cohabitation.[60] The bourgeois form of monogamy, based on private property, distorts and corrupts the love relation between man and woman and turns love into ideology. Marx sums this up in his statement that "[in] its highest development the *principle of private property contradicts* the *principle of the family*," which Hegel has taken to be love.[61]

In *The Communist Manifesto* (1848) Marx and Engels characterize the apparent self-destruction of the bourgeois family and contrast it to the real disintegration of the working-class family. They point to signs of the disintegration of bourgeois monogamy—the "private prostitution" of adultery (the secret "community of women") and public prostitution.[62] The bourgeois wife is revealed as an object, "a mere instrument of production" whose reproductive capacity is used to serve property interests. She is to bear and rear sons so that the family property will remain intact. While the bourgeoisie has "torn away from the

family its sentimental veil and has reduced the family relation
to a mere money relation," this inauthentic existence of the family is masked by the "holy concept of [the family] in official
phraseology and universal hypocrisy."[63] The bourgeoisie maintains this ideology because property, marriage, and the family
are linked together and are "the practical basis on which the
bourgeoisie has erected its domination." The bourgeois family
lives on because it "is made necessary by its connection with the
mode of production, which exists independently of the will of
bourgeois society."[64] Thus the disintegration of the bourgeois
family is only an apparent one. But capitalism leads to a real
disintegration of the family—"the practical absence of the
family"—among the proletariat: "The bourgeois claptrap about
the family and education, about the hallowed relationship between parent and child, becomes all the more disgusting, the
more that, as a result of modern industry, all family ties among
the proletarians are torn asunder and their children transformed
into simple articles of commerce and instruments of labor."[65]
The working-class family, as it provides the necessary labor
power for the system, is being destroyed.

With the subordination of the family to the sphere of civil
society the working-class woman is integrated into production.
Despite the initially murderous conditions of capitalist factory
life, Marx sees the entrance of woman into the realm of production as providing the preconditions for her liberation. Woman
is not to remain confined to the family, as in Hegel, but must
move into civil society in order to achieve freedom. She must
become a member of the community of producers. The historical
development of capitalism that entails the destruction of the
traditional family is progressive. The practical absence of the
family among the proletariat first noted in The Communist Manifesto is developed in Capital, where the disintegration of the
traditional working-class family is shown in a dialectical relation
to the possibility of creating a new and higher form of the family
and the relations between the sexes.

As the working-class woman moves out of the traditional
family into the factory she too must sell her labor power as a

commodity, and thus she participates in the ever-increasing socialization of production. The abstract equality between men and women workers in the sphere of production will transform the relations between the sexes outside of production:

> However terrible and disgusting the dissolution, under the capitalist system, of the old family ties may appear, nevertheless, modern industry, by assigning as it does an important part in the process of production, *outside the domestic sphere*, to women, to young persons, and to children of both sexes, creates a new economic foundation for a higher form of the family and of the relations between the sexes.[66]

Whereas "nature" created the first division of labor between the sexes in terms of procreation, and thereby created the initial inequality between men and women on which male domination is based, as human society develops beyond its embeddedness in nature it becomes possible to overcome patriarchal domination. The abstract equality between working-class men and women provides the basis for the abolition of capitalism and the abolition of male domination. Love as ideology will disappear in the realization of true monogamy in a free society. The family will change into a "higher form" in which the relations between the sexes and between parents and children will no longer maintain patriarchal domination. Thus *Capital* envisions the end to male domination through the abstract equality of men and women in commodity production.

In an 1868 letter to a friend Marx reveals his transformed understanding of woman's position in relation to social development: "Anybody who knows anything of history knows that great social changes are impossible without the feminine ferment. Social progress can be measured exactly by the social position of the fair sex (the ugly ones included)."[67] Leaving aside the misogyny of the parenthetical comment, we find here that woman is no longer seen primarily in terms of the heterosexual love relation but in terms of her own social standing. The position of woman *in society*, not her relation to man, reveals the extent of social progress. And the direct relation between man and woman depends on their relation within the process of production.

As the domination of nature through labor in civil society becomes the key to the understanding of history Marx transforms his concern with the intersubjective heterosexual love relationship in terms of the recognition of the Other (a relationship unmediated by a process of objectification) to a concentration on the intersubjective relations in civil society mediated by a process of objectification. True individuality as true intersubjectivity is to be found in relations mediated by the process of objectification. As I work (dominate nature), I find myself in another who is also working (dominating nature). In his later works Marx sees the domination of nature as progressive and thinks the dislocation of nature by capitalism will be transformed when that dislocation takes place under conscious human control in a free society. But the way to that free society is through the domination of nature, and the free society retains that domination. For Marx, critical consciousness comes from the experience of exploitation and the socialization of labor that accompanies the domination of nature. Woman's integration into this process provides the necessary conditions for her emancipation. That is, as woman enters the realm of the domination of nature she enters the realm of abstract economic equality where "universal individuality" may be realized.

Abandoning Hegel's tripartite structure of family, civil society, and state, Marx concentrates on civil society. He rejects Hegel's account of this sphere and transforms the Hegelian concern with consciousness as the recognition of the Other into a concern with the labor process as conscious activity; nevertheless, he retains the Hegelian understanding of ego development in that one must move out of the family to achieve true individuality as intersubjectivity. The position of the working class as "in but not of" civil society means that workers have the potential to realize themselves as universal individuals because they are in the sphere where true individuality is possible. Since individuality is achieved *outside* the family in the realm of waged labor, woman must move into civil society to gain a self-conscious identity. While this move is not sufficient (since Marx believes that civil society must ultimately be abolished as a separate sphere in the realization of communism) it is nevertheless *necessary*.

Woman is to move out of the family to gain her freedom, but her attempt to realize her individuality in civil society presents us with the same problem that we encountered earlier, the problem of freedom *in* labor versus freedom *from* labor. Moreover, if one extrapolates from Marx's position one can arrive at a form of technological determinism such as that articulated by Shulamith Firestone. Such a view sees woman's "revolution" as the abstract negation of her biology: the specificity of woman's unique relation to nature in reproduction is to be denied. The concept of freedom from reproductive labor, which is to be achieved through the development of artificial wombs and in vitro fertilization, is rooted in the concept of freedom from productive labor through the domination of nature.[68]

Marx exposes competitive or possessive individualism as historically specific to capitalism, but he has no fully developed model of ego development or individuality that recognizes the importance of the family in the formation of the psyche. That is, individuality as intersubjectivity is located within civil society between strangers and not within the family. This account of individuality as true intersubjectivity is central to Marx's "solution" to the woman question.

We have seen two forms of intersubjective relations in our analysis of Marx's project. The first is the direct relationship between man and woman outside the sphere of production in his early formulation of the dialectic in the *Economic and Philosophic Manuscripts*. The second is the relation between workers in the sphere of production as they dominate nature. These forms differ in that the relations of production are mediated by a process of objectification (subject–object–subject) whereas the early man-woman relation is a direct relation (subject-subject). Even if the Other is seen *as* an object in the direct man-woman relation it is not a relation mediated by a process of object creating in the way the production relation is. Unlike Hegel, Marx does not see the necessity for a child to mediate, or be the objectification of, the man-woman relation. (Indeed, if anything, the birth of a child creates a third form (subject–subject–subject) in which the child as the middle subject is not an equal Other.) Marx does not attempt to ground the relations of his early subject-subject form of intersubjectivity in a theory of social change. Rather, he moves away from the dialectic of nature and history that this relation represents. In his mature formulation what is at issue is the "necessary appearance" of the subject–object–subject relation as an object–subject–object relation in commodity fetishism.

From her participation in the labor process as a process of objectification (S-O-S) woman is to achieve equality with man in their direct relation (S-S) and all familial relations are to be transformed. This assumption of the dependence of the direct intersubjective relation on the relation of intersubjectivity mediated by the object contradicts Marx's own insight that each specific subject requires its own specific logic. The direct man-woman relation (S-S) and familial relations have their own specific logic based on human biological reproduction (S-s-S) in which patriarchal domination prevails over woman's reproductive potential and the development of her psyche within the family. While these relations are mediated by the social matrix, the sexual oppression of woman is qualitatively different from class exploitation.

The emphasis on the intersubjective relations of civil society, in which the social relations of production determine the social relations of the family, means that Marx cannot explain the way in which, in a patriarchal-capitalist society, we not only are dominated by others but suffer from self-domination. That is, Marx's analysis cannot explain the way in which domination is reproduced in self-consciousness. In order to understand how the domination of external nature entails the domination of internal nature we need to examine the development of the psyche within the family.

In summary, the failure in Marx's dialectical analyses of nature and history affects his approach to the woman question on several levels. In his early thought nature is an independent moment of the dialectic but woman is not seen as an historical actor. She is only an index of social domination and social progress. However, as Marx moves away from nature as an independent moment of the dialectic he shifts from a concern with the man-woman relation as a direct relation (S-S) to an analysis of the abstract equality between men and women in the sphere of production where nature is dominated (S-O-S). This later analysis ignores both the direct and abstract forms of patriarchy that have prevented woman from realizing equality in civil society. Here, Marx conflates woman's sexual oppression with class exploitation. And in his move away from Hegel's tripartite structure, Marx denies the specific logic of the family, as well as the specific logic of political life. He fails to mention, much less analyze, the way in which woman has come to represent nature as an abstract Other in patriarchal society and is, like nature, dominated as this Other. The transformation of Marx's analysis with its focus on civil society and the abstract negation of nature means that Marx cannot ask, much less "answer," the questions raised by the woman's movement concerning human sexuality, reproductive and domestic labor in the family of procreation, and the development of the female psyche within the family of origin.

Thus, neither of Marx's dialectical formulations is adequate for understanding woman's domination. Any attempt to frame an analysis of woman's liberation based on Marx's early work presents us with serious problems: while the "elemental" dialectic retains nature as an independent moment there is no developed concept of woman as an active historical being in this dialectic. The later formulation of the domination of nature sees woman as a historical agent but entails a technological determinism and the denial of the specificity of the man-woman relation. Both formulations accept the thesis that ego development or individuality develops within civil society between strangers, not in the family.

We cannot focus on an isolated comment in Marx's work where he explicitly refers to woman, nor can we extract concepts such as alienation or the labor theory of value from the context of his project and "apply" them to woman's situation.[69] Our primary task is to retain a dialectical analysis of nature and history that allows us to address the woman question in terms that reflect woman's unique biological potential and her unique history. A dialectic is not a dualism, as Marx so carefully articulated in *The Poverty of Philosophy*. Unfortunately, Marx seems to have forgotten this point in his later work where nature as the "bad side" of necessity is eliminated as an independent moment. We must reexamine the way in which the domination of nature entails social and self-domination. We must analyze how, from the dislocation of the present, we may maintain a dialectical understanding that will take us beyond the view of nature as merely the material for domination and yet not fall into a romantic idealization of nature.

PART II

Authority and the Family
in Critical Theory

CHAPTER THREE

Psyche and Society

THE CONCERN WITH THE SPECIFIC LOGIC OF THE FAMILY AND the necessity to rethink the dialectic of nature and history are central to an analysis of woman's domination. These issues are also central to the critical theory of Marcuse, Horkheimer, and Adorno. In their studies on authority and the family they focus on the family as the sphere in which the psyche is formed, and they attempt to resuscitate nature as an independent moment of the dialectic.

Since Marx's analysis cannot explain the way in which domination is reproduced in self-consciousness, these theorists turn to an examination of the non-identical in Freud's theory of the phylogenetic and ontogenetic development of humanity to explicate social and self-domination. They focus on the relation of ego to id and the way in which the libido theory reveals a fundamental contradiction between civilization (the reality principle) and gratification (the pleasure principle). Freud's theory of the libidinal base of human development implies that there is a level of our existence beyond immediate social domination that prevents a premature reconciliation of the conflict between psyche and society. Through a critical appropriation of Freud's theory these theorists integrate sexual repression into a Marxist critique of the necessity to labor in capitalist society. The necessity to labor elicits "a repressive organization of the instincts."[1] This project entails a reconceptualization of self-consciousness and a redefinition of "second nature": "second nature" is widened to include the psyche and is not confined to self-conscious political activity as in Hegel or self-conscious labor as in Marx.

We must begin with the general theoretical project of these critical theorists before examining what they say about woman's domination. Only in this way can we establish both the importance and the limits of this critical tradition for an analysis of the woman question. The schematic form of this synopsis will necessarily blur the differences among the three thinkers. I will clarify these differences with a more comprehensive examination of the conceptual framework of each thinker in part 3.

THE CRITICAL THEORY OF THE FRANKFURT SCHOOL

Initially, Marcuse, Horkheimer, and Adorno, as members of the Frankfurt school, attempt to adapt the Marxist framework to account theoretically for German fascism, anti-Semitism, and the destructive authoritarian character of twentieth-century society.[2] They do not appropriate Marxism as a closed theory of orthodox truth but believe that as concrete social reality changes Marxist theory must become self-reflective. They attempt to make Marx's theory adequate to the task Marx set for it as the "head" of the revolution in which the working class or proletariat is the "heart." Marx's critique of political economy as a critique of exchange society is central to their project: they see economic exploitation as the truth behind the appearance of equal exchange. However, within their analysis of fascism and the historical development of capitalism from its liberal to its authoritarian and totalitarian forms, they find Marx's epistemological assumption that all superstructural spheres simply mirror the autonomously developing economic substructure to be inadequate: Marx lacks a theory of the psyche that mediates between base and superstructure and he denies the specificity of various spheres of everyday life. The Frankfurt school therefore examines the specific logic of such spheres as the family, the state, and culture in order to develop a more comprehensive analysis of the relation between the economic substructure, the superstructure, and the individual psyche.[3]

Freud's theory of the individual becomes important in their attempt to explain how individuals internalize prevailing forms of domination through the reproduction of repression in the psyche. They expound the social psychology of fascism and late monopoly capitalism in terms of psychocultural regression as well as economic exploitation. As they develop their analysis of contemporary society they transform the thrust of critical theory from a critique of economic exploitation to a critique of domination. In their search for a basis for social relations free from domination, the domination of nature becomes a central theme: they attempt to resuscitate nature as an independent moment of the dialectic.

Within their conceptual frameworks Marcuse, Horkheimer, and Adorno theorize a historicized nature that is rooted in thought and knows itself to be thought. They hold that the domination of nature has been an important and necessary part of the development of the individual ego and human reason. But as nature comes to be viewed as *nothing but* the material for human domination, we come to see ourselves as "the measure of all things," and thus we lose our awareness of ourselves as part of nature. As a consequence we become blind to our true goals, those which will lead to self-realization and liberation.[4] More important, the denigration of nature leads to barbarism in the twentieth century with "the revolt of nature" that characterizes fascism.

In fascism "civilization" becomes "the victory of society over nature which changes everything into mere nature."[5] The Nazi ideology with its cry for a return to "blood and soil" is a turn toward the irrational, a return to mere particularity, mere nature. With the triumph of fascism history becomes nature, ego becomes id, and neither community nor individuality can be realized.[6] Fascism was first seen as a logical development of capitalism. That is, capitalism creates the preconditions for fascism, but when fascism emerges there is a qualitative, regressive transformation of society. Later, fascism was seen as only one form of the authoritarian state and not necessarily the most significant form.[7] Marcuse, Horkheimer, and Adorno turned their attention to the one-dimensional character of North American society; they described the decline of the autonomous subject and the development of the authoritarian personality within mass society.

Within their critique of the domination of nature the Frankfurt school theorists distinguish the rational mastery of nature from its irrational forms, and they contend that a new and qualitatively different relation between humanity and nature is possible.[8] This twofold formulation contains three interrelated critiques. First is the critique of the view of nature as a means, as the external, wholly alien and inferior Other to be dominated and the consequent loss of nature as an independent moment of the dialectic. Second is a critique of instrumental (formal/subjective) reason, the specific and partial form of reason through which nature is mastered. Reason has been transformed from critical insight into a tool for domination.[9] Discussion on this point expands Marx's analysis of commodity fetishism to show that the form of abstract domination peculiar to contemporary society is the reduction of all activities and relationships into depersonalized, instrumental forms. Finally, there is a critique of what Marcuse calls "the continuum of domination": the domination of external nature entails the domination of internal nature, the instinctual foundation of the psyche. That is, the repression or renunciation necessary for the domination of external nature rebounds on society through social and self-domination.[10]

Critical theory attempts to understand the domination of nature in terms of identity formation and intersubjectivity through an analysis of the family. Theorists see the decline of the family as central to the development of the authoritarian personality, a personality incapable of autonomy and necessary for a society based on instrumental rationality. As the father becomes an employee instead of an entrepreneur, and as the mother moves into civil society to become an employee, the socialization of the child changes. Professional "experts" on child care, mass culture, the schools, and state institutions all directly affect the formation of the psyche. There is a loss of conscience, consistency, and love, and a strong ego is not formed. The possibility of the individual judging and perhaps opposing our present society is lost. The result is a society of heteronomous individuals who experience intersubjectivity and intrasubjectivity as domination.[11]

The continuum of domination precludes the revolutionary break predicted by Marx. The development of capitalism with its eclipse of liberalism integrates the working class into mass society. The proletariat is no longer the "subject-object" of history whose interest is universal emancipation. The emergence of the authoritarian mass society creates a closed, one-dimensional, administered society. As reason is reduced to a tool for dominating nature, the corresponding loss of critical insight destroys autonomous subjectivity and therefore the revolutionary potential of those who are to achieve liberation through the transformation of nature.[12] While Marcuse is inclined to retain labor as the ground of self-realization, Horkheimer and Adorno eventually reject Marx's view of labor as the necessary source of liberation.

In the excursus on Odysseus in the *Dialectic of Enlightenment* Horkheimer and Adorno retell the encounter with the Sirens in terms of the master-slave dialectic. The interweaving of myth and history provides the critical ground for understanding the present by revealing the process of self-domination for both master and slave in the domination of nature. Here, "the servant remains enslaved in body and soul; the master regresses."[13] According to Horkheimer and Adorno, the female voice of the Sirens represents the song of the sensuous world of nature, the song of the pleasure principle. This song threatens the patriarchal-capitalist world order by threatening the male ego with disintegration. It does this by evoking the recent past, the time before the impulses of the id were forced to yield to the demands of the reality principle. In the given world order, the pleasure principle is repressed in the service of subjectivity so that the price paid for male subjectivity is happiness. However, to yield to the Sirens, to yield to the call of the pleasure principle through a self-abandonment to the sensuous, is to return to mere nature, and this return has its own price: the future. To forget oneself in the disintegration of the ego is capitulation, not true happiness or liberation.

Odysseus realizes that he cannot listen freely to the song of nature and sees only two ways of escape: either not to hear the song or to hear it without being free to respond to it. The first solution he prescribes for his men: they are to have their ears plugged with beeswax while they row the boat with all their strength through the dangerous passage past the Sirens. These men represent the slaves or modern workers who learn to survive through sacrifice. They are not allowed to hear the song of temptation rooted in the pleasurable past, not allowed to acknowledge the desire for gratification. Through this process of repression the workers become practical and continue to work but lose their access to freedom.

Odysseus, however, is the master. He therefore constructs a different situation for himself in which he maintains a contractual form of servitude to nature, but, like a good bourgeois, he finds an escape clause in the contract. Odysseus has himself bound to the mast of the boat. In bondage, which precludes his yielding to temptation, he listens to the song. Thus, he abandons himself to nature in such a way as to deny nature's power over him. He yields to nature only to betray it. In a dialectical turn, however, Horkheimer and Adorno show that through this domination of nature Odysseus comes to fear his own death (which prevents his triumph in the struggle for recognition) as he becomes hostile to his own happiness. He saves his life by denying himself fulfillment; in so doing, self-preservation is revealed as intricately bound up with self-denial. As Odysseus listens to the song of the Sirens his temptation to heed its call increases and he struggles to get free. But he himself has instructed his men to ignore his cries, and they respond to his plight by tightening his bonds. They will not free him to realize his desires. Thus what Odysseus hears changes nothing for him; the sacrifice of pleasure is the price of his subjectivity. Odysseus is revealed as the prototype of the bourgeois individual created by the dialectic of Enlightenment: a creature who seeks survival above all else and one who knows only renunciation, self-deception, and meaningless victories.

For Horkheimer and Adorno the story of Odysseus, as a myth of the master-slave dialectic, replaces the Freudian Oedipal drama and the myth of the primal horde. But in their version of this civilizing myth there is no journey through alienation to a happy return or reconciliation. Instead, the desire for reconciliation is revealed as a deception in which the ego's longing for a happy return causes the ego to become lost to its own future possibilities. Against Marcuse's claim in *Eros and Civilization* that a dialectical regression is not only possible but necessary for liberation, Horkheimer and Adorno assert that no dialectical regression is possible: there is only regression to mere nature. At the root of this regression is the separation of thought and action. Odysseus, as the master, has access to the song of the Sirens but cannot act on it; the oarsmen, as slaves/workers, labor without hearing the song of pleasure. Both master and slave are thus rendered impotent.

The Siren episode is a presentient myth of the master-slave dialectic of recognition in the modern world, in which intense forms of repression create instinctual fixation. According to Horkheimer and Adorno, the process of objectification is "performed under pressure, in desperation, with senses stopped by force."[14] This situation precludes the working class from freeing all humanity, as Marx had envisioned. In modern society human beings are yoked together in an industrial rhythm yet cannot speak to one another. The forced collectivity isolates the individual and reduces workers to "mere species-being," that is, each one is exactly like all the others and all are rendered impotent. Under these conditions, workers know only the dangers of the Sirens' song, none of its beauty; thus, the regression of the masses is revealed in their inability to hear the song of the Sirens, the song of the pleasure principle.

Through this excursus Horkheimer and Adorno argue that

the internal logic of the domination of nature does not lead to liberation, as Marx thought, but creates new and unique forms of subjugation in fascism and the technocratic barbarism of mass society: the traditional liberal ideology of freedom, autonomy, and equality is replaced by the demand for technical efficiency, which instrumental reason serves. Initially instrumental reason served the forces of enlightenment by allowing a distancing from the claims of mythical and religious traditions. But it was severed from enlightenment when it was confined to technical spheres and simultaneously became the dominant form of human reason. As a rationality of *means* instrumental reason eliminates the question of *ends*, and in doing so it distorts not only the ends but the means or techniques it uses by exalting them to ends.[15] The Frankfurt school's critique of instrumental reason attempts to counter the corrosive power of this form of reason. It does not attempt to replace instrumental or subjective reason with the "objective" reason of the ancient Greeks or German Idealism. Rather, both forms of reason are shown to have regressive and progressive tendencies. The goal is not to hypostatize one mode of reason over another but "to foster a mutual critique and thus, if possible, to prepare in the intellectual realm the reconciliation of the two in reality."[16]

Horkheimer and Adorno reject identity theory, the theory that latent in social contradictions is an ultimate unity of subject and object, essence and appearance, particular and universal, nature and history. With the rejection of identity theory and the rejection of the working class as the revolutionary class conceived by Marx, they formulate a critique in which liberatory potential is to be found in a changed relation to nature. (Marcuse is more committed to the possibilities of identity theory for social critique and more ambiguous about the role of the working class in revolutionary practice.)[17]

In terms of the changed relation to nature, aesthetic theory as well as psychoanalysis becomes important for critical theory. Autonomous art is thought to be *necessarily* critical. Adorno writes that "art's innermost principle, the utopian principle, re-volts against the principle of definition whose tendency is to dominate nature."[18] Within the development of their dialectical analyses Marcuse, Horkheimer, and Adorno root emancipatory promise in the necessity to remember nature: "By ... remembrance of nature in the subject, in whose fulfillment the unacknowledged truth of all culture lies hidden, enlightenment is universally opposed to domination."[19] While there is no single form of dialectical critique that emerges from the work of these three critical theorists, they all focus on the memory of nature— the memory of nature as suffering or as the utopian promise of freedom. Horkheimer and Adorno lament the missed possibilities of revolutionary change, and nature remembered is embodied finally in religion for Horkheimer and in "genuine" philosophy for Adorno.[20] Marcuse's more utopian outlook keeps him searching for the emancipatory potential in different social groups.

THE SPECIFIC LOGIC OF THE FAMILY

The focus on the specific logic of the family is important in the Frankfurt school's attempt to come to terms with Marx. As we have seen, Marx's critique of Hegel centers on Hegel's explicit principle that one must be immersed in the subject matter of one's analysis in order to let the logic of the material emerge without violation by predetermined thought. Nevertheless, in Hegel's work one continuously encounters the Hegelian logic whose "discovery" is merely a ruse since it has been placed there by Hegel himself. Marx initially proposes to redress Hegel's error by an immersion in history and the theory of political economy as the science of civil society. His focus on the logic of civil society shows that Hegel's dialectic is the logic of the specific social relations of capitalist production, not the logic of "everything." But Marx then goes on to claim that this economic logic permeates the whole of society: the other spheres of everyday life are formed by the expansion of economic logic into those spheres. In this way Marx carries over into his own conceptual formulation what he sees as the essential error of Hegel's philosophy—the elaboration of a theory of society as a monological development.

Critical theory exposes the limits of the focus on the logic of civil society. The emphasis on the economic base is shown to obscure the actual historical situation, which is a function not only of exchange but of the interface between an expanding logic of exchange and independent logics of other spheres such as the family, state, and culture. Marx's critique illuminates the central logic of civil society but falls short of a comprehensive critique of contemporary society. The conclusion, immanent in Marx's analysis but not drawn by Marx himself, is that there are many logics; thus social critique must turn to the problem of their interrelationship. An analysis of the interrelationship of the different social spheres requires first a detailed analysis of the specific logic of each. It is in this context that we must consider the Frankfurt school's studies on authority and the family.

In the 1930s Max Horkheimer and Herbert Marcuse, along with several other scholars at the Institute of Social Research in Germany, collaborated on a major project entitled *Studies on Authority and the Family*, which was published in 1936. These studies analyze the relation between the rise of fascism and anti-Semitism in Germany during the 1920s and 1930s and the decline of the European patriarchal family. Three theoretical pieces formed the first section of the study. Horkheimer wrote the introductory piece that established the rationale for the study; Erich Fromm wrote on the social psychology of authority; and Marcuse completed the section with an essay on the history of the idea of authority. The second section discussed results of the sociological surveys they conducted through questionnaires. The third section, under the editorial guidance of Leo Löwenthal, consisted of reports on special studies done on the family within different academic disciplines and in various countries.[21]

The initial investigation, in keeping with Marx's approach, was intended to develop a class analysis of family forms. However, the study concentrates on the bourgeois family for two reasons. First, most of the completed questionnaires focused on the bourgeois family. More important, the authors saw the bourgeois family becoming the model for the working-class family while simultaneously undergoing a transformation of proletarianization in which the male entrepreneur and his wife were becoming employees.[22] The tenacious ideology of the bourgeois family, which both reveals and distorts the truth, maintains its dominance even in the face of dramatic change. Thus, even though these theorists recognize that the bourgeois family is not a single uniform reality, they hold that the ideals of the bourgeois family prevail and must be analyzed for their critical and reactionary tendencies.[23]

There were several later studies on authority and the family. In 1949 Horkheimer published a piece entitled "Authoritarianism and the Family." In a footnote he gives credit to Adorno by acknowledging that this article is the result of their continuous collaboration.[24] Adorno contributed to a massive study of the authoritarian personality published in 1950.[25] While all this work is important I concentrate on Horkheimer's contribution because his essays give a theoretical critique and characterization of the specific logic of the contemporary family. He establishes the rationale for examining the specific logic of the cultural sphere of modern society and shows authority to be the "cement" of society.[26] In his 1936 essay on authority and the family he argues against both idealism and mechanical Marxism. He demonstrates that alterations in the psyche and the family are tied to the social relations of production while at the same time the psyche and mediating institutions such as the family have unique dynamics that must be understood in their specificity. He writes that it is necessary "to regard culture as a dynamic structure, that is, as a dependent but nonetheless special sphere within the social process as a whole." And "the psyche itself, like all the mediating institutions such as family, school, and church which form the psyche, has its own laws."[27] However, Horkheimer does not define the degree to which culture, the psyche, and the family are determining moments. He leaves the question open: the "answer" is rooted in the given historical situation. In the preface to *Critical Theory* he says that the 1936 essay on authority and the family, like all the essays in this collection, must be rethought and reflected upon in terms of the present social reality.[28]

For Horkheimer the patriarchal bourgeois family is an institution that serves the dual purposes of authority: it maintains
social and self-domination and at the same time contains liberatory potential. Here, Horkheimer distinguishes his analysis from
the abstract negation of authority characteristic of anarchism:
authority has liberatory potential as well as reactionary functions
in that it may ground our search for liberation even as it grounds
our submission to domination. "Only an analysis of the social
situation in its totality can provide an answer" to the question
of whether authority is functioning for "imprisonment or freedom."[29] He accepts the Freudian understanding that character
or psychic development is formed in early childhood within the
family, although he also considers adolescence to be a critical
period in the development of the authoritarian personality.[30] The
liberatory and reactionary dimensions of authority are located
within the specific logic of the family in terms of changes in the
socioeconomic roles of the father and mother, primarily as they
affect the development of the male child.

Critical theory claims that we live in a "society without the
father" due to the transformation of the economic role and image
of the father.[31] As the father becomes incapable of providing a
genuine model of paternal authority, consistency, and compe-
tence, his children become the helpless victims of manipulation
by mass society. They never internalize paternal authority and
therefore never develop into autonomous individuals able to critically assess society. Instead, they remain heteronomous creatures
easily manipulated into conformity.[32]

Society without the Father

Horkheimer believes that the family is the sphere in which the
child first learns to accept the dominant authority of society: in
bourgeois society the family's authoritarian structure is based on
patriarchal domination. The father's authority derives from his
greater physical strength and his economic position as the family
provider. This physical and economic power creates the foundation for the father's claim to moral superiority. The child learns

to respect the father's authority and simultaneously perceives the father's generalized superiority as "naturally" determined: "In consequence of the seeming naturalness of paternal power with its twofold foundation in the father's economic position and his physical strength with its legal backing, growing up in the restricted family is a first-rate schooling in the authority behavior specific to this society."[33] The child comes to accept that the only "reasonable" response to the father's superiority/authority is to adapt to it. In this way authority is internalized as a rational response to necessity. This process of coming to accept reason as a form of accommodation to necessity leads to the development of individuals who take responsibility for their fate: not the system but our abilities and deficiencies are believed to be the cause of our success or failure in life.[34]

According to Horkheimer, paternal authority had liberatory potential during the early stages of bourgeois society and was in fact necessary for the progressive development of society:

> The self-control of the individual, the disposition for work and discipline, the ability to hold firmly to certain ideas, consistency in practical life, application of reason, perseverance and pleasure in constructive activity could all be developed, in the circumstances, only under the dictation and guidance of the father whose own education had been won in the school of life.[35]

Horkheimer is primarily concerned with the development of the son in relation to the father. Thus, he claims that during the liberal phase of capitalism the patriarchal family structure, in which the father represents "the reality principle," not only prepares the son for the acceptance of authority but provides the basis for the development of the autonomous economic subject. The identification with the father within the Oedipal conflict is the precondition for the development of the son's autonomy: the son must identify with the father's strength in order to successfully rebel against him later to become self-directed. Thus the development of a strong ego and a conscience or superego requires "the internalization of the father image." Horkheimer sees the bourgeois individual as a partial and atomic individual; nevertheless, such individuality is a necessary, if insufficient, step in the progress of society.[36] While he is critical of the monadic character of the bourgeois individual, Horkheimer is also wary of the development of the "mass individual." He therefore attempts to retain and analyze a theory of individuality, which he sees as the precondition for the realization of freedom.

For Horkheimer the father's substantive economic power in bourgeois society was central to the father's authority and his critical role in the development of the son's psyche. The historical transformation of capitalism is therefore seen to undermine the father's authority by the dislocation of his role within the economy. The father is no longer the "genuine" authority figure whom the son can identify with and internalize, because he is no longer the independent entrepreneur but has become just another employee of the system. "With the disappearance of independent economic subjects, the subject as such disappears."[37] Authority is no longer experienced as the direct domination of a powerful father but rather as the abstract domination of instrumental reason. With no true paternal authority to internalize, we live in a "fatherless" society and the liberatory potential of that authority disappears.[38]

As instrumental reason comes to permeate all spheres of society, including the family, social and self-domination become increasingly inhuman and relentless. The functions of the family, including the conditioning for the acceptance of authority, are relegated to other institutions and the antiauthoritarian moments in the family are eclipsed. The development of the psyche is such that the child becomes a mass individual, a heteronomous social atom who is narcissistic, materialistic, and sadistic. Children fear authority and at the same time are attracted to those who exercise it; they become susceptible to mass conformity and submissive to leaders within totalitarian forms of authoritarian society.[39] Thus, society without the father means individuals without autonomy.

Nevertheless, Horkheimer is not without hope in his early

essays: the destruction of the bourgeois ego may open the way to freedom instead of barbarism. In "The End of Reason" he writes:

> Mutilated as men are, in the duration of a brief moment they can become aware that in the world which has been thoroughly rationalized they can dispense with the interests of self-preservation which still set them one against the other.... If the atomized and disintegrating men of today have become capable of living without property, without location, without time, they also have abandoned the ego in which all prudence and all stupidity of historical reason as well as its compliance with domination was sustained. The progress of reason that leads to its self-destruction has come to an end; there is nothing left but barbarism or freedom."[40]

Jessica Benjamin gives an excellent account of Horkheimer's analysis of the way in which domination in contemporary society expresses itself as abstract domination through instrumental reason. She then extrapolates from this analysis to explain the transformation of patriarchy from its direct to its abstract form: "However depersonalized or obscured, the new form of rationality which has superseded patriarchal religion and the visible role of *pater familias* should be understood as the embodiment of male domination in the culture as a whole.... We could think of this as patriarchy without the father.... Insofar as instrumental rationality prevails, we are far from fatherless."[41] While this is an interesting attempt to rethink the critique of instrumental reason in relation to the contemporary problem of woman's domination, Benjamin minimizes the fact that abstract patriarchal domination is *fundamentally* tied to the concept of woman *as* nature.

The view of woman as the alien, inferior Other to be dominated has been eloquently articulated by Simone de Beauvoir in *The Second Sex*. Man's assignment of the role of Other to woman is a way of mitigating the loneliness of his place in nature. He commandeers woman's services as intermediary between his conscious self and "first nature": "Man seeks in woman the Other as nature."[42] But nature inspires ambivalent feelings in man. This ambivalence is translated into a dualism in which man represents consciousness, transcendence, the spirit, and the self whereas woman represents matter, immanence, the flesh—the Other. The patriarchal concept of woman *as* nature and the socioeconomic legitimation of the domination *of* nature combine to form the basis of abstract patriarchy. While instrumental reason is *part* of this problem it is not the defining element.

Society without the Mother

Horkheimer analyzes familial relations to show how they may challenge the rationality of a society that aims at the complete domination of nature and the complete rationalization of all human relations. The most "natural" relations are shown to be mediated by historically concrete reality.

Woman as mother is seen in relation to nature, and this relation is either liberatory or reactionary, just as the father's relation to authority is liberatory or reactionary depending on the social matrix. The mother may represent the utopian promise of freedom or conformity to authority. For Horkheimer, mothering is not simply an immediate embeddedness in nature, a relation of mere particularity, rooted in woman's reproductive capacity. Rather, this biological embeddedness is reinforced by historical circumstances. The sexual division of labor leaves the bourgeois woman inside the family and unaffected by the harsher and more direct forms of domination in early capitalist society. If the father represents the reality principle to the child, the mother represents "a principle other than reality": she represents the dream of utopia. Maternal care contains liberatory potential because woman as mother keeps alive the promise of paradise. Horkheimer describes the family in the golden age of bourgeois society:

> Common concerns took a positive form in sexual love and especially in maternal care. The growth and happiness of the other are willed in such unions. A felt opposition therefore arises between them and hostile reality outside. To this extent, the family not only educates for authority in bourgeois society; it also cultivates the dream of a

better condition for [humanity]. In the yearning of many adults for the paradise of their childhood, in the way a mother can speak of her son even though he has come into conflict with the world, in the protective love of a wife for her husband, there are ideas and forces at work which admittedly are not dependent on the existence of the family in its present form and, in fact, are even in danger of shrivelling up in such a milieu, but which, nevertheless, in the bourgeois system of life rarely have any place but the family where they can survive at all.[43]

Because familial relations are not abstract or partial the family is a sphere in which one learns to accept the dominant social form of authority at a preconscious level. But for the same reason family relations are qualitatively different from the relations of society and one lives there "not as a mere function but as a human being."[44]

Here Horkheimer accepts the Hegelian analysis of the bourgeois family, which identifies "the principle of love for the whole person" with woman as she preserves and maintains the sphere of the family:

Hegel identified the principle of love for the whole person, such as it exists in the marital community, with "womanliness" and the principle of civic subordination with "manliness." ... To the extent that any principle besides that of subordination prevails in the modern family, the woman's maternal and sisterly love is keeping alive a social principle dating from before historical antiquity, a principle which Hegel conceives "as the law of the ancient gods, 'the gods of the underworld,' " that is, of prehistory.[45]

Thus, Horkheimer's view of woman in the ideal bourgeois family is rooted in the Hegelian schema, which sees the family as a sphere of life that has its own specific logic based on a unique form of recognition: recognition within the family is not grounded in the hostility of the risk of life. Hegel's philosophy of the family is the most significant analysis of bourgeois ideology, and Horkheimer believes that as such it contains premises for an immanent critique.

As critical theory appropriates Freud's analysis of the development of the psyche within the family it attempts to retain

Hegel's concept of the bourgeois family as a refuge while simultaneously maintaining Marx's conception of the historical character of the family as it is influenced by developments in the sphere of production. The development of the psyche is seen as a process that occurs primarily within the family, and the family, as well as the psyche, is seen as a sphere of second nature. For Hegel the individual is realized outside the family, in society; the family is a sphere of "unconscious" or "undifferentiated" unity in which the woman's relation to the universal offers man a "tranquil intuition of unity." For Marx, on the other hand, society is not a sphere of self-realization but one of human degradation. Horkheimer, attempting to unify Hegel and Marx, regards the bourgeois family as a refuge that renews and sustains the sense of worth in man denied him by society. The family resists the attempt to reduce all relations to relations of exchange: "In the family, each man is regarded for his own sake, whereas in society he merely represents a certain function, the neutral incorporation of a service, a replaceable cog in a great machine. But at home he is accepted as a definite, irreplaceable, and distinct individual. Thus the family becomes an institution which maintains and restores in man a consciousness of his own humanity which present-day society denies him."[46] The family, based on relations determined by woman, is not rationalized in the way society is; because the mother gives of herself without counting the cost, the family is a preserve of ethical love and human solidarity within a society ruled by exchange and atomic individualism.[47]

Woman retains the identification with the family as a preserve or refuge described by Hegel. The liberatory or critical potential in this traditional view of woman resounds through everything Horkheimer writes; for example:

> Formerly [the mother] endowed the child with a feeling of security which allowed him to develop a certain independence. He felt his love for his mother reciprocated and somehow lived on this emotional fund throughout his life. The mother, cut off from the community of the males and despite an unjustified idealization being herself forced into a dependent situation, represented a principle

other than reality; she could sincerely dream the dreams of utopia with the child, and she was his *natural* ally whether she wished it or not. Thus there was a force in his life which allowed him to develop his own individuality concomitantly with his adjustment to the external world.[48]

Love for the mother, who is dominated by the father, contains an antiauthoritarian moment and may sow the seeds of rebellion in the children.[49]

In accepting the Hegelian schema of the family Horkheimer laments only the fact that while Hegel sees the opposition between family and society he cannot conceive of the possibility that the individual as loved and understood in the family might be realized in society:

> Since Hegel absolutizes bourgeois society, he is not able really to develop the dialectic inherent in this opposition [between the family and the larger community].... Hegel was unable to think the possibility of a truly united and rational society in which "the individual as such," as understood and cherished within the family, could come into his own. He is forced, therefore, to regard this concrete individual entity, man in his totality, as being, even within the family, a "merely unreal insubstantial shadow."[50]

But Horkheimer misrepresents Hegel: "The individual in [Hegel's] philosophy, as in the society which corresponds to it, is 'not...this particular husband, this particular child, but...*a* husband, children *in general*,' and against the tensions and disruptive tendencies which arise out of the disregarded claims of particular men, war becomes a final, even if dangerous, act of wisdom."[51] The statement that Horkheimer quotes from *The Phenomenology of Spirit* is made within Hegel's discussion of the ethical household in the pagan world, not the modern world of capitalist production. Horkheimer may believe that the dualism of family and state in the pagan world is an apt description of contemporary society, just as Marx found the master-slave dialectic of that world an appropriate model for early bourgeois society. But Horkheimer does not explicitly state or justify such a position. More important for our analysis is the fact that in

The Phenomenology of Spirit Hegel is discussing *woman's* relation to husband and children. Horkheimer extracts the quote
from Hegel's work in such a way that the reference to woman
is obliterated. What Horkheimer laments is the fact that *men* are
"only replaceable representatives of economic functions, ex-
changeable cases and instances, and correspond wholly to examples of a concept as found in discursive logic."[52] He
completely overlooks the fact that Hegel subsequently describes
particularity (albeit unconscious) as achieved by the husband
within the family in the pagan world and the fact that in the
Philosophy of Right men achieve particularity in the sphere of
civil society. It is only woman who never achieves particularity
and remains the walking dead of "unreal insubstantial shadow."
Horkheimer wants to take the individual within the family as a
paradigm for individuality as such, but he disregards the fact
that this individuality within the Hegelian schema is *male* individuality, which is always realized at woman's expense: Hegel's
philosophy does not encompass a view of woman as a free and
equal Other.

Horkheimer accepts the claim that matriarchy preceded patriarchy and was defeated in the course of history. He quotes
Engels, who says that "the overthrow of mother-right was the
world historical defeat of the female sex."[53] The triumph of
patriarchy had emancipatory potential, according to Horkheimer, in terms of the development of the male child as an autonomous individual. However, Horkheimer is careful to detail the
reactionary side of patriarchal domination. He describes woman's historical domination in terms of the ideology that places
her on a pedestal only to humiliate her and regards her as a
necessarily evil and sinful creature. Medieval Christianity played
a central role in woman's domination by claiming that "woman's
subjection to man [is] the penalty for Eve's sin."[54]

What Horkheimer does not describe is the vision of woman
divided between the pit and the pedestal that the Church articulates in the opposition of Eve and the Virgin Mary. Christianity
invests woman with a frightening status; anxiety centers around
her sexuality: "vulgar eros" is blamed for all the world's ills.

Woman as Eve, the evil, erotic Other, is to be avoided because she lures man toward spiritual death by pulling him down into the pit of fleshly desire; she reduces him to mere nature. And woman as the once powerful mother-goddess is neutralized in the person of the Virgin Mary. With the advent of Christianity woman as potentially fearsome, fleshly mother is transfigured and enslaved in the Virgin Mary's supernatural/unnatural maternity. Mary's sexuality is denied and in her motherhood she is made subordinate: the mother Mary kneels before her son, Jesus. The medieval cult of the Virgin celebrated a supreme masculine victory. Woman, if she wishes to rise above her "sinful" nature, must bow to the will of a God that subordinates her to man. The only powerful mother—Mary—is never an erotic Other: she is an eternal virgin. Through her submissive role as nonsexual mother, woman may repent for her role as the evil, erotic Other exemplified by Eve.[55]

The virginity of Mary allows woman as mother to become the mediatrix of salvation, a creature to be revered, without disturbing the image of woman as erotic Other, the mediatrix of damnation, a creature to be reviled. That through which the flesh has been redeemed is not carnal. Mary knew neither the stain of sexuality nor the pains of childbirth. The aversion of the Christian ascetic to the feminine body is such that the Church spares the son of God the defilement of being born "between feces and urine."[56]

Woman was created after man according to Judeo-Christian thought. This time sequence in the original creation makes woman not only second in time but secondary—the second sex. This belief causes Isak Dinesen to lament: "I have always thought it unfair to woman that she has never been alone in the world. Adam had a time, whether long or short, when he could wander about on a fresh and peaceful earth, among the beasts, in full possession of his soul, and most men are born with a memory of that period. But poor Eve found him there, with all his claims upon her, the moment she looked into the world. That is a grudge that woman has always had against the Creator."[57] In the paradise myth as told in Genesis, woman as erotic Other personified

by Eve becomes the source of sexual challenge in this earthly
life—a living symbol of the flesh. Sexuality becomes, through
woman, the essence of temptation. It is a turbulence and a dis-
aster—a desire to fall, to fail, to lose one's autonomy.

While woman as the mother-goddess was neutralized in the
person of the Virgin Mary and vilified as the evil seductress Eve,
woman qua woman, a living female sexual being, was burnt as
a witch. Horkheimer describes the witch-hunts as "the most
frightful terrorism ever exercised against a sexual group," which
"was regarded as justified by the corruption of woman's nature."[58] The Church's doctrine endowed woman with a corrupt
and sinful nature, and the patriarchal world used this ideology
to rationalize a reign of terror against women. The witch-hunts
began in the fourteenth century and continued through to the
eighteenth: born in feudalism they lasted well into "the age of
reason." They took place in Europe, England, and North America. Some writers have estimated the total number of women
and female children killed in these hunts to be in the millions.
While witches were accused of every conceivable crime, their
primary "crime" was an active sexuality. In the eyes of the
Church a witch's power was ultimately derived from her sexuality; a woman's transformation into a witch supposedly began
with pleasurable sexual intercourse with the devil.[59]

According to Horkheimer patriarchy, which makes woman
dependent on man, has taken new and different forms through
the ages but in all cases it restricts woman's development: "In
the modern period woman's dependence has, indeed, taken other
forms due to the new mode of production, but the principle itself
remains unchanged as do its profound effects on the female
psyche."[60] Horkheimer does not elaborate on the psychological
consequences for woman under patriarchal domination.[61]
Rather, he focuses on the fact that her economic and social
dependence on man restricts the antiauthoritarian element in her
role within the family. More and more she comes to be someone
who reinforces obedience to authority and conformity.

As bourgeois monogamy in patriarchal society devalues sensual pleasure, sensuousness is necessarily repressed in the son's

attachment to his mother. She is therefore not seen as a concrete, particular, sexual human being but becomes a symbol of the dark side of motherhood: the all-powerful mother who threatens to engulf the male and deprive him of his autonomy.[62] Horkheimer says that protofascism is linked with either the lack of a genuine relation with the mother or a disturbed relation to her in which the boy rejects the mother as "different" and as a member of an inferior sex (instead of seeing her as "a principle other than reality" in a utopian or antiauthoritarian sense). In this way the son acquires a personality in which everything and everyone that is deemed "different" is subsequently rejected or persecuted.[63]

When she is not an active economic subject in civil society the bourgeois wife, more than her husband, regards it as a "natural" sphere that requires submission to its "laws." Insofar as her welfare and that of the children depend on her husband's success in the given society she reinforces and encourages his conformity to the status quo. As she becomes the spirit of devotion and adaptation to social authority she consolidates the children's conformity and obedience to the given.[64]

However, when woman does move into civil society as an active economic subject the problems increase, according to Horkheimer. The economic liberation of woman is a false promise in bourgeois society. In the first place, woman is socialized to focus on marriage as her primary goal so that any occupation she adopts is seen by her and by society as temporary and secondary. In the second place, woman suffers an economic and psychological disadvantage in civil society because it is a sphere created by and for men; she does not enter it as an equal. And finally, woman's economic "emancipation" has come at a time when unemployment is a permanent part of the structure of capitalism. While no one can be certain about his or her economic future today, woman, as last hired and therefore first fired, finds herself in an even less secure position than man. Given these conditions woman clings to the family as the one sphere of security and in so doing becomes a conservative force.[65] Excluded from civil society or allowed to enter it only on a marginal basis, in the present stages of patriarchal capitalism, woman is not only "backward" but "bigoted" according to Horkheimer. Here we see the beginnings of an analysis of the regressive element in woman's domination as nature, a theme which Horkheimer and Adorno will expand in their later works. While the mother once represented the dream of utopia, she now represents only conformity, obedience to authority, and nature as the alien, inferior Other. The mother has been replaced by "mom"—a mere mask of motherhood.[66]

The transformation of the bourgeois family affects the woman who remains confined to it insofar as she is reduced to a sex object or a domestic servant. However, most important in Horkheimer's analysis is the effect on the woman and her family as she moves into civil society to work. In order to function in civil society woman tends to become more and more like the atomic bourgeois male—cold and calculating. The focus of Horkheimer's argument against woman's move into civil society and the consequent changes in familial relations is primarily the effect not on woman but on her children, specifically her sons: "Women have paid for their limited admission into the economic world of the male by taking over the behavior patterns of a thoroughly reified society. The consequences reach into the most tender relations between mother and child. She ceases to be a *mitigating intermediary* between him and cold reality and becomes just another mouthpiece of the latter."[67]

As woman moves into civil society where instrumental reason prevails, motherhood is redefined by social "experts" according to the principles of scientific efficiency and hygiene. Thus instrumental rationality comes to permeate the family directly through woman as she learns to adapt to the sphere in which instrumental reason dominates and indirectly through the social redefinition of the mother-child relation. At the same time the functions of the family are surrendered more and more to the schools, the culture industry (the commodification of art in mass culture), and adolescent peer groups. The development of the child's psyche is adversely affected by these conditions. Since the mother no longer represents unconditional love, warmth, antiauthoritarianism, and utopia, an emotional coldness develops between the mother and child: "The spontaneity of the mother and her natural, unlimited protectiveness and warmth tend to be dissolved. Therefore, the image of the mother in the minds of children sheds its mystical aura, and the mother cult of adults turns from a mythology in the strict sense of the word into a set of rigid conventions."[68] In this way the critique of society without the father is extended to a critique of society without the mother. Fatherlessness creates a mass individual or authoritarian personality eager to conform and unable to challenge the status quo. Motherlessness reinforces this situation. But a society without the mother primarily means the loss of the utopian dream—the loss of a vision of the future lived in freedom. A motherless society is a society without love or hope.

In "The Concept of Man" (1957) Horkheimer continues to lament the transformation of the mother's role as woman is "pushed" into work in civil society, which makes new and different demands on her psyche. Mother love is not properly expressed because the mother is "pressed by other cares and occupations." Instead of being warm, friendly, and peaceful the mother is cold, indifferent, abrupt, restless, and openly displeased.[69]

In this essay the representation of woman as Other, as nature, is clearly articulated by Horkheimer. He again acknowledges that woman's role within the family has always been one of domination and enforced passivity. And again he says that even though woman's confinement was unfortunate it meant that she was "untouched" by the relations of civil society and could therefore represent the liberatory potential in her domination as nature:

> [Woman's] nature, unlike that of man, was not shaped by activity in the labor market and adapted to circumstances outside the home. Yet her passive role, which nothing could justify, also enabled her to avoid reduction to object-status and thus to represent, amid an evil society, another possibility. In the passage from the old serfdom to the new she could be regarded as a representation of nature, which eluded utilitarian calculation. This element, regardless of

whether woman was opposing society or submitting to it, determined her image for the bourgeois era.[70]

As woman moves into civil society to become an active economic subject, she becomes more and more like man. The "equation of woman and sex" begins to disappear, and men and women evaluate each other in terms of functions.

The economic activity of woman outside the home has led to a marriage of "partners," which Horkheimer characterizes as an "exchange between equals." Husband and wife begin to appraise each other according to principles that prevail in society. The relation between the sexes within the marriage increasingly comes to resemble the relations of society at large: each partner assesses the other to determine if he or she has made the best "deal" possible in selecting a mate. In this way the personal sphere becomes rationalized, prosaic, and utilitarian.[71]

Horkheimer's objection to a marriage of partners is rooted in the utopian promise he sees in romantic love, which is "the rebellion of eros against authority."[72] With the rationalization of family life, love becomes ideology and divorce becomes widespread. The prevalence of divorce makes us all replaceable, and the uniqueness of the individual disappears:

> No other institution of our society reveals so clearly the problematic nature of the modern family as the divorce.... Individuals are as exchangeable in marriage as they are in commercial relationships. One enters a new one if it promises to work out better. Each person is identified completely with his or her function for a particular purpose. Everyone remains an abstract center of interests and accomplishments.[73]

Divorce reflects the fact that "the social unit is no longer the family but the atomic individual."[74] However, the ideology of the family is intensified as the traditional family dissolves.

Horkheimer agrees with Marx that capitalism is destroying the family, but for Marx the apparent disintegration of the bourgeois family and the real disintegration of the working-class family were progressive. The working-class woman leaving her home to participate in production in civil society created the precon-

ditions for a higher form of the family and equal relations between the sexes. Abstract equality in civil society was to be the
foundation for overcoming patriarchal domination. For Marx,
the more the "natural" familial relations were revealed as socially
mediated, the more likely it was that we would achieve human
liberation. In contrast, Horkheimer sees the real disintegration
of the bourgeois family as a loss. The move of woman out of
the home destroys the family as a sphere of human love and
solidarity.

Here the ambiguity in critical theory's class analysis of the
family is most evident. The working-class woman was an active
economic subject in the nineteenth century during the so-called
golden age of capitalism. While she may have clung to the family
as a sphere of some security she was not necessarily reactionary.
Since her economic position and that of her husband often required active opposition to capitalism she participated in strikes
and riots. Her role in this resistance to capitalism was not always
revolutionary because of the hardships that would impose on
the family, but neither was she merely a conservative force.[75]
Horkheimer's comment that "the disintegration of the working-
class family represents a continuous danger to the existence of
society," creating a situation that "works counter to the conditions favoring respect for authority as found in the middle-
class family," seems to contradict critical theory's statements
concerning the way in which the proletarian family takes the
bourgeois family as its model.[76] On the one hand, Horkheimer
seems to accept Marx's analysis that the real disintegration of
the working-class family has revolutionary potential, but Horkheimer's focus on the bourgeois family obscures the actual role
and content of the working-class family. Within his analysis of
the family one cannot make sense of the activity of the working-
class woman outside the home in the nineteenth century; nor
can one understand how her activity affected familial relations
except to see it as part of the disintegration of the family. But
Horkheimer does not clarify why the disintegration of the working-class family has revolutionary potential whereas the disintegration of the bourgeois family spells defeat.

Clinging tenaciously to the notion of the golden age of the bourgeois family and woman's role as mother, he never examines the unique character of woman's domestic labor as an underpinning for capitalism: when woman moves into civil society she still has to do the housework. Having given no attention to the relation between waged and unwaged domestic labor, Horkheimer cannot analyze housework as exploitation.

Horkheimer examines the situation of bourgeois children in terms of the transformation of capitalism. He describes the decline of the family as an economic unit in the nineteenth century and claims that the sons of Victorian middle-class entrepreneurs were both indispensable to their fathers' businesses and unable to find comparable career opportunities outside the family business. Along with this the son's desire to inherit the family property kept him in line: "A son's future share in his father's property had been as powerful a motive for obedience as disinheritance was a menace."[77] Here Horkheimer seems to accept Marx's tenet that property concerns infect the family, but this belief does not lead him, as it did Marx, to a denunciation of the bourgeois family. Describing the situation of the daughter, Horkheimer says that she was needed in both the house and the shop in the nineteenth century. Today, however, the situation of both the son and the daughter of the middle class has changed in that we live in a world where everyone is an employee. The right of inheritance and fear of disinheritance of the family property/ business has lost much of its power over the son. The daughter, like the son, must move out of the home and the family business to earn a living. This move is now respectable for the daughter as well as the son.

Let us examine more closely the daughter's position. In early bourgeois society, the daughter never had the right of inheritance on her side—in fact, only the eldest son inherited the family property through primogeniture. The most a girl could hope for was a decent dowry to enable her to make a "good" (that is, financially secure) marriage. What ruled her life was not the possibility of inheritance nor the threat of disinheritance but the real control her father exercised over the choice of her husband:

the wrong husband could make her life a misery in a time when divorce was unacceptable. Furthermore, many a widower attempted, through direct or indirect coercion, to keep a daughter at home to replace his lost wife as domestic caretaker and emotional support.[78] The tyranny of the father over the daughter was not similar to that over the son any more than property concerns were similar. However, Horkheimer does not claim that conditions *were* similar but that with the transformation of capitalism they are now similar in that the "[rupture] with the family ... loses its terror for the girl as well as for the boy" as both must earn a living outside the home.[79] But woman's disadvantage in the marketplace, which Horkheimer himself has outlined, means that she cannot expect to achieve a high level of economic independence through waged labor and, in fact, regards such work as secondary to marriage. When and if she does marry and have children she is most likely to have to take responsibility for the children if the marriage dissolves through divorce. Given all these circumstances a daughter is more likely to fear a break with her family of origin than the son. The chance that she will be forced back into that family for support in times of economic and emotional stress is much higher for her than for her brother who has economic advantages as a wage earner and often becomes child-free if his marriage ends in divorce. Thus, similar conditions do not hold true for the son and daughter of the middle class, as Horkheimer claims, in terms of the ability to break away from the family of origin. In a patriarchal world the son always has advantages over the daughter.

Antigone Revisited

In his work on authority and the family Horkheimer analyzes woman's relation to her husband, her son, and her brother. He recognizes the critical difference between woman as wife, mother, and sister. While the mother-son bond offers the male infant the dream of utopia as he struggles to form an identity, this process of identity formation takes place within a triangle in which the child is not an equal Other. In contrast, both the husband-wife and brother-sister relations, in their ideal form, are relations of mutual recognition as elaborated by Hegel.

In "Authority and the Family" Horkheimer examines the brother-sister relation as Hegel interprets it. As we have seen, Hegel believes the ideal male-female relation is that between brother and sister as immortalized in *Antigone*. Horkheimer accepts the brother-sister relation as a paradigm of mutual recognition and says that if Hegel could have seen this relation not simply as one for mourning and remembering the dead but as taking "a more active form in the future, his dialectic with its closed, idealistic form would have broken through its socially conditioned limitations."[80] This is an interesting but undeveloped claim. His reference to Antigone is expanded a few pages later in a vision of sisterly love that describes her as the representative of woman's submission to patriarchal authority: "[Antigone] becomes an instrument for maintaining authority in society" by upholding the law of the patriarchal family. Horkheimer cites Antigone's final words as quoted by Hegel as proof that she "renounces all opposition" and "simultaneously accepts the principle of male-dominated bourgeois society: bad luck is your own fault."[81] Leaving aside the leap that Horkheimer makes from ancient Greece to the bourgeois era, let us recall the interpretation of *Antigone* in chapter 1 above. Contrary to Hegel's view of Antigone as a figure of female renunciation, Antigone does *not* bow to patriarchal authority. Rather, Hegel mistranslates her last spoken words and misconstrues her actions.

Antigone may be seen to submit to the gods (and one might make the claim that these gods are the divine representatives of patriarchal authority on earth); nevertheless, she does not admit guilt or submit to secular patriarchal domination as represented by Creon. Creon ends up admitting his guilt and suffering the fate he tried to inflict on Antigone. Thus, one sees Antigone's innocence revealed in the fate meted out to Creon. As I interpret Antigone's actions, her suicide is a form of defiance. She chooses a course of action even though it condemns her to death; and she takes her own life in order to refute Creon's power over her. Against Hegel and Horkheimer's interpretation, Antigone should be seen as representing opposition to patriarchal domination, not submission.

The existential concept of freedom underlying my interpretation of the *Antigone* is certainly not foreign to Horkheimer. In "Traditional and Critical Theory" he emphasizes the existential moment of critical theory.[82] And in both *Eclipse of Reason* and "The End of Reason" he writes of the development of the Greek hero and the role of woman in Greek society in a way that is quite inconsistent with his uncritical appropriation of Hegel's analysis of the *Antigone*. Antigone is fierce in her defiance and manifests all the characteristics of the male tragic hero in opposing the given as well as attempting "to reconcile the law with the good," which sometimes requires that one break the law.[83] Horkheimer's interpretation, like Hegel's, remains obscured by the glare of patriarchal domination in such a way that the situation of the sister is romanticized and misinterpreted. If the emphasis in Horkheimer's interpretation had fallen on Antigone's last *actions* rather than on her last words (as "interpreted" by Hegel), he might have seen that she stands firm in her opposition to authoritarian patriarchal rule. Her suicide was an honorable alternative to submission to male domination.

Robert Seidenberg and Evangelos Papathomopoulos attempt to understand Antigone's speech in which she defends her decision to bury her brother, Polyneices, saying that she would not make the same sacrifice for a husband or a son. Antigone's own defense of this position is that she could always find another husband or bear another child if hers were to die but, since her parents are dead, she cannot replace her brother. Seidenberg and Papathomopoulos take a Hegelian perspective within their psychoanalytic framework. That is, they focus on what, in Hegelian language, is the concept of recognition. Their interpretation of Antigone's speech is rooted in the fact that with a husband or a son a woman is in a position of actual or potential domination by virtue of patriarchal law and custom—she is not an equal Other. Although less obvious than the husband's authority over his wife, the son's domination of his mother is reflected in both cultural and religious texts: for example, Penelope must endure the patriarchal vigilance of Telemachus during Odysseus' absence just as later the Virgin Mary will bow before Jesus. A son, when grown to manhood in patriarchal society, rules the mother. Because the husband-wife and son-mother relationships are relations of male domination, a woman necessarily has ambivalent feelings about them. She finds her one glimpse of truly equal recognition with a male in the relation with her brother. Even if we challenge Hegel's claim that the brother and sister do not desire one another, we can see that it is a more equal male-female relation. If a brother mistreats or exploits his sister she has the option of drawing away from him. With a husband or a son such a retreat or abandonment is much more difficult: in these relationships there are legal and social encumbrances as well as the moral and religious ones attached to the brother-sister relation. Given the fact that it is easier to dissolve a relation with her brother a woman's love for a brother is less threatening to her freedom and her sense of identity. It is therefore the equality of the brother-sister relation that explains why Antigone would do for a brother what she would not do for a husband or a son.[84]

Woman qua Woman?

Here we should take Horkheimer's advice and rethink his analysis of the family. However, it must be rethought not just from the standpoint of the present but in terms of the history of the family and, most important, in terms of woman's domination. Much of Horkheimer's analysis has the ring of truth, most notably in his perception of the dehumanization of woman as she moves into civil society. However, this truth is *partial*: his concern with the family, and particularly with the son's development within the family, obscures the woman question. He ignores the emancipatory side of woman's escape from a family situation that is often oppressive, confining, and infantilizing. His focus on woman as mother is primarily a concern with the development of the male psyche and not with woman's domination per se.

As we have seen, Horkheimer accepts the Hegelian schema

of the family as a preserve or refuge based on woman's love as wife, mother, and sister. In her dominated position within the bourgeois patriarchal family she once retained traits that enabled her to avoid reduction to object status and thereby maintained the family as a unique sphere of human recognition. These traits were incorporated into the ideology of the family and had liberatory potential. The mother could dream the dreams of utopia with her son: she was and *had to be* his ally in the development of his ability to resist the demands of conformity and authoritarian rule. Woman as Other nourished the dreams of the developing male psyche through her unconditional love. But here woman is treated as an idealized Other in much the same way that Marcuse treats her in *Eros and Civilization*. That mothering might be an alienating experience for woman is never considered.

Horkheimer does not attempt to analyze Hegel's schema of the family from woman's perspective. Woman as mother is an ambiguous creature in Hegel's philosophy, for in the creation of another human life she is condemned to the shadows; she cannot personally grow, become an I, yet she spends her life creating the conditions for male autonomy. This partial treatment of woman limits Horkheimer's analysis just as it limits Hegel's philosophy. If man's awareness of his "wholeness" must be purchased at the cost of woman's development into a free and equal Other, the paradigm is obviously not liberatory for woman.

Horkheimer laments the loss of the traditional mother's role for the male child as woman moves into civil society. He sees woman's struggles to achieve equality in civil society, to be able to divorce herself from an unhappy marriage, and to gain control over her reproductive capacity through contraception and abortion as part of the dissolution of the family and the rationalization of life. Woman's movement out of the home and the traditional role that once confined her have, according to Horkheimer, worked against her own development and the development of her son. As "mom" replaces the mother, woman becomes the source of her son's neuroses. The fact that woman might have been oppressed and alienated by involuntary motherhood, as well as by the patriarchal domination that gave the grown son power over the mother, is not as important to Horkheimer as the fact that she was once her son's ally in the development of his autonomy "whether she wished it or not." This concern for the male child obscures woman's domination as mother.

The presentation of romantic love in Horkheimer's analysis is also partial. He makes an important and necessary distinction between bourgeois monogamy, which devalues sensual pleasure, and "true" monogamy based on romantic love as eros. True monogamy is a bond of mutual and unchanging fidelity, not the calculation of a bourgeois marriage of "partners." Horkheimer concedes that the bourgeois male has the upper hand in love relations: he is the one to choose and to determine the course of love. The only "choice" a woman may have is to refuse or accept the man who chooses her. Horkheimer identifies woman with love and sees love as central to a woman's life: love changes everything for her. Thus, a woman's "false step" in love is the basis of tragedy in literature. An unhappy and discontent woman may risk everything for love, but, like Madame Bovary or Anna Karenina, she will be destroyed in the process.[85] The fact that a real woman may be destroyed does not alter the critical content of romantic love for Horkheimer, because such love defies society. In fact, Horkheimer believes that a hindrance, some moment of tragedy, heightens human desire and longing. This belief led him to justify the Catholic church's refusal to sanction the use of artificial contraceptive devices. For him, part of a critical theorist's task is to analyze the human cost involved in social change. In this case, he argues that population control through technology (the domination of nature) entails the death of erotic love.[86]

But this position obscures several issues. The first is why *woman* should be identified with love and made to suffer tragic consequences if she errs in love. The second is that the fear of pregnancy does not heighten desire for woman. To think it does is to ignore the price woman has always paid for the lack of contraception and legal abortion— early and painful death from continuous pregnancies or illegal and unsafe abortions.[87] The price woman pays for the continuation of erotic love is very high indeed, but it finds no place in Horkheimer's analysis.

Romantic love has always been an ideological weapon used to induce woman to surrender herself to childbearing: it draws woman into the family of procreation and then the reality of motherhood keeps her there. As the love letters of Karl and Jenny Marx illustrate (see chap. 2, note 62), romantic love had a very different meaning for a man and woman even in the "golden age" of the nineteenth century. For Marx it was the realization of himself in another. For Jenny it was the fear of *losing* herself in another and then being abandoned. Given this, it is hard to see the liberatory potential in romantic love for woman.

In addition, Horkheimer fails to address the relation between bourgeois ideology, in which woman represents the utopian principle, and patriarchal ideology, which, long before the rise of capitalism, rejected woman as different and inferior even as it placed her on a pedestal. Horkheimer does show the patriarchal reverence for woman as the other side of her humiliation and as an ideology that vilifies woman as Other, as the evil seductress. The witch-hunts that preceded capitalism had their origins in the most reactionary forms of patriarchal ideology. On the other hand, he claims that with the development of capitalism the bourgeois woman's confinement to the home allowed her to escape reduction to "object-status." But this escape from the "object-status" of the worker in capitalist society does not necessarily overcome the patriarchal vision of woman as sex object (the Other/the second sex), which was a problem for woman before capitalism reduced humans to objects. The bourgeois ideology that has liberatory potential for the son is not necessarily liberating for woman. Or, if it is, Horkheimer does not explain how it is so.

The view of the family as a refuge or sanctuary in which woman represented and provided unconditional love and the tranquil intuition of unity is an idealization of nineteenth-century life. The struggles of women for reproductive rights, birth control, and the vote, as well as the economic struggles of working-class women, mean that this concept of the family has to be rethought in the light of historical evidence. Furthermore, the idea that divorce is simply an extension of capitalist relations of exchange, which are ruled by equivalence, ignores the fact that inside this "haven in a heartless world" the impossibility of divorce created a deadly situation. According to Ann Jones, during the nineteenth century there was a wave of homicides by women who wanted to end their marriages and could find no other way out. By 1850 this new "household fiend" was a very real social problem precisely because the double standard acted to her benefit. When a wife was tried for murder, the ambivalence of the male jurors—their fear of woman's fury when she sought revenge and their desire to disbelieve in its existence—helped her case. If she feigned innocence a woman was very likely to be found "not guilty" and set free. Thus, husband poisoning became the crime of the nineteenth century and acquittal practically routine. While men attempted to distinguish between the murderess and the "true" woman—the fiend and the angel—the early feminists attacked marriage and property laws and sought more liberal divorce laws. They argued that the institution of marriage often locked woman into a desperate situation; the very structure of marriage, without the possibility of divorce, created the potentially explosive conditions that sometimes led to murder.[88] The recent woman's movement for liberation has reexposed the underside of family life: the sexual and physical abuse endured by all classes of wives at the hands of their husbands (abuse which, until recently, was sanctioned by law and by custom) and the sexual abuse of daughters by their fathers.[89]

In summary, Horkheimer does acknowledge problems with woman's traditional role but his analysis of woman's situation is confined primarily to an examination of her mothering role within the bourgeois family. He focuses on the loss to the bourgeois family as woman moves into civil society. The references to woman's domination in his studies on authority and the family are secondary: the real regret is for the son who has lost his mother's unconditional love. The concern with woman as mother, as she represents another reality to her son, overrides any concern with woman qua woman.

Horkheimer's attempt to integrate the theories of Hegel, Marx, and Freud within an analysis of the specific logic of the family is seriously flawed by his failure to examine comprehensively woman's situation. The uncritical appropriation of the Hegelian view of the bourgeois family as a preserve or refuge leads to a theoretical closure. Horkheimer believes that as society becomes both fatherless and motherless the processes by which we are conditioned to accept authority and conform to the given are relegated to social institutions that eclipse the antiauthoritarian and utopian moments of the family. He ends in a lament for the male child in contemporary society who "imitates only performances and achievements: he accepts not ideas, but matters of fact," and he claims that the male individual is "without dream or history."[90] There is no account of how the dream was often a nightmare for woman who lived by, for, and through others.

The reliance on Marx in Horkheimer's early essays emphasizes the extent to which the relations of production determine the development of the family and the psyche even though both are said to have their own laws. Against Marx's view, however, Horkheimer sees woman's move into civil society as harmful, and he examines neither the social labor required by mothering nor the function of unwaged domestic labor. In addition, Horkheimer appropriates Freud's theory of male ego development in the Oedipal drama to analyze the specific logic of the psyche. The emphasis is on the relation between father and son in terms of the processes by which the son internalizes the father's authority to achieve autonomy. Thus, the autonomous ego remains the core of liberatory potential but the conceptualization of this ego is grounded in an idealization of bourgeois society and the Freudian concept of male ego development. The unique development of the female psyche is not addressed.

In Horkheimer's partial and fragmentary analysis, what is assumed as given or omitted reflects and reinforces woman's domination. The focus on woman as mother reproducing sons and on the sons' psyches obscures the unique forms of woman's social and self-domination. If Horkheimer had retained a dialectical approach to the family and woman's domination he might not have ended up grieving for the lost glories of the bourgeois family and the passing of romantic love. Most important, he might have seen that a woman not allowed to develop into a free and equal Other cannot foster true individuality in her son. What such a woman fosters is the continuation of patriarchal rule. Her son knows that someday he will be in a position of power over all women, including his mother.

The partial treatment of woman as wife, mother, and daughter limits the analysis of the specific logic of the family. The threads of woman's domination that Horkheimer picks up need to be woven into a comprehensive analysis of that domination. To begin such a project, we must consider the formation of the female psyche in Freud's theory before we turn to the dialectical development of critical theory in relation to the woman question.

> What woman essentially lacks today for
> doing great things is forgetfulness of
> herself; but to forget oneself it is
> first necessary to be firmly assured that
> now and for the future one has found
> oneself.
>
> SIMONE DE BEAUVOIR, *The Second Sex*

FREUD ON THE FEMALE PSYCHE

According to Freud it is within the context of coming to terms with the body's libidinal drives and the psychic dramas they entail that the ego is formed and adult sexuality, centered on procreation, is attained. We live embodied but there is nothing self-evident about this embodiment. How we understand, symbolize, represent, or fantasize about our anatomy is a complex process of development, not a simple result of biology. Freud attempts to demonstrate how psychosexual development within the family of origin transforms a bisexual, polymorphously perverse infant into a heterosexual, genitally oriented, monogamous adult. He analyzes the way in which gender identity is internalized so that boys appropriate masculine prerogatives while girls submit to the feminine destiny of subordination and passivity.[91]

Sexuality is central to human development because it reveals the contradiction between gratification and civilization, between the pleasure principle and the reality principle. Freud's understanding of this conflict undermines any belief in the simple identity of individual and society. Psychic pain and neuroses are shown to be closely related to "normality," the difference between the neurotic individual and the "normal" one depending on how successfully each sublimates libidinous drives.

In Freud's theory, therefore, normality is not something that happens—it is *achieved*. There is no given, essential self at the moment of birth. Rather, a fragmented self struggles for wholeness, from an undifferentiated identity with the mother to the recognition of difference that is the beginning of the recognition of the discrete self. This process moves through various stages of psychosexual development, the first three and most important of which are the oral, anal, and phallic stages. During the process of development, the psyche takes on a tripartite division into id, ego, and superego; with each integration of a new phase or stage there is a new awareness of self and other. Initially ruled by the id or the pleasure principle, the infant develops a sense of an "I" or ego that organizes sensations and experiences and distinguishes between the inner and outer worlds. In turn, a superego or conscience is developed, which represents the social ideal, and the reality principle prevails.

Both males and females find it difficult to live out in their mental life the fact that there are two separate and distinct sexes; both experience the conflict between libidinous desires and the demands of "civilization"; and both must make the journey from an undifferentiating, drive-dominated infant to an individuated, autonomous self. But this journey through the dialectic of inner drives and external social processes, during which the infant struggles to achieve a self, is different for males and females.

Therefore, Freud attempts to develop a specific logic of the male and female psyche within the family of origin, focusing on the libidinous relations between the child and its parents. However, while he sees female development as complex and unique, he ultimately conflates the universal with the male.[92] He does not describe the girl's development from the perspective of the presence of her unique biology; rather, she is seen primarily in terms of the absence of the penis.

Freud is often said to have answered the woman question with the phrase "anatomy is destiny." When he originally made this statement in 1912 it was not a reference to the fact that females have clitorises, vaginas, and wombs and males have penises. Rather, it was a comment on the animal nature of humanity, particularly the fact that excrement is "intimately and inseparably" bound up with sexuality. That is, he saw the position of the genitals "between urine and feces" as the decisive and immutable factor in human development. [93] However, in 1924 he does use this phrase to sum up the woman question:

> The female sex, too, develops an Oedipus complex, a super-ego and a latency period. May we also attribute a phallic organization and a castration complex to it? The answer is in the affirmative; but these things cannot be the same as they are in boys. Here the feminist demand for equal rights for the sexes does not take us far, for the morphological distinction is bound to find expression in differences of psychical development. "Anatomy is Destiny," to vary a saying of Napoleon's.[94]

Although Freud does not posit a simple correspondence between biology and psychology, he does claim there are universal psychic differences between the sexes due to anatomical differences. The perception of genital difference by the boy and girl entails libidinal reconstruction. Here anatomy, ego development, and concept formation converge. Freud expresses doubts about the strict biological basis and normative character of his observations, but ultimately he assumes that the female's lack of a penis makes her biologically and psychologically inferior—without a penis she simply cannot develop into a mature, autonomous, and rational individual.[95]

Oedipus and Castration

Juliet Mitchell details Freud's theory of male and female development in *Psychoanalysis and Feminism*, emphasizing the relation between the Oedipus complex and the castration complex in his formulations.[96] While the Oedipus complex is the touchstone of psychoanalysis for Freud, he considers the development and dissolution of that complex to be significantly different for males and females. This leads him to claim that males and females necessarily have a different relation to society and the family.

Both sexes begin life with a primary, exclusive, pre-Oedipal attachment to the mother that is highly ambivalent—the infant both loves and hates the mother, who seems to be the source of all pleasure and all pain. This libidinal relation to the mother is transformed from an oral attachment to an incestuous, genital desire for the mother.[97]

In describing the boy's development, Freud states that in the phallic stage the boy sees the father as a rival and desires to "do away with" the father in order to possess the mother. Out of the ambivalent love for the mother comes the separation of love and hate during this phase, so that the boy transfers hate to the father and retains a more "pure," that is, less ambivalent, love for the mother. During this phase the castration anxiety of the young male also develops. The boy fears castration by the father, the rival for his mother's love, and this fear becomes significant when he realizes the biological fact that females do not have penises: he sees the little girl's genitals and believes she is castrated. He then feels in danger of losing his own penis and remembers that the ban on masturbation was accompanied by threats of castration: "The castration complex arises after [boys] have learnt from the sight of the female genitals that the organ which they value so highly need not necessarily accompany the body. At this time the boy recalls to mind the threats he brought on himself by his doings with that organ, he begins to give credence to them and falls under the influence of castration."[98] Under the threat of castration the boy may become so frightened that he sets up a fetish as a substitute for the missing penis of the female while he simultaneously disavows the possibility of castration. Alternatively, he may accept castration in an inverted form and become a homosexual. Or, if all goes well, in the active form of the Oedipus complex the boy accepts the possibility of castration and develops into "manhood."

In the third and "normal" development the Oedipus complex is "destroyed" by the castration complex and a strong superego is formed. The threat of castration is perceived as emanating from the father even if it is the mother, or mother substitute, who actually threatens the child.[99] That is, boys come to fear castration by the father as a revenge on them for their incestuous desire for the mother. This fear of castration and the hate the boy initially feels for the father is transformed, with the aid of aggressive drives, into an identification with the father such that the boy incorporates into his own psyche the father's authority. Since he cannot have the mother the boy now wants to be the father. Through the renunciation of his incestuous desire for the mother he identifies with the father, creating a male bond. The father therefore breaks the dyad of mother and son to create the possibility of male solidarity. As Marcuse puts it, "the father . . . enforces the subordination of the pleasure principle to the reality principle" and the boy becomes a self "with but also *against* the other."[100]

The boy learns to accept his father's rights over the mother, in the process resolving his Oedipal complex by realizing that someday he will have the same rights over a woman of his own. The male child retains the female as his love object but generalizes his initial heterosexual attachment to his mother to all women. Thus, in normal development, the Oedipal complex is "destroyed" or dissolved for the small boy by the castration complex. The son learns to identify with the powerful father figure, thereby internalizing the father's authority. This creates in him a strong superego or conscience and simultaneously makes him part of the male community. As the male superego learns to exchange sexual goals for cultural ones it becomes the "heir" to the Oedipus complex. This formulation of the Oedipal drama is, as we have seen, a central point for the Frankfurt school's studies on authority and the family.

Freud believes that as a result of the Oedipus complex and its destruction by the castration complex, men tend to depreciate women, regarding them as castrates. In the mistitled article "On the Universal Tendency to Debasement in the Sphere of Love" (1912) Freud claims that the behavior of men in love relations with women bears the stamp of "psychic impotence" because men separate affection and sensuality: "The sensual current that has remained active seeks only objects which do not recall the incestuous figures forbidden to it. . . . Where [men] love they do not desire and where they desire [men] cannot love."[101] The man becomes impotent if the woman he has chosen as a love object with the intention of avoiding incestuous feelings somehow recalls the mother. Therefore, in order to maintain their virility and their equilibrium, men strive to keep the affectionate and sensual separate by debasing women who represent the sensual/sexual and overvaluing the mother and her representatives. However, in 1933, Freud changes his analysis and theorizes that it is precisely the male Oedipal love of the mother that creates the passion for a woman. That is, men desire precisely those women who represent the mother.[102]

The relation of the Oedipus complex and the castration complex in the girl's development is the opposite of the boy's: the girl does not move from an Oedipal complex to a castration complex but begins with a pre-Oedipal castration complex (or penis envy), which prepares her for entry into the Oedipus complex. Thus, the little girl's development is much more complex and less easily resolved. In the female psyche the Oedipal complex is a secondary formation, arising from the castration complex. Because of this, the girl lacks the motive (fear of castration) that leads the boy to overcome the Oedipus complex. Thus, the girl remains in the Oedipal phase for a longer time and never "de-stroys" or "dissolves" it in such a way as to create or achieve a strong superego:

> In the absence of fear of castration the chief motive is lacking which leads boys to surmount the Oedipus complex. Girls remain in it for an indeterminate length of time; they demolish it late and, even so, incompletely. In these circumstances the formation of the super-ego must suffer; it cannot attain the strength and independence which give it its cultural significance, and feminists are not pleased when we point out to them the effects of this factor upon the average feminine character.[103]

In the girl it is the pre-Oedipal *acceptance* of castration that is important whereas in the boy it is the Oedipal *fear* of castration that is crucial.

The asymmetry of the development of the male and female psyches has another dimension. During the phallic stage the girl must accomplish two tasks that find no parallel in the boy's development. She must shift away from the sex of the original love object (the mother) to take the father as the love object, and she must shift from the clitoris as her leading erogenous zone to the vagina. Since the girl, like the boy, begins life with the same incestuous love of the mother, Freud eventually rejects the idea of an Electra complex in which the girl begins with a straight-forward desire for her father and a wish to do away with her mother as the rival for the father's affection. The girl's primary attachment to the mother must be overcome, but, unlike the boy, the girl cannot separate the ambivalent love of the mother into love and hate and transfer the hate to the father in the process of identifying with him. Instead, the girl must take the father as the love object and retain an identification with the mother.

Just as the sight of the female genitals was critical for the development of the male psyche, the critical moment in the de-velopment of the female psyche occurs when the little girl sees the male genitals. According to Freud, when the little girl sees the penis of a young boy she immediately recognizes it as the superior form of her clitoris. Her self-esteem or narcissism receives a devastating blow when she realizes that she lacks a penis and she translates this lack into inferiority. From then on she suffers from penis envy, and this envy is the foundation of her future development.

At this point there are three alternative forms of development that the girl may follow. She may feel deprived and resentful that she has only a clitoris and no penis. In that case she withdraws in revulsion from all forms of sexuality and refuses to relate to others. Alternatively she may deny her "castration" and organize her sexuality around her clitoris, the "rudimentary" penis. In so doing she develops what Freud calls a "masculinity complex," which may later lead her to strive for professional or intellectual achievements; this complex often leads to the choice of a homo-sexual love object (lesbianism). In contrast to these two "im-mature" or neurotic forms of development is a third possibility, "normal femininity." Here, the female accepts her "castration" and gives up masturbatory activity, making the transition from the clitoris to the vagina as her leading erogenous zone.[104]

On this path to "normality" the girl blames the mother for depriving her of the penis and bringing her into the world female. The mother is also diminished in the girl's eyes for being a mem-ber of the inferior female sex. She turns from the mother to take the father as the love object in the hope of receiving a penis-baby from him. In this new situation the mother becomes the object of the girl's jealousy.

Thus, the move toward the father originates in resentment against the mother who did not give the girl a penis. The girl's turning away from the mother is therefore more than a mere change of object: it entails a hostility toward the mother and the transition from active to passive aims—from the desire to possess the mother to the desire to bear the father's son. This transfor-mation to passive aims favors the development of masochism in women, according to Freud. Here, as in the development of the boy, the father enters as a third element to break up the mother-child dyad. But the girl does not identify with the father. Rather, she takes him for her love object but retains an identification with the mother, who is seen as a rival and another member of the inferior sex. The girl, like the boy, becomes a self with and against an Other, but the Other is the mother, her first love. Given the deep-seated ambivalence of this love, the girl makes a more emotionally treacherous identification, if we are to believe Freud. In addition, the girl identifies with one she has come to regard as inferior and she therefore becomes self-deprecating.

Freud claims the male achieves instinctual sublimation because he is forced to overcome his desire for the mother through fear of castration by the father. Neither fearing castration nor identifying with the father, the girl never achieves the autonomy or resolve of the male. Therefore, according to Freud, the female has a different ethical or moral standard than the male's. Her conscience or superego is not as objective, as free of emotions as the male superego; she is less able to be just and less capable of postponed gratification. Fixated at narcissistic and masochistic stages of development, the female is "less able to manage the instinctual repressions necessary for intelligence, moral discipline and higher culture."[105] Thus, the move out of the mother-child dyad, which is seen as necessary for psychic health and which results from the entrance of the father as the third element, has different results for males and females.

When the female relinquishes her "masculine drive" and yields to her "feminine destiny" she receives the compensation she has been seeking—a baby. As penis envy is replaced with a wish for a penis-baby, the little girl turns into a little woman and her sexuality is thereafter centered in the vagina. (Freud qualifies the thesis of vaginal sexuality, saying that the woman remains responsive to clitoral stimulation.) The desire or wish for a baby is fundamentally a wish for a son. Through the son the woman may vicariously attain what she has been directly denied—access to the world outside the family:

> A mother is only brought unlimited satisfaction by her relation to a son; this is altogether the most perfect, the most free from ambivalence of all human relationships. A mother can transfer to her son the ambition which she has been obliged to suppress in herself, and she can expect from him the satisfaction of all that has been left over in her of her masculinity complex.[106]

We have seen this idealized view of the mother-son relationship echoed in Horkheimer's analysis of the bourgeois family. However, where Horkheimer sees the mother representing another reality to the son, Freud sees the son representing another reality to the mother.

To summarize, the female's path to normality in Freud's theory is a complicated one. It begins with acceptance of the biological fact that she has no penis, a fact that creates a fundamental difference between the female's castration trauma and the male's castration fear. The boy encounters the father as a menacing force ready to punish him for his incestuous desire to possess the mother. Fearing the loss of his penis the boy turns away from the mother and learns to identify with the father. In this process he gains the necessary self-control for sublimation, which allows him to achieve a sense of morality and to participate in the cultural projects of civilization. The girl's castration trauma, on the other hand, is not the overcoming of incestuous desire but the discovery that she lacks a penis. This discovery leads her to accept her status as the second sex, and she turns to the father in the hope of gaining a penis substitute—a baby. Accepting castration rather than fearing it, the girl does not gain the necessary self-control for sublimation.[107] She therefore is not equipped to participate in the cultural projects of civilization and she remains confined to the family.

Freud sees a correlation between the rule of the reality principle and the organization of the psyche in terms of reproduction. The sexual instincts of males and females undergo a transformation in which the original autoeroticism yields to an object love that serves the species need of procreation. The movement into and out of the Oedipus complex transforms the libidinous drives from their original polymorphous perversity to genital sexuality.[108] However, the male begins life with a heterosexual orientation due to his primary attachment to the mother whereas the girl's heterosexuality is acquired later. The boy's normal development moves from a pre-Oedipal situation in which his love object is female to a post-Oedipal situation in which his love object is still female. The little girl, on the other hand, must accomplish a radical shift in her object relation. She must give up her pre-Oedipal attachment to the mother and adopt a passive, "feminine" Oedipal attachment to the father in order to reach a post-Oedipal form of heterosexuality. Thus, the male begins as a little man while the girl must *become* a little woman, and the two sexes develop a different relation to love and work, to the family and society.

Work and Love

In *Civilization and Its Discontents* Freud writes of the critical role that professional work plays in the lives of men:

> No other technique for the conduct of life attaches the individual so firmly to reality as laying emphasis on work; for his work at least gives him a secure place in a portion of reality, in the human community. The possibility it offers of displacing a large amount of libidinal components, whether narcissistic, aggressive or even erotic, on to professional work and on the human relations connected with it lends it a value by no means second to what it enjoys as something indispensable to the preservation and justification of existence in society.[109]

Woman's work, however, is not a displacement of libido but the result either of a failure in development or her shame over the lack of a penis. If a woman attempts to have a career she is diagnosed as suffering from a "masculinity complex," which means that all her work and thinking result from frustration and envy. Even woman's historical inventions of braiding and weaving are interpreted as an attempt to hide the fact that she does not have a penis.

> Shame, which is considered to be a feminine characteristic *par excellence* but is far more a matter of convention than might be supposed, has as its purpose, we believe, concealment of genital deficiency.... It seems that women have made few contributions to the discoveries and inventions in the history of civilization; there is, however, one technique which they may have invented—that of plaiting and weaving.... Nature herself would seem to have given

the model which this achievement imitates by causing the growth at maturity of the pubic hair that conceals the genitals. The step that remained to be taken lay in making the threads adhere to one another, while on the body they stick into the skin and are only matted together.[110]

Braiding and weaving are two different processes, of course; and the notion that weaving cloth is a simple matter of "making threads adhere to one another" belies the intricate nature of the weaving process and belittles the creative intelligence behind its invention.

While man uses work to "test reality," displace libidinal drives, and maintain his identity, integrity, and sanity, woman has another destiny: her libidinal drives are to find full gratification in being loved and in loving her husband and her children. However, due to the process of her development, in which woman becomes more narcissistic than man, she needs to be loved more than she needs to love, according to Freud, even though she has come to represent loving rather than the need to be loved. Yet she finds that her husband's love for her is increasingly withdrawn as he pursues projects outside the family in the development of civilization.

> Women soon come into opposition to civilization and display their retarding and restraining influence—those very women who, in the beginning, laid the foundations of civilization by the claims of their love. Women represent the interests of the family and of sexual life. The work of civilization has become increasingly the business of men, it confronts them with ever more difficult tasks and compels them to carry out instinctual sublimations of which women are little capable. Since a man does not have unlimited quantities of psychical energy at his disposal, he has to accomplish his tasks by making an expedient distribution of his libido. What he employs for cultural aims he to a great extent withdraws from women and sexual life. His constant association with men, and his dependence on his relations with them, even estrange him from his duties as a husband and father. Thus the woman finds herself forced into the background by the claims of civilization and she adopts a hostile attitude towards it.[111]

Woman is identified with love and needs love yet she finds herself in a situation in which her need is not fulfilled. Here Freud goes one step beyond Hegel. He identifies woman with love and the family but recognizes that within the family woman's love remains unsatisfied.

Freud asserts that woman is unable to "carry out instinctual sublimations" and therefore *cannot* participate in "the work of civilization." However, he is closer to the truth when he sees her hostility coming from the fact that she is "forced into the background" by a patriarchal civilization that does not allow her to move outside the family to displace her libidinous needs into larger cultural projects. Denied access to cultural pursuits and living with a husband whose energy is channeled elsewhere, the bourgeois wife grows unhappy and neurotic. Freud's response to this problem is to suggest promiscuity as a potential, if not practical, solution: "Marriage under the present cultural standard has long ceased to be a panacea for the nervous sufferings of women; even if we physicians in such cases still advise matrimony, we are nevertheless aware that a girl must be very healthy to 'stand' marriage.... Marital unfaithfulness would... be a much more probable cure for the neurosis resulting from marriage."[112] What Freud fails to note here is that marital infidelity has always been the prerogative of the bourgeois male; the claim that all man's energy goes into cultural pursuits when it is withdrawn from the marriage is belied by the conventions of prostitution and adultery, which give the man access to sexual fulfillment while denying it to his wife.

Freud's last words on the development of the female psyche are revealing. He admits that while psychoanalysis describes the sexual function of the female it is perplexed by woman as a human being:

> That is all I had to say to you about femininity. It is certainly incomplete and fragmentary and does not always sound friendly. But do not forget that I have only been describing women in so far as their nature is determined by their sexual function. It is true that that influence extends very far; but we do not overlook the fact that

an individual woman may be a human being in other respects as well. If you want to know more about femininity, enquire from your own experiences of life, or turn to the poets, or wait until science can give you deeper and more coherent information.[113]

On another occasion Freud admits that with all his research and theorizing about the female psyche he has never been able to answer the question "What does woman want?"[114] Freud's confusion does not come from a lack of intellectual ingenuity. Rather, he does not approach the female *as* female, and therefore he cannot understand the uniquely female desire.[115] Instead of turning to poets or "science" as Freud suggests we must turn to woman herself as she tries to understand herself. From this perspective the answer to the question of what woman wants is quite simple: she wants to represent herself to herself and not be defined through the eyes and desires of man. She wants to be able to ask the question concerning her identity and her desire as the first step in attempting an answer.

Hysteria, Anorexia Nervosa, and Agoraphobia

In Freud's account the need for activity and control, which is a sign of maturity in male development, is devalued as a regression in female development. Those women who successfully repress any desire for autonomy so that they experience no distress over their enforced infantilism are considered to be mature, normal, and therefore "feminine" females. Those who experience psychic distress from the contradiction between their internal desire for autonomy and their social destiny of passivity become psychological casualties.[116] But if, as Marcuse claims, the neurotic individual puts civilization into question, and the private sickness "reveals itself to be a particular instance of the general destiny, of the traumatic wound that the repressive transformation of the instincts has inflicted on [humanity]," then the specifically "feminine" forms of neuroses may reveal the truth behind woman's "destiny" and show the psychic cost of woman's domination. In addition, Robert Seidenberg has suggested that neurosis is rebellion.[117] If we accept both definitions, we can see the uniquely "feminine" forms of neuroses as the female's attempt to struggle against her destiny of domination as well as the truth behind that destiny.

Freud began his psychoanalytic career treating hysteria—"the rising of the emotions of the womb"—an almost exclusively female neurosis that usually developed during puberty when the feminine destiny was first perceived with full force. Today, hysteria has almost vanished as a form of neurosis.[118] Where have all the hysterics gone? Where are all the middle-class adolescent girls who become ill at the thought of their future, who, when they realize what is in store for them, retreat from "womanhood" into neurosis? If hysteria was a way out of woman's destiny, a rebellion and the truth behind femininity, then today's equivalent is anorexia nervosa.[119]

The "haven in a heartless world," the affluent bourgeois family, produces intelligent daughters who, at puberty, find themselves unable to cope with the female destiny and rebel against it by starving themselves. Through starvation they not only lose weight but effectively stop menstruation. In *The Golden Cage: The Enigma of Anorexia Nervosa* C. Hilde Bruch observes that the incidence of this neurosis has increased in the last twenty years; to explain its aetiology, Bruch points to several factors, including the current cultural emphasis on slimness, the demands made on middle-class girls in terms of career goals, and the sexual "freedom" that becomes sexual coercion.

Within the family and at school, these girls are oversubmissive and overcompliant in their adaptation to others. Feeling no sense of autonomy or identity they attempt to gain some control over their lives through control over their bodies. Thus, they are often incredibly athletic as well as intellectually accomplished. Yet they act and feel as if their bodies and their actions were beyond their control. The anorexia, like almost everything else in their lives, seems to be determined by some external and mysterious force. Many of them experience themselves as divided—sometimes as one person split into two, sometimes as two distinct persons. Others experience the body as separate from the self. What is felt to "control" the situation is experienced as "a personification of everything that they have tried to hide or deny as not approved by themselves and others. *When they define this separate aspect, this different person seems always to be a male.*"[120] It is therefore the traditionally conceived "masculine" part of the self that is being denied. Though few of the girls Bruch discusses explicitly verbalize it, they all feel that being female is a disadvantage; they all wish to succeed at "masculine" pursuits, which get more respect and recognition.

The efforts made by the anorexics to achieve a slim body through feats of starvation and athletic prowess are attempts to control and transform the despised female body into a masculine one. Usually distress and alarm over bodily changes at the onset of puberty precipitate the anorexia. Normal changes and growth are construed as "fatness." However, this superficial interpretation of the body covers a deeper anxiety: the fear that with adult female size, adult female behavior will be required. Some physicians and therapists believe anorexics are afraid of becoming adults. Bruch thinks they are expressing a fear of becoming teenagers. But clearly if one examines this neurosis carefully, one finds they are expressing the fear of becoming *women*.

Anorexia nervosa is the return of the repressed "masculine" part of the female self. In their overt behavior these girls are totally submissive, dependent females who exhibit little or no sense of self-worth. But while behaving like compliant females through obedience and the denial of what they perceive as the masculine drive for autonomy, they simultaneously attempt to take control of their lives by making their bodies into male bodies—slim, athletic, nonmenstruous. With their concrete, indirect, unconscious thoughts and behavior they see the female body as the source of their distress and therefore try to solve their problem by transforming their bodies. Through their neurosis they punish themselves for being born female and rebel against the fate of the traditional female.

If an adolescent female manages to survive puberty without becoming anorexic her rebellion and inability to cope with the female destiny may occur later in the form of agoraphobia. Agoraphobia has been reconceived from the Greek term—fear of the marketplace or public sphere—to mean a fear of any open space. In this neurosis one is confronted with a paradox: originally denied entrance to the public arenas of human activity through custom and law, woman is now considered neurotic or phobic if she experiences anxiety when she enters them. The streets are often dangerous for woman and therefore a fear of the streets is a "normal" or appropriate response; nevertheless, the issue in agoraphobia is not whether a particular street or area is *actually* dangerous or not. Of greater significance than the external danger is woman's internal reaction of terror and alarm in public spaces, which leaves her unwilling and unable to leave home.[121] If one analyzes agoraphobia from woman's perspective one finds that she is simply acting out, with a vengeance, the traditional feminine destiny:

> The agoraphobic woman is actually abiding strictly by the rules of the game. She has learned the historical lesson and . . . is going by the book, much to the consternation of all concerned. . . . Agoraphobia [is] a very personalized sit-in strike, a metaphor of bold definition. If woman's place is indeed in the home, she will be there—with a vengeance. If being dependent and living vicariously is woman's lot in life, who is more womanly and feminine than the agoraphobe?[122]

In "The Trauma of Eventlessness" Seidenberg describes a case study of an agoraphobe and argues that trauma can result from the absence of stimuli as well as from a stimulus that overwhelms the ego. This housewife's neurosis developed when she realized that unless there was some change in her life her future would be a repetition of her past, a life characterized by "submission to authority, absence of choice, and a general exclusion and isolation from the significant stimuli of life." Leading an unchallenging and passionless existence, she feared the psychological death of the self that she saw approaching. Her anticipation of "more of the same eventlessness" caused her neurotic behavior. Seidenberg shows that the overriding danger in this woman's life came from the very "safety" of her existence. "The hostile elements of her environment were not the people of the street but her 'loved' ones who saw her as pure biology."[123]

Both the anorexic daughter and the traumatized housewife are rebelling against the traditional female destiny, attempting to find a way out. In the case of anorexia nervosa the adolescent female tries to escape her destiny by unconsciously denying the female body that is forcing her to confront her future as a woman. The agoraphobe is making a passive-aggressive assertion of the "feminine destiny." In order to understand the unique development of the female psyche we must go behind these neuroses to understand the female as she attempts to create a self in infancy, for it is the failure of this process that creates anorexics and agoraphobes.

Beyond Oedipus?

Autochthonism or self-creation is the central problem of the myth of Oedipus, in which Oedipus eliminates both his father, Laius (whom Oedipus kills), and his mother, Jocasta (who commits suicide when she realizes that she has engaged in an incestuous alliance). In addition, the Sphinx, who may be seen to represent matriarchal forms, is defeated by Oedipus and kills herself as a result of the encounter with him. When Oedipus answers the riddle of the Sphinx it is the answer of male self-creation: "a son grows to become a man and takes the place of his father." Thus, the myth centers on patrilineal descent: fathers are perpetuated in their sons and mothers are merely the vessels of reproduction who self-destruct when their sons grow to manhood.

Seen in this light, the Oedipus myth is a myth of male development within patriarchy and a denial of woman. For this reason, Freud found himself embroiled in difficulties when he tried to use the Oedipus complex to explain female development. If the Oedipus complex is the foundation of psychoanalysis, as Freud and many others believe, then it must be concluded that the foundation is essentially flawed: it may explain male development but it cannot explain female development as a process of self-creation.

Luce Irigaray claims that a logic of identity can be shown to permeate Freud's work insofar as woman as Other is defined only in terms of absence, want, defect, and envy. Woman is merely the reverse, the inferior copy of man and as such she is dominated. Thus, while suggesting that the female has a unique process of psychosexual development, Freud ultimately explains this process in terms of male biology. In *Speculum of the Other Woman* and *This Sex Which Is Not One*, Irigaray shows that Freud believes the little girl sees herself with the eyes of the little boy and does not see her "invisible" sex: the little girl supposedly looks upon herself as "not a boy," as castrated, when in fact she is not. Since the girl makes no attempt to symbolize the clitoris and vagina as unique and specific to her, the female as such does not exist for Freud. It is precisely because of her inability to represent her unique anatomy to herself that the Freudian female does not and cannot become an "I," an autonomous subject.[124]

If we take Freud's biologism seriously then the identification with the mother that the daughter achieves is more profound than any identification the son can ever have with the mother. As the female psyche is formed in relation to the mother, a unique relation of self to the first Other is achieved. The girl comes to know a physical correspondence with the mother and identifies this most significant Other with the self.

Freud does not confront female genitalia or the womb except to describe them as the context of hysteria and masochism. Childbirth is an experience of pleasure in pain, according to Freud, that along with "passive intercourse" confirms woman's masochism. While it is true that the pain associated with childbirth, menstruation, and defloration makes pain part of the female experience in a unique way, this does not necessarily mean that women enjoy or take pleasure in such pain. Women learn to live with pain and accept it as a "normal" part of life, but they experience pain as pain, as separate and distinct from the moment beyond pain, which may or may not be pleasurable.[125] From the mother's perspective, childbirth involves the recognition that life and growth cannot take place without pain since we are embodied, and therefore natural, beings: childbirth reminds us that pain is an integral part of human life. Despite the pervasiveness of the metaphor of birth for creative activity, the significance of pain in this respect is often overlooked. And, pain, if Horkheimer and Adorno are to be believed, is the foundation for the negation of the here and now as a process of the recognition of non-identity. With the pain of childbirth one sees the self in the Other but knows it to be Other. In the situation of involuntary motherhood this may be the source of alienation.

Some psychologists have theorized that the pain in male initiation rites allows men to achieve ego stability: men create situations of endurance to strengthen their egos. Such a syndrome of self-inflicted pain seems closer to masochism than the endurance of inevitable pain by women. If pain is the source of ego stability then woman's pain may provide her with a sound ego that requires no self-torture to confirm its strength.[126]

Most important, Freud does not integrate into his theory the fact that children of both sexes are profoundly affected by the significance of the womb. Robert Stoller asserts that while the female genitals are difficult to represent symbolically, because they are less visible than the penis, the swollen belly of a pregnant woman is no more difficult to "see" than the little boy's penis and "if measured by the mystery it creates, is more important even than the penis."[127] Without reducing womanhood to motherhood we must recognize the importance of the womb in the psychosexual development of both sexes. Ironically, Freud had the visual representation of woman's unique procreative power right in front of him during every analytic session in his office. A recent book on the birth symbol in traditional woman's art shows Freud's famous couch covered with a Persian rug woven with the schematic form of the ancient birth symbol. Freud did not recognize this and proceeded to weave his theories of the female psyche around the penis, not the womb or female genitalia.[128]

Irigaray's critique of Freud raises an important issue in terms of critical theory's appropriation of Freud, a problem which Monique Plaza articulates in " 'Phallomorphic' Power and the Psychology of 'Woman.' "[129] That is, if the non-identity of psyche and society in Freud's work is to be rescued within a critique of the domination of nature, it is necessary to come to terms with the fact that embedded in this formulation of non-identity is a rationality of identity that denies woman's uniqueness and simultaneously dominates her as "not male." Thus, the non-identity of psyche and society is collapsed into an identity theory in which the female as Other is not truly Other but merely the absence of self as male. The critique of identity theories made by Horkheimer and Adorno in their major works on Western philosophy is neglected in their emphasis on the liberatory potential of the male model of ego development in Freud.

Freud, like Hegel, conceives of woman as unable to develop into an autonomous self with a conscious sense of morality. Woman has to remain in the family—for Hegel, because she lacks a contradiction between herself and nature; for Freud, because she lacks a penis. Horkheimer reinforces both positions in his studies on authority and the family, by idealizing the role of woman as mother within the family in terms of her effect on the male psyche. Nowhere does Horkheimer suggest that the psychosexual development of the female is the same as that of the male; yet neither is there an attempt made to analyze the significance of the difference.

There does not yet exist a comprehensive psychoanalytic theory of the female psyche. That this is so undoubtedly helps to explain why whenever we encounter woman she is either a "question" or an "enigma." Many feminists have rejected Freud's theory because it lacks a sociohistorical analysis of patriarchy. However, as Juliet Mitchell points out in *Psychoanalysis and Feminism*, the attempt to come to terms with such an analysis leads feminists such as Shulamith Firestone, Germaine Greer, and Kate Millett to assume a simplistic approach to the relation between social reality and the development of the individual psyche. In the "social realism" of these feminist critiques there is no place for the dynamics of desire, fantasy, infantile sexuality, or unconscious drives. They disregard the non-identity of psyche and society, claiming that social actuality and conscious choice rule over human development. They construct theories in which the infant is immediately confronted by the reality principle and penis envy is derived from the fact that patriarchal civilization values the male (symbolized by the penis) and devalues the female.[130]

Mitchell herself interprets penis envy as symbolic of patriarchal domination but she approaches Freud differently. She defends Freud for having given us an analysis of the way in which infants unconsciously internalize gender identity and argues that it is impossible to explain gender differences through a sociohistorical analysis that denies the unconscious. At the same time she shows that there are socially specific processes that inform the development of gender identity. Thus she attempts to make the dynamics of the unconscious subject to critical analysis while pointing to the possibility of historical transformation.

However, Mitchell does not come to terms with Freud's analysis of sexual differentiation as an identity theory in which woman's unique biology is denied. In addition, Mitchell's attempt to integrate Lévi-Strauss and Lacan into her analysis of Freud leads to confused and confusing statements concerning incest and exogamy. If instead she had turned to the work of Marcuse, Horkheimer, and Adorno she might have gained some insight into the problem of non-identity and provided an important critique of their failure to develop an analysis of the Freudian female psyche.

The unique development of the female psyche cannot be understood without reference to the experiences of female embodiment in which the female seeks a sense of self through her conflict and identification with the mother. Woman's embodiment must be redefined so that it is no longer seen in terms of the Oedipal drama nor in terms of male biology, as the absence of the penis; rather, it must be seen as the female experiences it—as the presence of the clitoris, vagina, womb, and breasts through which the identification with and against the mother is made. We must reconstitute the theory of psychosexual development based on the non-identity of libidinous drives and the demands of culture. With this in mind we turn now to the dialectical development in the theories of Marcuse, Horkheimer, and Adorno as it relates to the woman question.

PART III

Dialectical Development: Woman and Nature in Critical Theory

CHAPTER FOUR

The Domination of Nature

> Through reason man frees himself
> of the fetters of nature. This liber-
> ation, however, does not entitle
> man to dominate nature...but to
> comprehend it.
>
> MAX HORKHEIMER,
> "The End of Reason"

THE WOMAN QUESTION IS CENTRAL TO THE PROJECT OF MAKING
critical theory self-reflective since it is situated at the intersection
of two important themes: intersubjective recognition and the
relation of humanity and nature.

In Hegel the family is the sphere that guarantees the preservation of natural immediacy in human life, thereby providing
the foundation for intersubjective recognition in civil society and
political life. Yet Hegel's account comes at woman's expense:
she is confined to immediacy, reduced to nature, and therefore
cannot achieve intersubjective recognition. The framework of
the early Marx seemed more fruitful insofar as it focused on
heterosexual love as the paradigm of intersubjective relations
and the reconciliation of nature with human society. However,
there is no conception of woman as a social actor in this formulation. The later Marx moves away from the analysis of the
specific logic of the family and heterosexual relations to a theory
in which the logic of civil society is taken to be the dominant
logic of historic development; consequently, the idea of a reconciliation of society and nature is replaced by the acceptance
of the domination of nature as the basis for intersubjective relations in the sphere of production. Thus, for Marx ego development occurs in civil society. And in his theory, as in Hegel's,
the fundamental issue of patriarchal domination—its personal,

direct form within the family and its abstract, social form within society at large— is ignored.

Horkheimer, Marcuse, and Adorno attempt to appropriate critically the work of Hegel and Marx by resuscitating nature as an independent moment of the dialectic. They investigate the specific logic of the family but, departing from Hegel and Marx, they focus on the psychic development of the ego within the family. To do this they turn to Freud. Their studies on authority indicate that the domination of nature does not lead to inter-subjective recognition, as Marx maintained. Rather, the psychic prerequisites of domination tend to reproduce authoritarian social relations. Thus, the Freudian account of ego development within the family provides the basis for an analysis of the relation between the domination of external nature, social domination, and self-domination.

The turn to Freud within a focus on the specific logic of the family entails a consideration of woman's situation. Particularly in Horkheimer's analysis, woman as mother represents unconditional love to the son, which leaves him with a memory of the liberatory potential of nature that can ground social critique. But there is a fundamental problem with Horkheimer's analysis: the woman question is interpreted as the symbolic function of woman as mother for the son. Woman qua woman—woman as a self-conscious social actor—still does not appear. This is all the more serious since Horkheimer appropriates Freud's analysis of ego development through the Oedipus complex but ignores the unique development of the daughter. Here Freud is more to the point since he at least gives a separate account of female ego development within the family. The daughter's conflict and identification with the mother is rightly formulated as essential to this development. However, Freud's account is vitiated by a male bias evident in the claim that the girl views *herself* as lacking a penis. At the crucial point in his theory of female psychic development Freud substitutes an *other's* view (the boy's) for the self-experience of the girl.

At each step in the tradition of critical theory, including the incorporation of Freud, a view *of* the female supplants a view *by* the female. Woman's lived experience is overreached in the tradition as woman is defined as different and associated with nature. Therefore, a consideration of the woman question is crucial to the concern with the domination of nature, which critical theory has rightly identified as the central theme in its critique of contemporary society. The intersection of intersubjectivity and nature in the family underscores the role of woman as an index of the domination of nature—and an articulation of woman's experience is a necessary link in the attempt to make critical theory self-reflective.

Critical theory's attempt to resuscitate nature as an independent moment of the dialectic, that is, to develop a critique of the domination of nature, is examined in this chapter primarily through the work of Herbert Marcuse. Marcuse's thought moves away from the identification of woman and mother within the family to focus on the "feminine principle" as an analysis of woman qua woman. Relevant positions of Horkheimer and Adorno can be situated with respect to Marcuse's work. Thus, Marcuse's conception of woman in terms of the "return of the repressed" is directly related to the view of woman in the authority and the family studies, and through the concept of "repressive desublimation" his work leads back to Horkheimer's "revolt of nature" and the excursus on Odysseus by Horkheimer and Adorno in the *Dialectic of Enlightenment*. In addition, the development of a dialectical analysis leads to Adorno's attempt at a comprehensive formulation of the dialectic as a theory of non-identity in *Negative Dialectics*.

Marcuse's utopian vision in *Eros and Civilization*, like that of Horkheimer's in the authority studies, depends on woman as mother providing a utopian vision for the son. Marcuse extends this analysis through Freud's instinct theory. His later works move away from this position but still bear traces of the treatment of woman in the authority and the family studies insofar as the feminine principle is based on woman's historical distance from civil society and the ethic of production. While the move away from the identification of woman and mother in Marcuse's work is an important step in the attempt by critical theory to theorize woman's domination in relation to the domination of nature, it tends to elide the importance of potential motherhood in the development of "feminine" traits and again to miss the experience of woman as a historical actor. In addition, the non-identity of woman and mother depends on an analysis of repression that ties all the distortion of repressed instincts to sociohistoric factors rather than the mechanics of repression. The latter alternative is maintained by Freud and is represented within critical theory by Horkheimer and Adorno.

There are two alternative poles around which the critical theory of contemporary society revolves: utopian regression and regressive barbarism. They are rooted in the ontogenetic and phylogenetic dimensions of memory that revivify images of happiness and suffering. Woman's experience, as the intersection of intersubjectivity and nature, provides the nexus for reinterpreting both images within a critique of the domination of nature.

RETURN OF THE REPRESSED

As we saw in part 2, woman's domination as nature was thought to offer liberatory potential to the son in the Frankfurt school's studies on authority and the family. Marcuse's analysis of Freud in *Eros and Civilization* begins from these studies and attempts to go beyond them. He proclaims Freud's theory "obsolete" insofar as the transformation of capitalism has changed family dynamics. But for Marcuse psychoanalysis draws its strength from its obsolescence—from its insistence on the individual's need and potential for gratification. "That which is obsolete is not, by this token, false.... The Freudian concepts invoke not only a past left behind but also a future to be recaptured."[1] With the historical obsolescence of established society, the growth of its inner antagonisms may potentially release repressed instincts in an undistorted form. Libidinal forces would then change their social function and, rather than preserving the old society, lead to the creation of new social formations.

Beginning from the theses of fatherlessness and motherlessness Marcuse attempts to show that a "society without the father" has utopian promise. "Society without the mother," how-ever, remains defined as a society without hope or love, since it is maternal Eros as the female principle of gratification ("the return of the repressed") that is central to the project of liberation that *Eros and Civilization* outlines.

Marcuse attempts to rescue the liberatory potential embedded in Freud's theory of the instincts. He interprets the basic Freudian conflict between the pleasure principle (first nature) and the real-ity principle (second nature) as a sociohistoric conflict. Contem-porary society enforces a surplus repression, repression beyond that required by the current stage of civilization. Marcuse calls this the performance principle, which is "a Reality Principle based on the efficiency and prowess in the fulfillment of com-petitive economic and acquisitive functions."[2] This historical form of the reality principle defeats the pleasure principle and thereby maintains society as a system of social and self-domi-nation. However, the objectives of the defeated pleasure principle are retained in the unconscious. What civilization represses in the interest of economic performance is retained in the individ-ual's unconscious psyche as a desire for gratification. The project of human liberation is therefore to establish a society beyond the rule of the performance principle, where libidinal satisfaction, not domination, will be the foundation of human relations.[3]

In the attempt to specify those aspects of instinctual life that are the basis of a *new* reality principle, Marcuse resuscitates nature as an independent moment within a dialectical theory that points to the possibility of a reconciliation of man and nature. (This is "the humanization of nature and the naturalization of man" central to Marx's early work, although Marx is never cited in *Eros and Civilization*.)

Marcuse recounts the fact that "according to Freud, the his-tory of man is the history of his repression." Marcuse widens the term *repression* in his own discussion: " 'Repression,' and 'repressive' are used in the non-technical sense to designate both conscious and unconscious, external and internal processes of restraint, constraint, and suppression."[4] In Freud's theory the concept of repression usually means an unconscious and unsuccessful defense, and a return of the repressed is always a return of infantile wishes characterized by distortion. In *Moses and Monotheism* Freud explains that when an instinctual demand goes unsatisfied it is repressed. However,

> either the instinct has kept its strength, or it will regain it, or it is reawakened by a new situation. It renews its claim and—since the way to normal satisfaction is barred by what we may call the scar tissue of repression—it gains at some weak point new access to a so-called substitutive satisfaction which now appears as a symptom. ... All phenomena of symptom-formation can be fairly described as "the return of the repressed." The distinctive character of them, however, lies in the extensive distortion the returning elements have undergone, compared with their original form.[5]

For Marcuse, the return of the repressed is the return of the undistorted desire for liberation. Thus, Marcuse draws on Freud but goes "beyond" him by redefining significant concepts. This produces what Marcuse calls an "extrapolation" of Freud.

After redefining the concept of repression Marcuse claims that even in Freud's theory there is the basis for a distinction between basic repression (the necessary control of the instincts for the survival of humanity) and surplus repression (the unnecessary and avoidable repression required by the given form of social domination). Marcuse attempts to show that a non-surplus-repressive society is possible; he bases this possibility on a "rescuing" of Freud by continually recalling Freud's statement that the nature of the instincts is "historically acquired" and by showing that Freud seems to forget this at significant junctures in his theory. Freud's acknowledgment of the historical modification of the instincts is vitiated by his equation of the reality principle with the norms of patriarchal-capitalist society.

Marcuse's theory of liberation is rooted in a "dialectical regression," which is a critical regression behind the mystifying forms of the given that would revive yet transcend early stages of libido:

> The emergence of a non-repressive reality principle involving instinctual liberation would *regress* behind the attained level of civilized rationality. This regression would be psychical as well as social;

it would reactivate early stages of libido which were surpassed in the development of the reality ego, and it would dissolve the institutions of society in which the reality ego exists. In terms of these institutions, instinctual liberation is a relapse into barbarism. However, occurring at the height of civilization, as a consequence not of defeat but of victory in the struggle for existence, and supported by a free society, such liberation might have very different results.... [In freedom] the libido would not simply reactivate precivilized and infantile stages, but would also transform the perverted content of these stages.[6]

The dialectical regression is to realize the transformation of sexuality into Eros, that is, to transform sexuality from a partial drive that focuses on genital sexuality to Eros as the "intensification, gratification and unification of life and of the life environment."[7] According to Marcuse, under changed social and existential conditions, the dynamics of the sex instincts will generate enduring erotic relations among mature human beings. No longer focused on genital, procreative sexuality under male domination, a higher stage of polymorphous eroticism will be activated through the regressive dialectic. The re-eroticized body will become a true source of gratification as libido is not simply released but transformed.

The precondition for freedom based on a new reality principle is the quantitative reduction in work time facilitated by automation. That is, qualitative change in human existence emerges from quantitative change. Marcuse's position that a quantitative reduction of labor time is necessary to the qualitative change from an unfree to a free society reflects the problematic relation between freedom from labor and freedom in labor that we find in Marx. In contemporary society work is the realm of unfreedom, and freedom can be realized only outside labor: "No matter how justly and rationally the material production may be organized, it can never be a realm of freedom and gratification; but it can release time and energy for the free play of human faculties *outside* the realm of alienated labor. The more complete the alienation of labor, the greater the potential of freedom: total automation would be the optimum. It is the sphere outside labor which defines freedom and fulfillment."[8] However, Marcuse envisions a future society in which work will be libidinally satisfying and freedom will be realized *in* labor through the reconciliation of work and play: "If work were accompanied by a reactivation of pregenital polymorphous eroticism, it would tend to become gratifying in itself without losing its *work* content. . . . The altered societal conditions would therefore create an instinctual basis for the transformation of work into play."[9]

In Marcuse's extrapolation of Freud's theory of repression what is repressed is the message of liberation contained in the pleasure principle. Marcuse ties this to the Oedipal wish as a desire for the mother, which is really the desire for gratification, in terms of Freud's phylogenetic account of the development of civilization.[10] Freud's theory is both ontogenetic and phylogenetic: the ontogenetic account traces the psychosexual development of the individual through the oral, anal, and phallic phases, especially through the relation of the Oedipus and castration complexes; the phylogenetic account focuses on the killing of the father by the primal horde. Marcuse deemphasizes the Oedipus complex and does not analyze Freud's ontogenetic account. Instead, he uses Freud's phylogenetic approach to reconstruct an ontogeny in terms of the domination of the pleasure principle (represented by the mother) by the reality principle (represented by the father).

As Marcuse points out, the understanding of reality that prevails in Freud's work and that is condensed in his concept of the reality principle is tied to the image of the father. Since this reality confronts the developing ego as an external and antagonistic power, the father is seen primarily as a hostile figure. The castration threat symbolizes the father's power and asserts itself against the infant's attempt to gratify its libidinous desire for the mother. The decisive step then in the development of the ego is the compliance with a hostile force: submission to the threat of castration.[11] (All of this pertains only to male development, as we saw in part 2, since the role of castration is quite different in the development of the female psyche.)

However, for Marcuse the rebellion of Eros against domination is kept alive through the return of the repressed as the memory of gratification: "Eros...is moved by remembrance." Critical remembrance, rooted in our psychosexual development, is the impetus for liberation. Memory preserves the promises and potentialities for freedom that are embedded in our childhood. Even if these memories are betrayed or denied by the adult they are never completely forgotten: "The psychoanalytic liberation of memory explodes the rationality of the repressed individual. ... The forbidden images and impulses of childhood begin to tell the truth.... Regression assumes a progressive function.... The *recherche du temps perdu* becomes the vehicle of future liberation."[12] Thus memory emerges as the mediation between the psychological and the political spheres of life. The memory of gratification fuels representations in fantasy, aesthetic and mythic images, and sexual "perversions" that contain intimations of a liberated future. In these domains, which remain relatively untouched by the reality principle, subterranean impulses safeguard their subversive content. These representations of the return of the repressed as the memory of liberation are rooted in the image of woman as mother in *Eros and Civilization*.

Maternal Eros

Marcuse realizes that the phylogenetic account of the primal horde advanced by Freud has been strongly objected to, if not completely rejected, on the ground that the thesis has not been anthropologically substantiated. However, he defends his reliance on the theory of the primal horde by claiming that despite its lack of scientific verification and logical consistency "it telescopes...the historical dialectic of domination and thereby elucidates aspects of civilization hitherto unexplained."[13] Thus, Marcuse emphasizes the symbolic value of this theory, not its historical reality.

In *Totem and Taboo* and *Moses and Monotheism* Freud reconstructs the prehistory of "mankind" from the primal horde through patricide to the brother clan of civilization. According to Freud, the original human group was formed and sustained by the domination of one man over all others. The father supposedly kept for himself the women who represented supreme pleasure (sexual gratification) and forced the other male members of the horde to submit to his power. The women bore the father's children and maintained them. All the other work was done by the sons, whose instinctual energy was "free" to be channeled into unpleasant but necessary labor since it was not allowed direct gratification in sexual relations with the women. If the sons made the father jealous, they were killed, castrated, or driven out of the group. In this way, the father's control over the sons' desire for gratification created the psychological preconditions for maintaining domination.

The original patriarch was both father and tyrant. Through him sex and order, pleasure and reality were united. In his functions and his person he incorporated the necessity and the internal logic of the reality principle. By establishing a social order based on reproductive sexuality the father secured the sociological and biological basis of history. Granted, the father established his domination in terms of his own interest; nevertheless, this domination was "justified" by his biological function, his age, and, most important, by his success: he created the "order" necessary to retain group cohesion.

The "effective" social order established by primal patriarchal tyranny evoked both love and hatred of the father. In Freud's theory, the hatred that results from patriarchal suppression culminates in the rebellion of those sons who had been exiled from the primal horde—they collectively kill and devour the father. But this rebellion is a rebellion against "justified" authority. Therefore, the crime against the father is also a crime against group life. As a crime against the whole, the killing of the father rebounds as a crime against the very sons who have committed it. That is, the assassination of the father threatens to destroy the permanence of group life and to restore the destructive rule of the subhistoric and prehistoric pleasure principle represented by the woman/mother: sexual need begins to divide the brothers, who become rivals for the women.

However, the sons, like the father, want sustained satisfaction. They can achieve this goal only by duplicating, albeit in a new form, the order of domination that preserved the group by inhibiting pleasure. Therefore the sons establish themselves as the brother clan, which deifies the assassinated father and reintroduces taboos and restraints on the pursuit of sexual pleasure. Rules concerning the acquisition of women, such as the incest taboo and exogamy, are restored. Consequently, civilization begins with the brother clan, since it is here that self-domination is established as necessary for social order. Thus, according to Freud, it is necessary both to overthrow the primal father (as external domination) and restore him (as internalized domination). The move from the primal horde to "civilization" is effected by a feeling of guilt: the rebel sons are guilty in their own eyes as they are guilty in the eyes of the others. Through their guilt they internalize taboos and inhibitions and develop the ability to accept delayed gratification, all of which are necessary to civilization.

According to Freud the primal crime and the guilt it entails "return" in altered forms throughout history. Marcuse interprets this to mean that the crime may be seen in the conflict between generations, in the rebellion against the given system of authority, and in the subsequent restoration and justification of authority. The decisive difference is that domination is normally no longer personal, but abstract—it resides in the society as a whole.[14]

Within his recounting of Freud's theory, Marcuse details the role of woman/mother in the primal horde: "In the primal horde, the image of the desired woman, the mistress-wife of the father, was Eros and Thanatos in immediate, natural union. She was the aim of the sex instincts, and she was the mother in whom the son once had that integral peace which is the absence of all need and desire—the Nirvana before birth." Because woman was Eros/Thanatos/Nirvana in "immediate" union she represented the threat of "mere nature"—"the regressive impulse for peace which stood in the way of progress, of Life itself."[15] (Marcuse then speculates that this may explain the taboo on incest with the mother. He does not mention a father-daughter taboo.) However, Marcuse interprets this "regressive" impulse as the locus of liberatory possibility in an advanced civilization. He argues that maternal Eros only retains a regressive association with "mere nature" due to the continuing supremacy of the patriarchal performance principle.[16] A dialectical regression beyond surplus repression would be a return of the desire for liberation tied to the memory of infantile gratification, which is rooted in the relation to the mother.

The argument that such a "return" would be the realization of freedom rather than a regression to mere nature rests on Marcuse's reinterpretation and extrapolation of the relation between Eros, Thanatos, and the Nirvana principle. For Marcuse, the historic development of the conflict between the pleasure principle (the mother) and the reality principle (the father) transforms the domination of the father from personal to abstract domination. Within this development the image of the mother is also transformed. In his phylogenetic account, Freud claims that the taboo on incest instituted by the brother clan differentiated the image of woman into mother and wife. With this separation "the fatal identity of Eros and Thanatos was...dissolved."[17] Love for the mother became aim-inhibited, transformed into tenderness or affection. Thus, sexual/sensual love and affection were divorced.

As we have noted, Freud first argues that this separation led to "psychic impotence" in men. Later he claims that affection and sensual love are rejoined in the man's love for his wife. However, this unity in the love for the wife is, as I have argued in connection with Hegel's theory of the family, at the expense of woman as a self-determining and recognizing individual. And, as Freud himself observes, it leaves woman's need for love unsatisfied. Marcuse is not concerned with the situation of woman as wife; instead he focuses on the representation of the mother. The mother is said to represent "another reality," as she did in Horkheimer's studies, but for Marcuse this conception is grounded in the fact that she represents maternal Eros.

Marcuse interprets the pleasure principle as a desire for liberation from want and pain; it is associated with woman who, as mother, provides integral gratification. In the initial stages of the infant's development, "the relation between 'pre-ego' and

reality, the Narcissistic and the maternal Eros seem to be one
and the primary experience of reality is that of libidinous union."
Marcuse sees the Oedipal wish as a perpetual infantile protest
against the separation from the mother, from the source of satisfaction, and as the desire for the archetypical form of freedom,
freedom from want. It is the sex instinct that retains the memory
of this archetypical freedom, and therefore the desire for the
mother is a sexual desire. Thus, the desire for liberation as a
reconciliation with nature is contained in the "return" to the
mother in the Oedipal wish as a sexual craving for the mother
as woman.[18]

Marcuse fuels his extrapolation of the mother as the image
of Eros/Thanatos/Nirvana by claiming that the main objective
of the Nirvana principle is not necessarily death but rather the
absence of want.

> The death instinct operates under the Nirvana principle: it tends
> toward that state of "constant gratification" where no tension is
> felt—a state without want. This trend of the instinct implies that its
> *destructive* manifestations would be minimized as it approached
> such a state. If the instinct's basic objective is not the termination
> of life but of pain—the absence of tension—then . . . the conflict be-
> tween life and death is the more reduced, the closer life approximates
> the state of gratification.[19]

Here Marcuse argues that a change in the conditions of civilization would directly affect the "formed" human instincts—sex
and aggression—while the "natural" base of human life—Eros
and the Nirvana principle—would remain constant. This natural
base would provide itself with its own limitations. Thus, in a
free society the pleasure principle and the Nirvana principle
would converge not as a reversion to mere nature but as the
reconciliation of humanity and nature. Through a dialectical
regression the early stages of the libidinous relation to the mother
would "return" as a new reality principle beyond the immediate
identity of Eros/Thanatos/Nirvana, which is destructive and
devouring.

According to Marcuse, with the elimination of surplus repres-

sion and through a dialectical regression, a "sensuous rationality" containing its own moral laws would develop to sustain
freedom. This "libidinal morality" is tied to the mother in Marcuse's conception of the "maternal super-id," which is meant to
show how the instincts themselves, in a free society, might har-
monize the apparently contradictory claims of the pleasure principle and the reality principle. Taking his clues from Charles
Odier, Marcuse points out that the superego, as the representative of conscience or morality, has an alliance with the id
(mother/pleasure principle) as well as an alliance with the father/
reality principle. Therefore, he agrees with Odier's claim that the
superego retains within it "a primitive phase, during which morality [has] not yet freed itself from the pleasure principle."[20]
This "pregenital, prehistoric, preoedipal 'pseudo morality' " is
suggested by the identification with the mother, which is expressed, in Marcuse's account, by a castration *wish*. This substitution of a castration wish for Freud's castration threat could
be illuminating insofar as girls get this wish but boys do not.
Unfortunately, this insight is left unexplored because Marcuse
does not analyze Freud's ontogenetic account of the specifically
female psyche.

Within his analysis of a new reality principle rooted in maternal Eros and a maternal superid, Marcuse examines Freud's
theory of the primal horde as it relates to the development of
matriarchy. Both Freud and Marcuse associate matriarchy with
erotic freedom. However, because he believes that freedom is
possible only as liberation from an original state of domination,
Freud believes that in the development of civilization matriarchy
comes after patriarchy. Matriarchy is replaced by a counterrevolution in which patriarchal domination is reinstated and
stablized by institutionalized religion. Marcuse is not primarily
concerned with the historical question of whether matriarchy
precedes or follows patriarchy. For him the significant issue is
the *interpretation* of matriarchy. Against Freud, he accepts Erich
Fromm's thesis that matriarchy precedes patriarchy insofar as
matriarchy represents an original state of freedom. Here again

the emphasis is on a "natural," "unrepressed" freedom that lies undistorted beneath the forms of domination.

The Feminine Principle

In *Counterrevolution and Revolt*, as well as in his later essay "Marxism and Feminism," Marcuse overrules his original theory of woman as mother by recognizing that the identification of womanhood with motherhood is not necessarily liberatory. The woman-as-mother linkage is based in the social valuation of woman as merely a biological being. It is a link in the chain of domination that connects woman to a nature to be dominated: "The image of the woman as mother is itself repressive; it transforms a biological fact into an ethical and cultural value and thus it supports and justifies her social repression."[21] Within this framework there is no liberatory potential to be found in a consideration of the symbolic value of matriarchy.

Whatever we may have thought of the analysis of woman as mother in *Eros and Civilization*, it is invalidated in *Counterrevolution and Revolt*. What is now seen as central to the project of liberation is "the ascent of Eros over aggression, in men *and* women," which is tied to the "feminine principle" as the definite negation of the male performance principle. In this discussion explicit references are made to the conception of the reconciliation with nature in the early Marx. Here, characteristics that have been designated as feminine in the ontogenetic and phylogenetic processes of civilization are seen as necessary to the overturning of the repressive domination of nature: "The faculty of being 'receptive,' 'passive,' is a precondition of freedom: it is the ability to see things in their own right, to experience the joy enclosed in them, the erotic energy of nature—an energy which is there to be liberated; nature, too, awaits the revolution!" Passivity and receptivity, tenderness, and sensitivity—all traditionally feminine traits—are essential to the vision of liberation. Here it is woman's *distance* from civil society, her embeddedness in the specific logic of the family, that allows her to represent a vision of liberation: "Isolation (separation) from the alienated work world of capitalism enabled the woman to remain less brutalized by the Performance Principle, to remain closer to her sensibility: more human than men."[22] As in the earlier formulation in *Eros and Civilization*, this vision is grounded in memory—but not remembrance of a Golden Age (which never existed) of childhood innocence or primitive society. Rather, memory is a synthesis of fragments that can be found within distorted humanity and nature. Remembered fragments of liberatory potential, which are less distorted in woman, are imaginatively reassembled in aesthetic visions of utopia. Thus, Marcuse recalls the painting by Delacroix in which a beautiful, bare-breasted woman leads the revolution. Such visions may not be really actualizable, but they are the precondition for a consciousness that strives for freedom.

With his emphasis on the feminine principle Marcuse has rejected the bourgeois notion that "equality" is the solution to the domination of woman. Horkheimer and Adorno point out in *Dialectic of Enlightenment* that "bourgeois society is ruled by equivalence. It makes the dissimilar comparable by reducing it to abstract quantities."[23] Woman becoming like man would merely be the expression of a commodity society that treats differences as abstractly comparable. In other words, woman could be "equal" to man only at the price of ignoring the specific differences rooted in her condition.

Marcuse's rejection of the equivalence logic of civil society leads him to value the specific difference of femininity. The free society would therefore recognize both masculine and feminine qualities—its ideal would be an androgynous fusion of historically separated differences. For Marcuse sexual and biological difference has been appropriated and institutionalized by society (first nature has become second nature): "The feminine characteristics are socially conditioned. However, the long process of thousands of years of social conditioning means that they may become 'second nature' which is not changed automatically by the establishment of new social institutions." Even though second nature is historically mutable it is not merely a product of the ego's conscious intentions; in this sense, feminine characteristics are "natural" to the beings who acquire them through the process of identity formation. Nevertheless, even if a free society can eliminate gender differences based on expedience, a difference based on nature will remain:

> But, no degree of androgynous fusion could ever abolish the natural differences between male and female as individuals. All joy, and all sorrow are rooted in this difference, in this relation to the other, of whom you want to become part, and who you want to become part of yourself, and who never can and never will become such a part of yourself. Feminist socialism would thus continue to be riddled with conflicts arising from this condition, the ineradicable conflicts of needs and values, but the androgynous character of society might gradually diminish the violence and humiliation in the resolution of these conflicts.[24]

In other words a new social order could *recognize* different qualities such that the traditional masculine/feminine dichotomy would break down, but society would remain divided by a fundamental *natural* difference between male and female that could never be entirely overcome by social and historical mutation. Marcuse's formulation situates the problem of intersubjective recognition of difference within that of the domination of nature, but it refuses to let nature disappear as an independent moment of the dialectic.

Criticism of contemporary society based on the domination of nature has conferred a central significance on the sexual, biological, natural configuration of intersubjective social relations. Within this configuration the association of woman with nature implies that feminine characteristics are important for creating a free society. As Marcuse says, woman literally embodies "the promise of peace, of joy, of the end of violence."[25] However, we must ask: embodies for whom? In *Eros and Civilization* the answer is clear—for the son, who remembers the initial gratifying attachment to the selfless figure of the mother. This analysis is identical in its major axes with that of Horkheimer (see part 2). The unconditional love of the mother is a utopian moment in the son's psychical development. But of course this does not

speak at all to the daughter's development, which turns on identification and conflict with the mother. Both Horkheimer and
Marcuse ignore Freud's theory of the psychosexual development
of the daughter. Consequently, this utopian vision of the mother
cannot comprehend the effect of the domination of nature on
woman's psyche.

In his later works Marcuse abandons the identification of
woman and mother. Society without the mother retains utopian
promise through the ascent of the feminine principle. This is an
important step toward a critical theory of woman's liberation
insofar as it both recognizes the liberatory potential of feminine
characteristics and yet refuses to chain them to motherhood as
a merely biological and natural function, which would then be
without universal significance for the transformation of society.
However, Marcuse abandons the identification of woman and
mother because he views the family as a repressive institution
solidifying natural differences. True enough. But again there is
no account of the development of the female psyche within the
family. While its focus on the domination of nature turns critical
theory toward the specific logic of the family, within this analysis
the female psyche is assimilated to the male—an error not present
in Freud, whatever the insufficiencies of his account. In Marcuse's
earlier theory, woman as mother entered the son's psyche as the
vision of liberatory potential. Given the abandonment of the
woman-mother equation and the absence of *any* account of female psychic development, the question reasserts itself with a
vengeance: for *whom* does woman embody utopia? No longer
for the son, and there is no theoretical basis elaborated on which
it could be the daughter—woman herself.

This lacuna in Marcuse's theory is widened even further when
we ask *why* woman embodies utopia. The earlier theory gave
an answer based on Freud's instinct theory: woman as mother
represented maternal Eros as utopian promise to the son. Having
abandoned the liberatory potential of the identification of
woman and mother, the later theory of the feminine principle
rests on the distance of woman from the productive logic of civil
society. But this distance depends upon woman's institutionali-

zation within the family—her continuing identification with nature as mother, which Marcuse does not acknowledge.

If woman literally "embodies" liberatory traits such as receptivity, passivity, and nonviolence and if a "natural" difference will always remain between woman and man, then it seems that Marcuse's theory is rooted in the problem of woman's embodiment. Woman is not to be identified with mothering; nevertheless, the way in which the daughter comes to "live" within a body based on potential motherhood cannot be ignored. In addition, mothering is a human project as well as a natural function. It solidifies domination or offers liberatory potential depending on the sociohistoric circumstances in which it takes place. Since Marcuse simply dismisses motherhood as repressive and provides no account of the unique development of the female psyche, he cannot go beyond the mere assertion of sexual difference to a theory of its critical foundation.

The androgynous vision of society that Marcuse puts forward has been criticized by many feminists as sexist since it depends upon the acceptance of sex-role stereotyping. Marcuse would probably respond that these stereotypes are historically conditioned and must be combined in an androgynous individual—though not completely. But his understanding of androgyny is conceptually incoherent. As Kathryn Morgan points out, one of the assumptions behind any theory of androgyny is that "masculinity and femininity refer to the kinds of opposites which, when combined, will yield a proper balance of moderation" resulting in the "good" of each being combined.[26] Because Marcuse's argument for androgyny does not address this problem it lacks a theoretical foundation and amounts merely to a polemical statement against "masculine" aggressiveness.

REPRESSIVE DESUBLIMATION

Marcuse's analysis of the return of the repressed in *Eros and Civilization* seeks to ground the critique of the domination of nature in the memory of utopia underlying the psychoanalytic account of repression. Through a dialectical regression the return of the repressed will transform sexuality into Eros. This theory differs fundamentally from Freud's discussion, in which the return is always distorted by "the scar tissue of repression." However, Marcuse does not see all forms of sexual release as liberating. In *One-Dimensional Man: Studies in the Ideology of Advanced Industrial Society*, he details both the potential and the limitations imposed on our ability to transform our lives through the project of sexual liberty. This analysis shows how society is able to use both our recognition of the liberating potential of our sexuality and our attempts at sexual liberation as instruments *for maintaining* the status quo of general repression while simultaneously indicating it as "liberation." By allowing expression of what he terms "institutionalized desublimated sexuality," the range of socially permissible and desperate satisfaction is increased. However, this kind of satisfaction in sexual pleasure is not liberating. It cannot generate the radical social change necessary for liberation because it is "adjusted" to the society and in fact generates submission: "Loss of conscience due to the satisfactory liberties granted by an unfree society makes for a *happy consciousness* which facilitates acceptance of the misdeeds of this society."[27]

In our advanced industrial society, the body, without ceasing to be an instrument of labor, is allowed to be "sexual" in the work world; sexuality is integrated into work with the result that it is made more susceptible to *controlled* satisfaction: "Technical progress and more comfortable living permit the systematic inclusion of libidinal components into the realm of commodity production and exchange."[28] This perverted form of "sexual liberty" eliminates much of the unhappiness and discontent that are necessary to elucidate the repressive power of the society and, in fact, weakens the chances for real sexual liberation.

Marcuse calls the extension of social control through the weakening of sexual taboos "repressive desublimation." Desublimation replaces mediated gratification with immediate gratification. In its repressive form desublimation is integrated into society through the process of self-domination. That is, the internal drives and satisfactions of individuals are such that they accept forms of sexuality that promote social conformity and contentment: "The Pleasure Principle absorbs the Reality Principle."[29]

The ability to maintain social control by simultaneously extending sexual license and intensifying domination is rooted in our technological society. While earlier social forms of the domination of nature required repression of erotic instincts, the consumer society in an era of high productivity requires libidinal energy to be directed to the acquisition of goods. Moreover, the desublimation of repressed eroticism reproduces the separation of sexual pleasure from love and spontaneity.[30] Sex takes increasingly calculated forms and is increasingly isolated from the whole of emotional life. Sexual pleasure is not liberated; it becomes an obsession. The original unity of psyche and body, rather than being restored, is denied and the dissociation is extended by institutionalized desublimation. It is a further step in the domination of nature, not its undoing.

Repressive desublimation, by releasing the distorted libidinal instincts, binds the individual at a preconscious level to the established institutions of society and undermines the capacity for critical reflection. In a later essay, Marcuse documents the replacement of the individual by the "social atom" who introjects the dominating structure of society.

> The mediation between the self and the other gives way to immediate identification. In the social structure, the individual becomes the conscious and unconscious object of administration and obtains his freedom and satisfaction in his role as such as object; in the mental structure, the ego shrinks to such an extent that it seems no longer capable of sustaining itself, as a self, in distinction from id and superego. The multi-dimensional dynamic . . . has given way to a one-dimensional static identification with the others and with the administered reality principle.[31]

Here Marcuse moves away from the utopian conception of the fatherless society grounded in maternal Eros to return to the original thesis of a fatherless society that makes possible the extinction of the individual and libidinal attachment to established authority. This possibility is buttressed by the entrenched powers of society, which are extending the domination of nature to new psychic dimensions.

Notably in *One-Dimensional Man* but also in other works, Marcuse theorizes the possibility of the *distortion* of instincts in the "return of the repressed" through the concept of repressive desublimation. The factors that tend to enforce this possibility are mass culture, technological rationality, and the replacement of private and family enterprise by large-scale economic institutions.[32] These factors could be described and documented at great length; what is significant here is that they are all social and historical factors: the distortion in the return of the repressed is introduced by the prevailing configuration of sociohistoric forces. Distortion is not necessary. It is not rooted in the process of repression itself, as it is for Freud. Consequently, the decisive factor in determining the direction of the society without the father is the attitude taken by individuals to the structure of society as a whole. Marcuse's "Great Refusal" is the individual choice to struggle to make the utopian vision prevail—there is no theoretical thesis/premise that precludes the outcome of historical tasks. While Marcuse will not assure us that the circle of domination can be broken, he has given an account of how it is "thinkable": the theoretical foundation for thinking the possibility of utopia is the denial of the necessity of distortion in repressed instincts.

THE REVOLT OF NATURE

In contrast to Marcuse, and based on a more faithful reading of Freud, Horkheimer and Adorno emphasize the distortion of instinctual desires by repression. Repressed desires expelled from the ego generate a resentment against civilization and against the ego itself, which grows to the extent that society dominates nature.[33] In the *Eclipse of Reason* Horkheimer details the way in which this resentment bursts forth in what he calls "the revolt of nature." The distortion of instinct through repression turns nature's revolt into a destructive, regressive rebellion. Since it possesses no utopian vision of any experience prior to, or undistorted by, repression, this revolt is utilized by existing institutional powers to justify and maintain their domination:

> Resistance and revulsion arising from this repression of nature have beset civilization from its beginnings, in the form of social rebellions ... as well as in the form of individual crime and mental derangement. Typical of our present era is the manipulation of this revolt by the prevailing forces of civilization itself, the use of the revolt as a means of perpetuating the very conditions by which it is stirred up and against which it is directed. Civilization as rationalized irrationality integrates the revolt of nature as another means or instrument.[34]

Due to the inherent distortion of instincts by repression, their revolt against civilization is complicit with, and tends to extend, those very aspects of civilization that maintain domination. Thus, the domination of nature calls forth psychic and social revolt, as it does for Marcuse, but this revolt serves only to extend the domination of nature as social and self-domination.

Adorno's account of femininity in *Minima Moralia* links the revolt of nature to the woman question. Here, in contradistinction to Marcuse's formulation, the association of repression with distortion undermines the turn to the feminine as a critique of domination.

> The feminine character, and the ideal of femininity on which it is modelled, are products of masculine society. The image of undistorted nature arises only in distortion, as its opposite. Where it claims to be humane, masculine society imperiously breeds in woman its own corrective, and shows itself through this limitation implacably the master. The feminine character is a negative imprint of domination. But therefore equally bad.... Glorification of the feminine character implies the humiliation of all who bear it.[35]

Woman's domination creates feminine characteristics that lead to an abnegative reconciliation with nature, a reconciliation that does not challenge domination but reinforces it.

The key issue in assessing the liberatory potential of "femininity" or the "feminine character" is the relationship of distortion and repression. Marcuse attributes all distortion to sociohistoric factors. Thus, psychic distortion is not necessary, and the female image becomes the repository of a utopian vision whose fortunes are decided on the political stage. Horkheimer and Adorno, who follow Freud in attributing a necessary distortion to repression, see in femininity and the revolt of nature the means for the further consolidation of domination, not liberatory potential.

> Dominant practice and its inescapable alternatives are not threatened by nature, which tends rather to coincide with them, but by the fact that nature is remembered.
>
> HORKHEIMER AND ADORNO,
> *Dialectic of Enlightenment*

MEMORY: HAPPINESS OR SUFFERING?

The domination of nature means that the historical process of domination recreates within the psychic structure of individuals a second nature that presents historical domination as natural and unchangeable. Consequently, there is a difficulty at the center of the theory: how is it possible to recognize internalized domination and still maintain that motives and experiences that demand a free society are possible? Critical theory turns to memory to ground the possibility of the critique of the domination of nature. Memory, in both ontogenetic and phylogenetic dimensions, breaks the vicious circle of dominated consciousness and opens the vision of a free future.

The experience of woman has always been a struggle against the psychic reproduction of domination—internal self-domination—as well as a struggle against external social domination. Since woman is tied more fundamentally to the family than to civil or political life and since the family is the sphere that solidifies natural differences through the reproduction of psychic structures, critical theory's concern with the specific logic of the family and the resuscitation of nature as an independent moment of the dialectic speaks to the central theme of woman's liberation. It is virtually axiomatic for woman that the domination of nature can lead only to an abstract equality with man that denies the sexual difference of first nature and the psychic overlay of second nature rather than recognizing this difference.

Following the trajectory of critical theory, the *given* consciousness of woman is immersed in self-domination. Woman's liberation must therefore incorporate "consciousness raising " as a process that re-forms second nature and recognizes natural difference. The motive and ground for the critique of empirical consciousness is to be found in the ontogenetic and phylogenetic traces of memory. But memory does not refer to a lapsed utopian moment, or Golden Age, supposed to have empirically existed in individual or social life (although there are indeed many feminist accounts that try to locate such ages in an empirical experience of matriarchy).[36] Rather, in critical theory, memory, as temporal continuity, is a function of reason and imagination. The past as recaptured in the present: only this is memory, not that which has ineluctably gone.[37]

Critical theory offers two versions of the function of memory, corresponding to the two versions of repression, which center on the question of whether distortion necessarily accompanies repression or is imposed by revocable historical circumstances. In emphasis, the memory of happiness is associated with Marcuse—it grounds his utopian vision. Memory of suffering and pain is associated with Horkheimer and Adorno. However, both views can be found in Marcuse; what is important here is the distinctiveness of the two views, not their contentious presence in the work of each thinker.

For Marcuse, memory recalls happiness, which in turn evokes a utopian vision that criticizes the domination of nature in the present. Since happiness is a state of union of subjective experience with its object, utopia is characterized by a reconciliation of humanity with nature, a unity of subject and object that recalls Hegel's absolute knowledge. While these moments of happiness may have been only passing and fragmentary, memory is not simply a latent echo of actual occurrences but an active process:

"Recollection as an epistemological faculty rather is synthesis, reassembling the bits and fragments which can be found in the distorted humanity and distorted nature. This recollected material has become the domain of the imagination."[38] The fragmentary experiences of happiness in history motivate the vision of reconciliation with nature in which historical pain can be erased. Since happiness is timeless, utopia implies the conquest of time—an end to history. Even if utopia is not realizable, and the redemption of past suffering can never be actually achieved, the motive and ground of critical theory for Marcuse is precisely such a vision of redemption based on the memory of happiness.[39]

In the *Dialectic of Enlightenment*, Horkheimer and Adorno articulate the contrasting version of the function of memory: "Hope for better circumstances—if it is not a mere illusion—is not so much based on the assurance that these circumstances would be guaranteed, durable, and final, but on the lack of respect for all that is so firmly rooted in the general suffering."[40] The first part of this statement is rather a polemical exaggeration. Here it is not a question of the realizability of utopia but of the epistemological and psychological basis of the vision. Nevertheless, the second part shows an orientation opposite to Marcuse's. The memory of *suffering* motivates the critique of the domination of nature. Adorno writes, "The need to lend a voice to suffering is a condition of all truth"; and Horkheimer declares that nature is "a text to be interpreted by philosophy, that if rightly read will unfold a tale of infinite suffering."[41] This view of suffering nature recalls Edvard Munch's lithograph *The Scream* with its telling inscription, "I listened to the great, infinite cry of Nature."

Since it is the memory of suffering that gives rise to thought and social change, Horkheimer and Adorno's future society, however utopian, would not reconcile itself with the past or with nature. The domination of nature distorts repressed instincts, and the fragments of this distorted nature, though they give rise to the vision of utopia, cannot erase the suffering of historical and psychological experience. While for Marcuse distortion of instinct is a product of historical circumstances, distortion, for Horkheimer and Adorno, is rooted in nature itself. Adorno de-

EDVARD MUNCH, *The Scream*, Oslo Kommunes Kunstsamlinger, Munch-Museet.

clares: "The suppression of nature for human ends is a mere natural relationship, which is why the supremacy of nature-controlling reason and its principle is a delusion.... The subject's desperate self-exaltation is its reaction to the experience of its impotence, which prevents self-reflection."[42] Thus, the domination of nature is a consequence *of* nature. It is therefore only the memory of distortion and suffering resulting from this domination that animates critical theory—not nature "itself."[43] Given this analysis, Horkheimer declares: "The sole way of assisting nature is to unshackle its seeming opposite, independent thought."[44]

The memory of suffering gives rise to the infinite value of individuals, who are distorted by treating them as merely "one of a type." The domination of nature is *essentially* the treating of individuals as dispensable for the good of the whole. Thus, the critique of the domination of nature relies on a utopian vision that rests on unlocking the non-identity of the individual with any other. Adorno attempts to give a comprehensive formulation of the theory of non-identity, rooted in the memory of suffering as the negation of the here and now. In *Negative Dialectics* Adorno claims there is no direct access to the non-identical since such access would assume the sovereign power of thought that has been shown to be an expression of the domination of nature:

> The history locked in the object can only be delivered by a knowledge mindful of the historic positional value of the object in its relation to other objects—by the actualization and concentration of something which is already known and is transformed by that knowledge. Cognition of the object in its constellation is cognition of the process stored in the object.[45]

The two versions of the function of memory in critical theory articulate the significance of happiness and suffering in human experience. For Marcuse, the memory of happiness provides a vision of utopia as the reconciliation of nature and human society. For Horkheimer and Adorno, utopia is an opening to the possibility of freedom found in the memory of suffering. This memory grounds a vision of the recognition and acceptance of non-identity.

When Marcuse, Horkheimer, and Adorno turn to memory to ground the possibility of critique, the concept of history as understood in the modern emancipatory project of Hegel and Marx is challenged. Hegel and Marx understand historical movement as a progression from domination to freedom in which the domination of nature is the precondition for the passage from nature to history. Marx intensifies this concept by claiming that all time past is merely prehistory and truly human history has yet to be achieved. For the Frankfurt school, the concept of memory is a reclaiming of important aspects of the past in a "now" that breaks the historical continuum. Past times (of happiness for Marcuse, of suffering for Horkheimer and Adorno) are experienced in memory as present: every "now" is filled with revolutionary possibility. In this way the emancipatory project moves beyond historical necessity, and the assumption of historical progress is challenged.[46]

The analysis of the dialectic of nature and history done by the Frankfurt school begins by questioning the concept of the domination of nature in the modern emancipatory project and proceeds by questioning the concept of historical progress. This analysis provides a more comprehensive framework for understanding the project of woman's liberation. The question that emerges here most urgently is to what extent the project of woman's liberation fulfills the emancipatory project of modernity and to what extent it "reverses" or criticizes the domination of nature and the concept of historical progress on which this project rests. That is, to what extent does it accept the Hegelian-Marxist understanding of the movement of history as the movement from domination to freedom as it reclaims woman's history and struggles with the problem of equality, and to what extent does it challenge the given, challenge the domination of nature, to move beyond the issue of "formal" equality in civil society by focusing on the intersubjective significance of sexual difference. Intersubjective recognition involves a relation between self and Other that allows for concrete differences but does not on that account render them unequal. This Hegelian problem of identity and non-identity is at the heart of the modern project to create a free and equal society. Alternatively put, it is the search for *concrete* equality. Marx's mature work accepts the position that the domination of nature is the basis for intersubjective recognition in civil society: only by drawing humans out of nature can they be fully recognized as human subjects and regarded as equals. In their productive relations humans can mutually recognize each other based on the social process of forming objects. In the case of woman, she must enter the sphere of civil society and join the struggle for economic, productive liberation as a worker, not specifically as a woman. Any reference to the "natural" differences between man and woman would detract from the *historical* project of overcoming the limitations imposed by nature.

With the rise of fascism and the development of the culture industry, the philosophers of the Frankfurt school turn their attention to the psychic processes of internalizing domination. Rather than society becoming increasingly transparent to its members (in particular the members of the working class), social authority structures are shown to become increasingly powerful *within* the individual's consciousness. Through the process of ego development or identity formation within the family, social domination establishes itself as "second nature" and occludes the possibility of critical consciousness. Consequently, Marx's project is renewed in a critique of the domination of nature that attempts to uncover the psychic and social basis of the solidification of repressive society and tries to generate new possibilities of critical consciousness. This reconceives the dialectic of nature and history by challenging the concept of history as progress as well as analyzing the domination of nature. Attention is focused on the specific logic of the family through a critical appropriation of Freud.

The Frankfurt school theorists' turn to the Freudian account of psychic development is not intended to *replace* Marx's account of the domination of nature in the sphere of production but to *supplement* the focus on civil society, as the sphere of object-forming activity, with a theory of ego development within the family. Nevertheless, this supplement displaces the central locus of critical consciousness. Rather than being situated as an internal contradiction of capitalist production, which turns object-creating activity into a commodity, it devolves upon the problem of the domination of nature itself. Both in the sphere of production and in the family, the domination of nature entails effects that perpetuate domination. Given this, critical theory must find a motive for a limitation of the domination of nature in order to ground social change.

The dialectical development in critical theory comprehends the psychic internalization of domination and also focuses on experiences that demonstrate the limits and inadequacies of domination. These experiences are crucially related to a view of nature as more than the "stuff" of domination. This widens the Marxist project beyond the critique of capitalism to a critique of Western civilization as such. While the ecological crisis can be taken as the index of limits to the domination of external nature, the limits of internal domination are most clearly evident in the domination of woman.[47] Woman has been associated with nature due to the biological attributes that distinguish her from man. Patriarchal domination, which preceded capitalist society, denies to woman the psychic as well as the social capacities for action and intersubjective recognition that the domination of nature was supposed to introduce. In addition, it creates a problem of female desire as subjugated desire. While the theorists of the Frankfurt school acknowledge woman's domination, the oversights and assumptions concerning woman in their analyses of the civilizing dialectic of desire and recognition call for a feminist critique.

CHAPTER FIVE

Woman's Experience: Renaming the Dialectic of Desire and Recognition

THE TWO VERSIONS OF MEMORY IN CRITICAL THEORY, WHICH articulate the significance of suffering and happiness in human experience, have a parallel in the two civilizing myths used to explicate the dialectic of desire and recognition. For Horkheimer and Adorno Homer's *Odyssey* provides an account of the development of self-consciousness that reveals reconciliation as a mythic deception. Homer's tale of alienation, adventure, and return is used in the *Dialectic of Enlightenment* to show the limits of recognition rooted in a process of the subjugation of desire through self-denial, suffering, and pain: here the ego is defeated by a desire for self-preservation. In contrast to this, Marcuse invokes the myth of the primal horde in *Eros and Civilization* to elucidate the dialectic of desire as familial, incestuous desire in which the memory of happiness remains tied to the memory of the mother. Marcuse argues for a dialectical regression based on the Oedipal desire for gratification; he argues for a "return" to the mother through the sexual craving for mother as woman. In reclaiming these two myths the Frankfurt school appropriates Freud and simultaneously, through Marx, recalls Hegel. Both Hegel and Freud analyze the relation between civilization and desire by focusing on desire as fundamental to the formation of self-consciousness: both trace the formation of self-consciousness as an ontogenetic (individual) and phylogenetic (historical) process.

The attempt by critical theorists to appropriate both Freud and Hegel raises a fundamental question concerning the arena of ego development. Though the mechanism is in each case desire, for Freud, it is incestuous desire within the family that, in direct intersubjective relations with others, is repressed and forms the basis for civilized life. For Hegel, desire (initially for objects and then for others) within civil society is central to the development of self-consciousness, and the master-slave dialectic prepares the way for intersubjective recognition through object-creating, productive activity. Freud's intersubjective situation is not the same as Hegel's understanding of intersubjectivity, which requires that two consciousnesses *first* confront each other as equals. The inequality of the master-slave dialectic is a *result*, not the ground, of the encounter. Thus, the slave enters the dialectic as an equal by risking death for recognition, and he has the potential to recognize the Other. Master and slave are not predetermined— it is only in the conflict that one concedes and becomes the slave. Conversely, the parent-child relationship begins as a relationship of inequality: the Freudian child does not enter the Oedipal conflict as an equal Other able to confer recognition. Parent and child are predetermined. The question that must be addressed is whether ego development is a process that occurs primarily in the family, as Freud claims, or between strangers in civil society, as Hegel claims. Furthermore, we must ask if there is a relation between the two arenas that has yet to be articulated.

Paul Ricoeur attempts a comprehensive analysis of the relation between the Hegelian and Freudian models of ego development. The civilizing project that these models share and that gives credence to the attempt to unite them is explicitly outlined in his book *Freud and Philosophy: An Essay on Interpretation.*[1] Most important for Ricoeur is the relation between desire and intersubjectivity, which is rooted in the infinite character of desire in both theories. He attempts to place Hegel's master-slave dialectic at the heart of the Oedipal complex by observing that in both accounts the division of consciousness is not egalitarian. But this entire project is grounded in Ricoeur's confusing an intersubjective situation with Hegel's concept of intersubjectivity. In a later work, "Fatherhood: From Phantasm to Symbol," in which he examines the concept of fatherhood (as differentiated from simple biological fatherhood), Ricoeur acknowledges some of the difficulties due to the confusion concerning intersubjectivity in his earlier work, and he sets limitations on the attempt to place the Hegelian reduplication of consciousness at the center of the Freudian drama.[2] Here he places the master-slave dialectic *after* the Oedipal drama as the content of the latency period in Freud. However, this comes up against the same dilemma at the heart of critical theory's appropriation of Hegel and Freud: what is the arena of ego development, the family or civil society? And what is the relation between the two arenas? The later essay cuts the ground out from the original analysis by introducing a contractual relation into the father-son relationship. This introduces a relation of civil society into the familial tie and negates the analysis of desire that is central to Ricoeur's major work.

In critical theory, Freud's theory of ego development within the family is seen as crucial, but the Hegelian paradigm of intersubjectivity, as a relation between free and equal Others outside the family, is the goal. The exact nature of the intersection between the two theories is not clearly defined, and the implicit assumption is that using the two models together to describe ego development does not pose a problem. This assumption is certainly questionable and becomes even more so when we focus on the differing processes of ego development for males and females in Hegel and Freud.

As I have argued, Hegel and Freud both try to develop a theory that gives full due to the non-identity of nature and history, psyche and society, but in each case the theory collapses back into identity due to an internal failure to come to grips with woman's experience. In Hegel natural immediacy is overreached by the dialectic of recognition in society: nature collapses into society/history. In Freud society is ultimately reduced to nature since sexual difference is collapsed into a signal polarity: the absence/presence of a penis. For both, female experience is a moment in male experience, which is reckoned to be fully human.

Woman is confined to the family in both Hegel and Freud. She is not an equal Other; she does not attain intersubjective recognition or an independent ego and her desire remains subject to and defined by male desire. Woman is dominated both by recognizing her difference and confining it within the family and by denying this difference in civil society. This raises the Hegelian problem of the relation between identity and non-identity, which is central to the tradition of critical theory. While the theorists of the Frankfurt school acknowledge woman's domination, there are significant oversights and assumptions concerning woman in their appropriation of the two civilizing myths.

Both myths fail to understand woman as a historical actor and fail to analyze the specificity of the female psyche in terms of desire and recognition. Both focus on the relations between men and on the relations between man and woman from the perspective of the man. Neither addresses the relations between women or the relations between woman and man from woman's perspective. Horkheimer and Adorno treat the myth of Odysseus primarily in terms of male recognition; female desire is discussed only insofar as it relates to promiscuous heterosexual desire and represents the domination of nature. For this reason their use of the myth distorts an understanding of woman's desire and her role in the process of recognition. Marcuse treats the myth of the primal horde as a myth of male homoerotic bonding; the question of female desire is simply ignored. Female difference is written out of the myth, although the heterosexual couple is portrayed in conflict with the male group. The insufficiencies that derive from the omission of woman's self-experience of desire reveal that neither of the civilizing myths can be universalized. The myth of male desire and the myth of male recognition cannot be used to describe female desire or female recognition. However, a reconsideration of these myths from woman's perspective unmasks important aspects of male domination.

WOMAN AS MOTHER, LOVER, AND WIFE

The Odyssey Revamped

Against Marcuse's analysis of the sacrifice of the father in the primal horde, which initiates the possibility of liberation, Horkheimer and Adorno see the introduction of sacrifice into the human community and the human psyche as a catastrophe affecting humanity and nature alike. They disregard the myth of the primal horde of equality in favor of the phylogenetic account provided by Homer's *Odyssey* as interpreted through the master-slave dialectic. Odysseus' mythic journey represents the recognition story that is central to the development of human self-consciousness. Horkheimer and Adorno retell this myth as a reconception of the master-slave dialectic by focusing on the role of labor—male labor— and thus they give an account of male development. Odysseus is the atomic individual forced into exile to find himself. He leaves Ithaca and battles nature to achieve a self, but in the process he denies his own nature for the sake of self-preservation. He retreats from the risk of death necessary for the master's conquest in the process of recognition. The workers, on the other hand, are reduced to mere species being through the repression of the desire for gratification, and they are rendered as impotent as the master.

While Horkheimer and Adorno interpret Odysseus' travels as a journey of alienation and return, a journey of recognition, they omit significant elements concerning woman's situation in their narration of this tale. There is only cursory attention given to the female psyche in the shorthand account of the relation between the domination of woman, female self-alienation, and the domination of nature. What is muted is the subjugation of female desire and the role of woman in the dialectic of recognition. By focusing on Odysseus' relation to the Sirens, Circe, and Penelope, we can critically appropriate the analysis of woman as mother, lover, and wife for a more comprehensive analysis of the domination of woman.

As we noted earlier, Horkheimer and Adorno interpret the Sirens' song as the call of the pleasure principle, the call of sexuality. However, as I see it, the voice of the Sirens, as the call of mere nature, is the male's perception of woman as the ancient all-engulfing mother symbolized by the close association of womb and tomb. Thus, the Sirens represent for the male the all-powerful mother figure. The desire to yield to the Sirens is the male's desire to give up responsibility for the self—a desire that signals death to the male ego.

Horkheimer and Adorno remind us that we do not know what happens to the Sirens once Odysseus manages to resist their power and sail past them. But, as they say, we may surmise that, like the Sphinx in the Oedipal myth, once defeated, once heard without compelling surrender, they self-destruct. To Horkheimer and Adorno, this self-destruction affects song and language: following this defeat, songs proclaim the power of the aesthetic impulse yet remain impotent, and language shifts from formalism to nominalism.[3]

However, if we see the Sirens' song as the call of the all-engulfing mother—the first (M)Other—then we may interpret the self-destruction quite differently, as the way in which woman as mother is sacrificed to the development of the male ego. Just as the maternal figures of Jocasta and the Sphinx self-destruct because of their encounters with Oedipus, the Sirens are defeated by the developing male ego represented by Odysseus. In contrast to Horkheimer and Adorno's view of this encounter as a threat of death for the male ego, from woman's perspective this encounter signals the death of the female as mother, the loss of female power as mother.

The death of matriarchal power is clearly illustrated in Odysseus' trip to Hades, where he views the mother figures that have become "impotent, blind, and dumb." Horkheimer and Adorno claim that the matriarchal images have been banished to Hades by "the religion of light."[4] But the religious domination of the matriarchal figures is an ideological overlay of the social domination of woman by which woman, even as mother, is subordinate to man. From a psychoanalytic point of view the visit to

Hades may be seen as Odysseus' descent to the realm of the unconscious, where a final death blow is dealt to the mother's power to allow a rebirth of the male. Thus, Odysseus descends to the land of the unconscious, the land of the mother, and emerges from this land reborn beyond her power.

Horkheimer and Adorno explicate Odysseus' interlude with Circe as a general account of the renunciation of pleasure in heterosexual sex and the development of heterosexual love as ideology in exchange society. Circe is described as the prototype of the prostitute or courtesan (hetaera), a figure of nondifferentiation: she is the progeny of fire and water and in her these elements are not separated. This nondifferentiation is the defining characteristic of promiscuity, so that Circe represents woman's desire as fickle and indiscriminate. In this reading of Circe we see the Hegelian influence, in that woman's confinement to immediacy or nondifferentiation is said to make her a representative of desire as capricious and contingent, a principle of subversion in the patriarchal world.

For Horkheimer and Adorno woman as prostitute represents the return of repressed nature, but only as a deceptive representation of nature as "idealized prehistory": the prostitute promises pleasure but delivers only degradation. Circe tempts Odysseus' men into giving themselves up to sexual pleasure and then she turns them into pigs—creatures whose association with the sense of smell evokes an association with debased forms of sexuality. But these creatures retain their consciousness of once having been men. Thus, to succumb to Circe is to lose oneself in a reversion to the animal in which one remembers having been an autonomous individual, an ego or an "I." Since Horkheimer and Adorno believe that repression or self-domination is necessary for the development of self-consciousness, any "return" to nature is seen as regressive, not redemptive. They criticize the association of woman and nature and see Circe's transformation of men into pigs as a reduplication of the transformation inflicted on woman in patriarchal society. Just as woman is reduced to mere animal nature, an animal defined by sex and forced to "smell out" sex for her survival, so Circe reduces the male to sex, to mere animal nature, yet leaves him conscious of his humanity.

Taking the initiative in her encounter with Odysseus, Circe invites him to her bed. Thus, as I see it, Circe represents woman, not as mother, as womb, but woman as sex, as the lover with the *vagina dentata*, the bitch/witch who lures men into her trap and through the power of her sexuality changes them into animals. Odysseus has been given an antidote by Hermes (the god of commerce and the market) that nullifies Circe's power. Thus, through an act of male solidarity Odysseus becomes immune to Circe's magic, the magic of female sexuality. But to man Circe's sexuality is so powerful that it creates a form of male castration anxiety, which remains alive even after he has successfully resisted her. Thus, Odysseus confronts Circe with sword in hand, making her swear that if he has sex with her she will not take away his courage or his manhood. This oath, according to Horkheimer and Adorno, is intended to protect man from mutilation, from revenge for curtailing promiscuity and installing male domination. But they miss the double standard in the oath, for what is clearly prohibited is *female* promiscuity. Odysseus indulges in sex with Circe and curtails her relations with other men, even though he is married to Penelope.

For Horkheimer and Adorno the relation between Circe and Odysseus presages the "civilized" marriage contract of bourgeois society, which transforms the love relation between woman and man into a contractual relation of exchange. Here the relation between desire and command reveals a "deprivation of instinct" as the prerequisite for relations between the sexes. Circe is said to renounce her power over Odysseus, the power of female desire, while Odysseus renounces the pleasure of sexual surrender. Circe foreshadows woman's contribution to the frigidity of love in bourgeois patriarchal society in that she gives herself to the man who can resist her. Within the framework of love as ideology the lover is always at fault because to give more than one gets is always wrong in the world of commercial exchange. The incapacity for self-domination and the domination over the Other, the inability to mask one's love along with the inability to force the Other to submit to it, ultimately denies fulfillment to the lover. What is created and recreated is a society that "reproduces and extends solitariness."[5] Thus, Circe gets Odysseus into bed with her but it is a loveless encounter based on the loss of pleasure and female power. However, Horkheimer and Adorno's analysis does not acknowledge that female frigidity is not caused merely by male resistance but by the male's threat of physical violence coupled with the threat of his withdrawal from the encounter unless woman does as she is told.

According to the *Dialectic of Enlightenment* the encounter with Circe reveals love as ideology that masks the hatred of the sex war. What is not mentioned is that man and woman have never been equal in love in patriarchal society; love as ideology has always been more deadly for woman than for man. The defeat of female desire, the defeat of female power in love, is extracted from Circe through trickery and the threat of violence. This episode recalls the fact that the right to ask a man into bed has been taken from all women and given back only to those who sell pleasure for a living: it recalls the mutilating chastity that man requires of woman. In the patriarchal world any woman who "seduces" a man is seen as a whore, a hooker, a prostitute; the seduction succeeds only at a great price—woman's submission to male domination.

What Odysseus wants to ensure with Circe's oath is that he will not be mutilated for *his* acts of promiscuity. In sex outside social laws, in illicit sex with prostitutes, the male fears a reversion to the animal, a symbolic mutilation and death of the self. What woman risks in illicit sex in patriarchal society is actual death. We see this clearly in the account of Odysseus' return home when he orders his son, Telemachus, to kill all the women who have engaged in sex with Penelope's suitors. Horkheimer and Adorno refer to these women as prostitutes, yet they have not done anything more than Odysseus has done with Circe. In fact, they have done less, since they were not bound by marriage vows when they engaged in unlawful sex. Odysseus instructs Telemachus to kill the women by running them through with a sword. But Telemachus invents an ignoble death for them, ending in their hanging. Horkheimer and Adorno see this episode as an account of atrocity in which we cannot forget the victims or their agony, but this is to see a generalized brutality in what is a specifically female death inflicted on women for violating codes of sexual behavior set up by men. Horkheimer and Adorno ignore the fact that Telemachus creates a gruesome punishment for these women by forcing them to clean up the blood and corpses of their lovers, the suitors slaughtered by himself and Odysseus. Thus, the women are made to do their "housework," their domestic cleaning, before they are herded together to face death for the little bit of pleasure they have had in Odysseus' absence.

I see Circe's encounter with Odysseus as an episode in which male castration anxiety is turned against woman to subjugate her desire. The male constructs a situation that allows him both marriage and adulterous liaisons yet limits woman to a restricted and enforced monogamy. From man's perspective Odysseus' encounter with Circe is the defeat of promiscuous female desire, which allows him to behave promiscuously without responsibility or guilt. From woman's perspective this encounter depicts monogamous heterosexuality as sex without love in which woman has no power to determine the grounds of the encounter. Man sets limits on woman's desire by threatening her with death.

Horkheimer and Adorno understand Circe's relation to Odysseus as being "ultimately of advantage only to male survival," and they talk of the prostitute as one who maligns her own sex.[6] After she has been conquered by Odysseus, Circe tells him how he may sail past the Sirens and escape the power of their song. If we interpret the Sirens as the powerful mother figure then we see here the prostitute making the patriarchal world her own by betraying the mother, the female representative of sex for procreation.[7]

Horkheimer and Adorno pronounce a judgment on the relation between prostitute and wife that is similar to that made explicit more recently by the woman's liberation movement. They write that "prostitute and wife are the complements of female self-alienation in the patriarchal world-order: the wife denotes pleasure in the fixed order of life and property, whereas the prostitute takes what the wife's right of possession leaves free, and—as the wife's secret collaborator—subjects it again to the order of possession: she sells pleasure."[8] While I argue that the prostitute is the *husband's* secret collaborator, it is true nevertheless that this complementary relation between prostitute and wife ultimately divides and degrades all women and renders them powerless. Thus, Circe, the supposedly powerful seductress, is actually "weak, obsolete, and defenseless."[9] As a representative of nature, she symbolizes for man both sexual irresistibility and powerlessness. In this way she is a reflection of the domination of nature.

Penelope, the prototypical bourgeois wife, is woman in relation to property and recognition, the defining terms for woman in Hegel's philosophy. But, in contrast to Hegel's claims, Horkheimer and Adorno acknowledge that woman as wife is denied fulfillment in the patriarchal world order. For them the problem lies in the fact that the bourgeois world links sex and property so that no woman can afford a spontaneous reaction to any man: she must always size a man up as a potential husband before reacting. Given that a woman's life rests in the hands of the man she marries, she cannot afford to choose carelessly nor can she afford any mistakes after marriage. Thus, woman is not an equal Other as lover but must strive for equality in a relation of exchange in which she exchanges her chastity for economic security.

As we have seen, woman, according to Hegel, represents the possibility of a "tranquil intuition of unity" between man and woman. Horkheimer and Adorno refer obliquely to this when they describe the marriage between Penelope and Odysseus as a unity that promises permanence in life and solidarity in the face of death. This kind of union is the mythic basis of civilization that transcends myth: it offers a haven in a heartless world. However, Odysseus conceals his identity from Penelope, for she is to be tested. But he reveals himself to his son in a reversal of the recognition problem of paternity (that is, the father can never be absolutely sure of his son); here, the son cannot recognize the father. After Odysseus' revelation, father and son conspire to keep Odysseus' return secret. Thus, the male bond is reasserted while the male-female bond is to be tested. Penelope does not, in this situation, represent first nature, nature as the tranquil intuition of unity, the immediate recognition between woman and man as Hegel conceives it.[10] Nor does she represent woman as mother. Rather, she represents woman as alienated nature defined in terms of property and female chastity. It is precisely because Penelope represents *alienated* nature that Odysseus denies his identity to her in order to test her. But this denial of himself only intensifies his own alienation. Penelope responds to Odysseus' test with a test of her own. She says: "If this is Odysseus we two shall surely recognize each other ... for there are tokens between us which only we two know and no one else has heard of."[11] Penelope proceeds to describe their marriage bed as if it could be moved. This makes Odysseus furious because he himself has made the bed immovable by carving it from an olive tree and building the bedroom around it. Here the Hegelian moment of substantial unity is revealed as a union based on property. There is no direct subject-subject relation between husband and wife but only a subject-object-subject relation; the object that mediates the relation is the bed as a symbol of the bond between sex and property.

This encounter reveals the reality beneath the appearance of the Hegelian dialectic of male-female recognition. Where Hegel sees a moment of contingency introduced into the relation between man and woman by male desire, Horkheimer and Adorno see a moment of contingency introduced into this relation by the fact that woman represents nature as property linked to her subjugated sexuality.

Prior to his return to Ithaca Odysseus visits his mother, Anticleia, in Hades and asks after Penelope. His mother answers, "Penelope has schooled her heart to patience, though her eyes are never free from tears as the slow nights and days pass sorrowfully by."[12] Why does Penelope cry all the time? Edna St. Vincent Millay points to Penelope's loneliness and unceasing toil as the source of her tears.[13] Since Penelope is powerless to confront male power directly she does it indirectly, by telling her suitors that she cannot choose a husband until she has finished the burial shroud for her father-in-law, Laertes. Then she proceeds to weave the shroud all day and unweave it at night. Through this subversion she keeps the suitors at bay. But in addition to her loneliness and toil, Penelope suffers from eventlessness, the trauma of woman trapped at home doing the same thing day after day. While Odysseus journeys toward the unknown in search of himself, Penelope's future is known: it is the "given" of family life as predictable and routine. The weaving and unweaving of the shroud in this tale represents the rhythm and tedium of woman's domesticated life.

Home figures as a source of identity for man, but it is a place that he must leave; for woman home signifies denial of the self, yet it is a place she cannot leave. Thus, whereas Ithaca marks a point of departure and arrival in the mythic development of Odysseus' self-consciousness, it represents a fixed landscape of work and domination for Penelope. Man encounters the pain of exile, of alienation; woman endures the pain of place, of coerced immobility. If the journey gains meaning for Odysseus from the return, it is because Penelope remains home to recognize him on his return. Penelope makes no journey—she is allowed no journey—and her self-consciousness is not nurtured or sustained by Odysseus: she achieves no recognition.[14]

In critical theory's appropriation of the *Odyssey*, as in Hegel's philosophy, man's mobility and recognition require woman's immobility. The myth of male recognition requires woman's confinement to the family, the private realm, and does not allow for the development of a female self through and with an Other. If Penelope were to journey with a crew of women to find herself, if she were to move out of the private realm into the public, Odysseus' journey would have neither source nor goal, neither origin nor telos. Thus, the quest of male recognition, the journey through alienation to a return, requires that woman not experience the journey. How-

ever, woman's mobility, her move into the public world of exchange, will make her "the same as" man—an atomic individual: it will destroy the pre-atomic base of identity only to
create woman as a mirror image of man.

Horkheimer and Adorno ignore the repression of woman's
desire in the interest of self-preservation. Penelope has lived without sexual pleasure for nineteen years and knows that she cannot
act on any desire she might feel for any one of the suitors without
risking death. While Odysseus spends a year in an adulterous
liaison with Circe, Penelope's chastity is strictly enforced. The
exchange relation, in which Penelope must remain faithful to
Odysseus in order to ensure his return, is an unequal exchange
in which her desire is sacrificed on the altar of marriage.

Both Circe and Penelope are weavers. Freud, as we have seen,
interprets woman's weaving as an attempt to hide the fact that
she does not have a penis: shame over her sexual inadequacy
leads woman to discover ways to weave and braid covers for
her genitalia. Karl Kerényi, the distinguished mythologist, points
out that for the ancient Greeks weaving was an act of creation,
a metaphor for the continuous processes by which "life is spun
and woven."[15] Thus, woman as weaver is, for the Greeks, woman
as the creator and recreator of human life, not woman as shamed
by male genitalia. The defeat of Circe and Penelope represents,
in this context, not only the defeat of female desire but the defeat
of female desire as a creative force.

After Odysseus is convinced of Penelope's loyalty and fidelity he finally embraces her as his own. But within this embrace
the echo of the death cries of the servant women rings in her
ears. The death of these women, women who have died for
their pleasure, comes as no surprise to Penelope; she has made
her bargain with the patriarchal world and knows its rules and
its limits. Although Penelope betrays no woman she has no
particular allegiance to womankind. Her fate, like the fate of
every bourgeois wife loyal to her husband, is one of alienation,
repression, and isolation, a fate for which she sheds incessant
tears.

Medea: The Female Odysseus?

The recognition myth requires that someone be home when man returns from exile or alienation, and in the tradition of critical theory from Hegel through Marx and the Frankfurt school that someone has always been woman, whose self is not nurtured or sustained but denied by man. However, Greek mythology does portray two women who leave their "proper" place, and both suffer for it. Antigone, as we have seen, leaves home insofar as she enters the public realm on behalf of the private; there is no male to provide her with recognition and she dies for her audacity. But a more provocative example of the woman who defies the patriarchal world order emerges in the myth of Medea.

Medea is the female equivalent of Odysseus in that she is the female exile, but she can never return home and no one there waits for her. Medea is not Greek; she is a stranger from Colchis, whose exile from home stems from her passionate, all-consuming love of Jason. She betrays her father to help Jason obtain the golden fleece, and her brother is killed when he pursues the couple in their flight from her homeland. Euripides has Medea claim responsibility for the fratricide, which portends the infanticide she later commits. In other versions of the myth she is only Jason's accomplice in the murder. Nonetheless, Medea's love for Jason clearly transcends her love for, and loyalty to, her family of origin. And Medea accepts the fate of eternal exile as the condition of this love. Thus, she represents the fate of woman in patriarchal society who, in the name of love, must leave her parents' home to become a stranger in her husband's house.

Medea follows Jason to Corinth and has two sons by him. But once she has become a mother, accepting motherhood as a consequence of her great love, Jason betrays her by marrying the daughter of the king of Corinth. This king fears Medea's powerful magic and, with Jason's consent, condemns Medea to a second exile. She is now to be exiled with the responsibility for two helpless children. Medea foresees only slavery for herself and her sons. She refuses this fate and takes her revenge. After the king of Athens agrees to accept her into his city she kills Jason's bride and her own children.

In her plight Medea appeals to the women of Corinth for support. She knows and delineates the situation of domination that the women share.

> We women are the most unfortunate creatures.
> Firstly, with an excess of wealth it is required
> For us to buy a husband and take for our bodies
> A master; for not to take one is even worse.[16]

Not only are women forced into marriage, a marriage for which they must have a dowry, but once married they are condemned to the life of the family while man moves freely in the public world. Contradicting Hegel's claims regarding woman's experience in the pagan world, Medea articulates the separation of the public and private spheres and her dissatisfaction with it.

> A man, when he's tired of the company of his home,
> Goes out of the house and puts an end to his boredom
> And turns to a friend or companion of his own age.
> But we are forced to keep our eyes on one alone.
> What they say of us is that we have a peaceful time
> Living at home, while they do the fighting in war.
> How wrong they are! I would very much rather stand
> Three times in the front of battle than bear one child.[17]

Medea finds no solace in motherhood or family life in a patriarchal world. She prefers a battle of recognition in the public world to the solitary pain of the private realm, which offers woman no recognition of the self.

The fact that Medea is not Greek is central to this mythic drama. True, she appeals to the Greek women by making common cause with their domination, but she sees the fate of Greek women only to refuse it: she will not be an idiot condemned to home and hearth.

> Let no one think me a weak one, feeble-spirited,
> A stay-at-home, but rather just the opposite,
> One who can hurt my enemies and help my friends;
> For the lives of such persons are most remembered.[18]

Woman's desire and passion have been tamed in the Greek world to allow for male promiscuity. In their subjugated forms, contained and confined within marriage, they no longer threaten the male. But Medea represents the sexually assertive woman who seeks her own pleasure. Jason accuses her with these words: " 'For the sake of pleasure in the bed you killed [the children] / No Greek woman would have done this.' "[19] When Euripides tells Medea's story he places the infanticide at the center of the drama. Medea is depicted as a wild woman, "mad" with revenge, a woman willing and able to kill her family when roused to anger. She portrays for man the violence of female passion that has not been "civilized," female passion prior to male domination. In a patriarchal world that subjugates woman's desire and denies her recognition, woman's rebellion takes on terrifying overtones for the male.

Although Medea acts on her desire for the Other, she does not kill her children for the sake of her *sexual* satisfaction. What is central to the myth, from woman's perspective, is man's betrayal of woman in *love*. Jason's betrayal creates a violent separation that destroys the unity of the marriage. Medea responds by destroying the children who objectify this unity. Out of the pain of betrayal Medea searches for a way to inflict pain on the one who has betrayed her. When Jason says that he cannot believe that she was motivated by pain to kill their sons, she asks: " 'Is love so small a pain, do you think, for woman?' " Medea kills the children to create the same violent rupture between Jason and his children that he created between him and her.[20] Rather than kill him or internalize her "madness" in a self-destructive manner, she externalizes her pain and seeks to recreate within Jason the pain she experiences.

Medea represents monogamous married love, the union of two into one. But this does not mean that she accepts female chastity prior to marriage. She mocks Jason for seeking a "virgin" bride, implying that she was no virgin when they married. She stands for the free rein of woman's desire prior to marriage and for monogamous marriage. Jason, on the other hand, stands for female chastity before and after marriage and for male promiscuity. Here we see a fundamental conflict between male and female perspectives on female desire and marriage. And we find a challenge to the idea that *woman's* desire is promiscuous: in this myth it is man who is fickle and inconstant.

Medea loves Jason and sacrifices everything for him; her love is without bounds. Jason's love is a calculated gesture to ensure the success of his quest for the golden fleece. This gesture is abandoned when he has the opportunity to realize his ambition to move up in the world by marrying into the royal family of Corinth. Because Medea has chosen Jason for her lover and not waited to be chosen first, betrayal is her fate. Since Jason's betrayal of Medea all women fear to choose first, and all male claims of fidelity and love are suspect.

Woman's Desire and the Primal Horde of Brothers

The reconsideration of the myth of recognition in Horkheimer and Adorno's *Dialectic of Enlightenment* leads us back to the question of female desire. While Circe and Penelope illustrate the defeat of female desire through subjugation, Medea illustrates its defeat through betrayal. When we turn to the other civilizing myth in critical theory, Marcuse's appropriation of Freud's phylogenetic account of the primal horde in *Eros and Civilization*, we find that he too overlooks the problem of woman's self-experience of desire. The formation of a *human* group is traced to male desire; the phylogenetic account ignores woman except insofar as she is desired by man.

Within the primal horde the brothers kill the father to gain access to the women, but then, in order to maintain group solidarity, the brothers reinstitute sexual taboos concerning women. According to Marcuse, the original patricide "promises a society without the father—that is, without suppression and domination" but the brothers "re-establish domination by substituting many fathers for one, and then by deifying and internalizing the one father."[21] That is, the guilt over the killing and eating of the father establishes civilization through self-domination. The father now lives within the sons and the mother is desexualized.

Woman is not guilty of either the patricide or the betrayal of liberation since it is the brother clan that murders the father, feels guilt, and establishes taboos. The brothers renounce sexual claims on the mother and sister, instituting the taboo on incest and the law of exogamy.[22] This forces the males to find women outside the clan, a requirement which helps preserve the life of the group since it removes all heterosexual bonds that are not aim-inhibited from relations between members. Direct satisfaction of sexual pleasure is banished from group relations to become established only in relationships with non-members, women who are strangers. Civilization is constituted on the basis of a fundamental repression of the unity between affectionate love and sexual love. In support of this point, Marcuse quotes from *Group Psychology and the Analysis of the Ego*, where Freud writes: "The primal father had prevented his sons from satisfying their directly sexual tendencies; he forced them into abstinence and consequently into the emotional ties with him and with one another which could arise out of those of their tendencies that were inhibited in their sexual aims. He forced them, so to speak, into group psychology."[23] Now what Marcuse misses here, in the leap from the relation to woman to the establishment of "lasting" group relations, is that the group is entirely male. This is an analysis not of group psychology per se but of male bonding. In fact, the continuation of Freud's commentary, which Marcuse does not quote, is quite explicit on this point: "It may also be assumed that the sons, when they were driven out and separated from their father, advanced from identification with one another to homosexual object-love and in this way won freedom to kill their father."[24] Marcuse's goal of describing a vision of non-surplus-repressive civilization is not adequately met, because Marcuse fails to give a comprehensive analysis of the role of woman in the erotic bonding of the group. That is, he fails to emphasize the male homoerotic nature of the group. Even though Freud notes the homoerotic nature of the brother clan, he nevertheless speaks of civilization as the development from the group of the family to the group of humanity as a whole.

Neither Freud nor Marcuse inquires how we move from the

primal male horde to humanity as a group of men and women. Women appear only as the desired and taboo within the group and as strangers. The group bond is a male/homosexual one. How the sexual bond between men and women as couples relates to this is only discussed by Marcuse insofar as it presents an "ambiguity" in Freud's discussion of Eros as uniting and destroying group relations.

Eros is said to unite males in the group and to unite individual men and women. Neither Freud nor Marcuse explains how Eros may unite women or how it may unite men and women outside a couple relationship to form a heterosexual group. Woman's relation to the group is made *only* via the individual male to whom she is erotically tied. Marcuse quotes Freud again: "The conflict between civilization and sexuality is caused by the circumstance that sexual love is a relationship between two people, in which a third can only be superfluous or disturbing, whereas civilization is founded on relations between larger groups of persons."[25] Monogamous heterosexuality is seen as an essentially explosive force in conflict with civilization, which is seen as an effort to "combine organic substances into ever larger unities."[26] However, Marcuse does not note that the conflict between civilization and desire here is a conflict between heterosexual desire and a male homoerotic bond. Rather, he tries to address this conflict as the effort to combine many into one. He claims that the tension in Freud between sexuality and civilization, the supposedly "biological" conflict between the pleasure principle and the reality principle, is actually a historical conflict that can be reconciled by a *free* Eros.[27] However, once the male homoerotic basis of civilization is recalled, this conflict must be regarded as a conflict between male bonding, female bonding, and heterosexual love; to address the conflict in this way requires an analysis of female desire, something that is entirely absent from the theory of the primal horde.

Woman is not seen as an active historical agent in either Freud or Marcuse's version of the development of civilization. She is an object of pleasure or the "principle" of gratification rather than a desiring subject. Even if it were true that woman acts only once, in accepting or rejecting the love object, the theory of the primal horde requires that this one act be brought into the analysis. Until it is, the conflict between civilization and sexuality that is fundamental to Freud's theory and to Marcuse's critique of the domination of nature cannot be comprehended.

The blindness concerning woman leads Marcuse to a strange reinterpretation of the myths of Narcissus and Orpheus. He attempts to show that these myths contain images of freedom beyond the logic of domination, in that Narcissus rejects "normal Eros" or heterosexuality for self-love, as a "oneness with the universe," and Orpheus shuns all women to embrace homosexuality. But how can the *denial* of woman, the denial of heterosexuality, be the embracing of a fuller Eros? Surely there must be self-love, male homosexual and lesbian love, as well as heterosexual love for Eros to be realized.[28]

The lack of attention to female desire and the development of the female psyche in the theory of the primal horde means that the daughter's relationships with the father and the mother are not addressed. There is no exploration of the psychological effects on the female who lives in an incestuous relation with the father. The incest taboo refers only to that between mother and son. The mother is seen as the primary source of gratification, and the son's "progress" and "Life itself" are "saved" from the mother's power (to engulf, to swallow). The daughter is simply sacrificed to the father. Even if one accepts the idea that the incestuous relation between father and daughter *may* not be as treacherous because, as Freud and Marcuse claim, this relation lacks the pre-ego relation to the Nirvana principle that the mother represents, the most significant point is that *nothing is said* of the father-daughter relation.

What is implied in the myth of the primal horde is that women are sexually satisfied by the father and therefore they have no motive for killing him. Women are the *reason* for the patricide—they are the desired objects—not the killers. The killing that unites the brothers in a new way destroys the female group built around the father. It is not possible to place the sisters into a primal horde as equals to the brothers because then the brothers would have sexual access to them and the motive for the patricide would evaporate.

What would a psychology of daughters, as a group of sisters all in incestuous relations with the father, entail? What happens to the female psyche when, as daughter, the female is seduced/raped/impregnated by the father? Is the daughter separated by rivalry from the mother? Or do mother and daughter unite against the father? And what happens to woman when the primal father is overthrown? When suddenly she must leave the group of women formed around the father to begin individual relations with men who are strangers? These speculative questions, which may have no more of an anthropological foundation than Freud's theory of the primal horde, do however, call for a reconsideration of the symbolic content of critical theory, which, as Marcuse argues, telescopes the dialectic of domination.[29]

The impossibility of using the traditional civilizing myths to explain woman's experience has led some feminists to search for "new" myths. Luce Irigaray, for example, calls for an investigation of the dialectic of female desire through the myth of Demeter and Persephone, the myth of the relation between mother and daughter. This would displace the emphasis on the myth of Oedipus to ground the feminist concern with the pre-Oedipal relation between mother and daughter. Such a focus is meant to refute the theory that males and females have "the same" experience of the mother and to show that in order to understand difference or non-identity it is first necessary to understand "sameness" as homoeroticism.[30] Susan Cavin, on the other hand, challenges the anthropological grounds of the myth of the primal horde from a feminist perspective in her book *Lesbian Origins*. Where Freud's theory begins from the belief that the first human group was formed primarily through relations between men, the relations between father and sons in terms of their desire for the wife/mother, Cavin focuses on the bonding between women in the original group and argues that the primal horde was a group formed by lesbian relations in which the first male lover was the son, not the husband.[31] Given my analysis of the traditional civilizing myths, which shows the impossibility of universalizing them to apply to woman's experience, the logic behind the appropriation and reconstruction of "new" myths by feminists becomes clear. However, my argument is not to be construed as a call for new myths but as an immanent critique of critical theory's analysis of the civilizing process.

MOTHERHOOD AND SISTERHOOD RECONSIDERED

The analysis of the dialectic of desire and recognition is central to critical theory as theory and as emancipatory project. The omission and distortion of woman's experience of this dialectic calls for a consideration of woman's *self*-experience of desire and a consideration of the relations between women. Feminists have pointed to the importance of sisterhood and motherhood as female-female relationships. However, within the contemporary woman's liberation movement there has been a shift from a focus on sisterhood to a focus on motherhood. My analysis of critical theory makes it possible to understand this shift in a new way, a way that gives form to the diverse strains of feminist theory, by clarifying and making explicit what has remained, up to now, only implicit in the feminist project: that within the feminist critique of society, female desire, as a desiring relation between daughter and mother, is seen as the origin or ground of woman's experience while recognition between women (sisterhood) is the goal or telos.

Woman's desire has been written out of the modern emancipatory project of critical theory except as promiscuous heterosexual desire, which has been dominated by man to establish heterosexual monogamy. Because of woman's identification with nature as immediacy, her desire has been seen as not fixed on a specific (love) object. In this sense, woman's desire has been discussed only from the male perspective. For centuries the question of woman's experience has been posed as "the woman question"—a question asked by man about woman. Today feminists have made an axial turn, as Adorno would say, to ask "the question of woman"—a question of self-understanding posed by woman herself. From a feminist perspective, the motive for marriage and monogamy as discussed in critical theory appears to be the male need to contain female desire, to limit desire that is not merely a moment of male experience. Woman's active heterosexual desire is feared by man, as we see in the myth of Medea. As active lover and mother, as a combination of vagina and womb, woman is perceived as deadly. She is then psychically castrated in a form of reversal: fearing castration, man proceeds to "castrate" woman. This psychic castration is accompanied by social domination through rape and incest. The male assertion of power that is not manifested in direct, overt violence against woman turns into a male assertion of power through the threat of withdrawal from the male-female union. Here male impotence may be seen as passive aggression, as the most dramatic form of male protest against female sexual assertiveness. The burning of witches at the stake is transmuted into the slow burning of woman by unfulfilled desire.[32] Through this analysis patriarchy is revealed as a system of domination in which woman's desire is repressed, distorted, and denied fulfillment.

In order to understand woman's *self*-experience of desire, feminists have turned to an analysis of the development of the female psyche in terms of the Freudian, and sometimes neo-Freudian, account of incestuous desire. However, the reconsideration of female desire from the daughter's perspective has not led to a new theory of heterosexual desire insofar as the focus is on female relations (daughter-mother); the father is either ignored or remains understood as the "third" Other who enters the mother-infant dyad to break the oceanic consciousness. There is no *new* account of the daughter-father relation articulated based on the transformed understanding of the pre-Oedipal relation between daughter and mother. This psychoanalytic analysis culminates in a reconsideration of homosexual desire as female-female desire, but it leaves in place the Freudian account in which female heterosexual desire can only be interpreted as a desire for the authoritarian father. There is, in this respect, no basis for a redefinition of heterosexual *desire* from the daughter's perspective as a female-male relation. Woman's desire for man, as anything more than the desire for domination, remains to be named.[33]

Given this, there has been within contemporary feminist theory, either explicitly or implicitly, the substitution of the mother-daughter pre-Oedipal paradigm (S-s) for both the Oedipal mother–infant–father paradigm (S-s-S) and the man-woman paradigm (S-S) as the focus of the search for a libidinal union that cannot be broken. The concern with female desire from the mother's perspective has become a concern with a desire for the Other as a desire for the child, and, more importantly though not always explicitly, a desire for the child as daughter.[34]

The analyses of desire as incestuous desire between daughter and mother are analyses of desire within a relation of inequality, a vertical relation in which who is daughter and who is mother is predetermined. Yet this vertical relation of inequality has become the implicit ground of the analysis of relations of equality, of horizontal relations between women. The analysis of woman's desire has become a reclaiming of motherhood, but women came together in the movement not as mothers but as sisters. The telos of the movement has been, and remains, sisterhood as recognition.

Sisterhood is a concept taken from the private realm, the realm of the family; it was initially used in the public realm by the woman's liberation movement to *challenge* the family by pointing to the fact that women have a bond that, like the family, is a bond not chosen.[35] From a shared social position of domination women created a solidarity and a vision of liberation through consciousness raising. Sisterhood, in this context, represents a relation of mutual recognition outside the family, civil society, and the state in that it is not a true blood-tie, it is not mediated by a process of object creating, and it is not based on each woman being free and equal. It represents, rather, a non-desiring relation of recognition between women, one which focuses on the political potential of a universal community of women.[36]

This concept of sisterhood has been confronted with the desiring relationship between women—lesbianism—not only as a personal preference but as a political choice. This moves the concern with the nondesiring relationship between all women (S-S-S) to the desiring relationship between two women (S-S). The eroticization of feminism by lesbianism assumes that free intersubjective relations require an Other that is the "same as" the self, and this assumption obscures the problem of non-identity. Freedom of sexual choice is a necessary part of feminism; nevertheless, lesbianism is not the same as feminism, and the analysis of lesbian desire is not a comprehensive response to the question of female desire.

What we find from this consideration of the relation between motherhood and sisterhood is that the feminist inquiry into the development of the female psyche in terms of the dialectic of desire and recognition is a necessary corrective to the focus on the relations between men and the relations between man and woman from man's perspective. However, there are significant problems in feminist theory that emerge with greater clarity when seen within the project of critical theory's analysis of the civilizing process.

First, the relation between motherhood and sisterhood implies the same problem made explicit in my analysis of critical theory concerning the arena of ego development. As we have seen, the attempt to ground the dialectic of desire and recognition in both Freud and Hegel remains problematic in critical theory: no passage from Freud to Hegel is articulated that can ground the enterprise of using Freud's theory of desire as a theory of origin and Hegel's theory of intersubjectivity as the goal. This problem has an analogue in the feminist enterprise in which motherhood as a theory of desire is the origin and sisterhood as a theory of intersubjectivity is the goal.[37] That is, is female identity formation or ego development a process that occurs primarily in the vertical incestuous relations of the family, as Freud claims, or is it a process that occurs in horizontal relations between strangers in the public world, as Hegel claims? Or, is there a relation between these two accounts that has yet to be articulated? The "answers" to these questions imply different political strategies centering either on the family or civil society as the arena for social change. Put somewhat simplistically, they become either a politics of childhood socialization or a politics of equal opportunity/affirmative action.

Second, we find that nothing new is said about heterosexuality as a relation of female *desire* insofar as the Freudian father as the "third" remains in place or is simply ignored. Feminist theory often attempts to ground the intersubjective recognition of the Other in "identity"; that is, the intersubjective paradigm is based on female-female relations as daughter-mother or sister-sister relations. Within this analysis relations between females are the basis for defining and restructuring female-male relations. The desiring relationship between women is seen as important to the development of the group, but there is no analysis of the relation between homosexuality and heterosexuality, the problem which emerges in my analysis of Marcuse's appropriation of Freud. If the group is founded on homoerotic desire between women, how does that relate to the question of heterosexual desire and the formation of the heterosexual group? The underlying question in feminist theory emerges here as the underlying question in critical theory: the relation between identity and nonidentity in the dialectic of desire and recognition.

IDENTITY, NON-IDENTITY, AND NAMING

In order to criticize the domination of nature, Marcuse retains the Hegelian notion of identity-in-difference as a utopian vision. The redemptive vision of the reconciliation of nature and history, subject and object, provides the motive and ground for his critique. However, although he supports the movement for woman's liberation in a political sense, he provides no theoretical conception of woman as historical actor based on the specificity of the female psyche. Woman remains a "principle" or representation of liberation: "patriarchal society has created a female image, a female counter-force, which may still become one of the grave-diggers of patriarchal society. In this sense too, the woman holds the promise of liberation. It is the woman who, in Delacroix' painting, holding the flag of the revolution, leads the people on the barricades. She wears no uniform; her breasts are bare, and her beautiful face shows no trace of violence."[38] Thus, the reconciliation of identity and non-identity in Marcuse's work ends by romanticizing woman and swallowing her into an identitarian framework that privileges male experience.

The Hegelian problem of the relation between identity and non-identity is central to the feminist project of creating a free and equal society. That is, theorists search for a form of inter-subjective recognition (a relation between self and Other) that allows for concrete differences but does not, on that account, render women unequal. However, as Adorno has shown, Hegel's notion of reconciliation presents us with a false identity of subject and object, nature and history, particular and universal. The ontological and epistemic claims of universality and the reconciliation with the Other have always meant the domination of the particular. Where Adorno argues that identity philosophy is animated by a hostility to the Other and necessarily excludes certain forms of experience, feminists have argued that woman as Other has been "feared, idealized, and negated" as the Other: she has been defined as different from man, and as the ontological principle of difference itself, to be dominated and excluded.[39] Thus, a theory of non-identity is a prerequisite for a theory of woman's liberation. Adorno argues for such a theory in *Negative Dialectics*, where the non-identity of nature and history, subject and object, particular and universal does not mean an absolute dualism but a dialectic whose "reconciliation" avoids the annihilation of the Other: "The reconciled condition would not be the philosophical imperialism of annexing the alien [the Other]. Instead, its happiness would lie in the fact that the alien, in the proximity it is granted, remains what is distant and different, beyond the heterogeneous and beyond that which is one's own."[40] Here the recognition of non-identity, which would allow for the rescue of woman as Other, as the particular, the different not to be dominated, seems most firmly grounded. And whereas he formulates a critique of abstract equality ("equality in which differences perish secretly serves to promote inequality") he also rejects direct access to difference, which would simply confine

woman to her "own" sphere ("The illusion of taking direct hold
of the Many would be a mimetic regression...a recoil into
mythology").[41]

But for Adorno access to the non-identical comes indirectly
through the construction of "constellations." These constellations are philosophical "texts" that juxtapose concepts around
the object so that no single concept is identical with the object.
"Properly written texts are like spiders' webs: tight, concentric,
transparent, well-spun and firm" in which the object, the concrete particular, is interpreted through its many representations.[42] It is an infinity caught in the web of everyday life, and
Adorno's metaphor recalls woman's weaving as creation activity.

The question that emerges here, however, is how the concern
with conceptual thought, which relies on such an indirect route
to the non-identical (the weaving of constellations), relates to
the project of the historical actor. As we have seen, Adorno rejects
the notion that there is a given class or group that is necessarily
the source of liberation: any group can be ideologically corrupted
under the prevailing system of domination, no matter how much
its social location may point it to truth. In his schema the domination of woman has created her as a symptom and representation of distorted nature. As actor she would either be
destructively regressive by emphasizing her difference, which is
the "scar tissue" of repressed nature, or she would be dominating, by accepting the identitarian logic that *denies* her difference
in the name of abstract equality. The social component of Adorno's theory is removed from the realm of politics to the aesthetic
realm. It is in artistic creation that a liberatory moment is to be
found: "It is now virtually in art alone that suffering can still
find its own voice, consolation, without immediately being betrayed by it."[43] Thus, Adorno's negative dialectics saves non-
identity by severing it from an historical actor.

What emerges from my critique is a polarity between the
work of Marcuse and the work of Adorno, which is a polarity
between the project of universal reconciliation and a defense of
non-identity. Where the non-identical is secured in the philosophy of Adorno, the historical project of liberation is lost: it is

removed to the realm of thought and imagination, severed from the realm of action. And where the historical project of liberation is secured in the work of Marcuse, the philosophical grounding in Hegelian reconciliation undermines the project of woman's liberation. In the last analysis, Marcuse and Adorno both fail to provide an analysis for woman as historical actor.

Thus, Marcuse and Adorno do not solve the problem in which woman is dominated both by recognizing her difference and denying it. In Marcuse the vision of woman formed within the family is the ideal of civil society insofar as woman represents freedom for man. However, this solution rests on woman's confinement to the family to secure her difference. In Adorno woman represents not freedom but the domination of nature. Her representation as "Other" secures her domination such that any attempt to act only reinforces domination, either through the emphasis on difference or its denial.

From woman's perspective it is simply not enough to be the aesthetic or psychic representation of liberation for man (Marcuse) or to be the conceptual representation of the domination of nature (Adorno). The dilemma for woman, in which she needs to find herself as historical actor without denying her non-identity, is a dilemma at the heart of critical theory. It calls for a move beyond the polarity of Marcuse and Adorno in order to understand the dialectic of civilization as a dialectic of identity and non-identity. Thus, we find an initial basis for renewing the critique of the domination of nature in reflecting upon and articulating woman's experience.

Woman's experience is to be found in the traces of memory reformed through the process of "naming." Although naming can never capture the immediacy of the experience—what is articulated is never *the same as* the experience—we must name experience in order to understand it; without naming, experience is simply passed through or endured. When concepts are linked to experience so that experience is understood, not just undergone, we are led to a rediscovery of philosophy as critical theory. The importance of naming is underscored by Horkheimer: "Philosophy is the conscious effort to knit all our knowledge and insight into a linguistic structure in which things are called by their right names."[44] The philosophical articulation of domination rescues the particular, the non-identical, and initiates a vision of liberation and historical action: it gives an image to the name that transcends the present to become the future.

The naming of woman's experience within the civilizing myths that explicate the philosophical ground of critical theory remains silent on the relations between women and on woman's self-experience of desire. In this way, woman's experience is distorted and denied. Woman's voicelessness reveals reification as silencing. By giving voice to her experience, by naming the unnamed for herself, woman challenges the reification of the name through silence and she initiates the political project.

The effort to find the right names for woman's experience has been central to the woman's liberation movement from the very beginning. In the 1960s woman's domination was described as "the problem with no name."[45] Soon after this, radical women began meeting in consciousness-raising groups to articulate and analyze the ubiquitous but amorphous sense of male domination. Along with this new political practice of naming one's experience for oneself, the traces of memory reformed through naming created feminist theories of domination and liberation. The feminist critique of the male-female relations embedded in a patriarchal-capitalist system of power expresses theories of liberation in the naming of motherhood and sisterhood. But the feminist theories of motherhood and sisterhood are only partial: they focus on relations between women and woman's self-experience of desire. As essential as this new naming is to the political project of liberation it may become reified into new mythologies that themselves obscure aspects of woman's experience; mythologies are names subjected to a reified universal that obstructs the necessity to *name for oneself.*

Critical theory has occluded woman's experience within its analysis of the domination of nature; nevertheless, within this tradition the attempt to find the right names, to name woman's self-experience is not an arbitrary intrusion but a self-reflective turn called forth by the theory itself. Critical theory undoes reified universals by tracing them back to the experiences from which they arise; simultaneously, it carries partial insights forward into a universal reflection. As the contemporary expression of the critical and civilizing task of philosophy, critical theory makes it possible for woman to rename her experience of motherhood and sisterhood as experiences of the dialectic of desire and recognition within the civilizing process.

Notes

CHAPTER 1. HEGEL: RECOGNITION, INTERSUBJECTIVITY, AND DESIRE

1. Earlier versions of this chapter were published as "Hegel and 'The Woman Question': Recognition and Intersubjectivity" in *The Sexism of Social and Political Theory: Women and Reproduction from Plato to Nietzsche*, ed. Lorenne M. G. Clark and Lynda Lange (Toronto: University of Toronto Press, 1979), pp. 74–98; and "Hegel's *Antigone*" in *The Owl of Minerva: Journal of the Hegel Society of America* 17 (Spring 1986): 131–52.

2. G. W. F. Hegel, *Phenomenology of Spirit*, trans. A. V. Miller (Oxford: Oxford University Press, 1979), p. 263, paragraph 438.

3. Jean Hyppolite, *Studies on Marx and Hegel*, trans. John O'Neill (New York: Harper Torchbooks, 1973), p. 76.

4. For my sketch of Hegel's project I found the following works particularly helpful: Richard J. Bernstein, *Praxis and Action* (Philadelphia: University of Pennsylvania Press, 1971); Frederick Copleston, S.J., *A History of Philosophy*, vol. 7 (Garden City: Image Books, 1963); Jean Hyppolite, *Studies on Marx and Hegel* (see note 3 above); John Herman Randall, Jr., *The Career of Philosophy*, vol. 2 (New York: Columbia University Press, 1965); Georg Lukács, *The Young Hegel*, trans. Rodney Livingstone (London: Merlin Press, 1975); Edith Wyschogrod, *Spirit in Ashes: Hegel, Heidegger, and Man-Made Mass Death* (New Haven: Yale University Press, 1985).

5. Hyppolite, *Marx and Hegel*, p. 27.

6. Ibid., pp. 469–72.

7. Ibid., pp. 161–64.

8. Ibid., pp. 26–28; Wyschogrod, *Spirit in Ashes*, pp. 106–07.

9. Hegel, *Phenomenology of Spirit*, p. 114, paragraph 187.

10. Ibid., p. 115, paragraph 189.

11. Ibid., p. 117, paragraph 193, and p. 115, paragraph 190.

12. Ibid., p. 117, paragraph 194.

13. Hyppolite, *Marx and Hegel*, pp. 29 and 163; Wyschogrod, *Spirit in Ashes*, pp. 106–10.

14. Mary O'Brien, *The Politics of Reproduction* (Boston: Routledge & Kegan Paul, 1981), pp. 67–73.

15. G. W. F. Hegel, *Philosophy of Mind*, trans. A. V. Miller and J. N. Findlay (Oxford: Clarendon Press, 1971), pp. 176–77.

16. Hegel, *Phenomenology of Spirit*, p. 110, paragraph 177.

17. Robert Graves, *The White Goddess* (New York: Farrar, Straus and Giroux, 1976), p. 11.

18. Jessica Benjamin, "Authority and the Family Revisited: or, A World without Fathers?", *New German Critique* 13 (Winter 1978): 55; Caroline Whitbeck, "A Different Reality: Feminist Ontology," in *Beyond Domination: New Perspectives on Women and Philosophy*, ed. Carol C. Gould (Totowa, N.J.: Rowman & Allanheld, 1984), pp. 64–88. Mary O'Brien, "The Politics of Impotence," in *Contemporary Issues in Political Philosophy*, ed. William Shea and J. King-Farlow (New York: Science History Publications, 1976), p. 158; O'Brien, *The Politics of Reproduction*, p. 70.

Dorothy Dinnerstein gives the most profound account of the mother as first witness conferring recognition on the infant and the problems this entails; see Dinnerstein, *The Mermaid and the Minotaur: Sexual Arrangements and Human Malaise* (New York: Harper & Row, 1976).

19. This discussion of Hegel's philosophy of nature is based on the following works: Copleston, *A History of Philosophy* (see note 4 above); Alexandre Kojève, *Introduction to the Reading of Hegel*, trans. James H. Nichols, Jr., (New York: Basic Books, 1969); Emil Fackenheim, *The Religious Dimension in Hegel's Thought* (Boston: Beacon Press, 1970).

20. Kojève, *Reading Hegel*, p. 58.

21. Ibid., pp. 58–61.

22. Hegel, *Phenomenology of Spirit*, p. 270, paragraph 451 (amended translation). Miller's translation of *marklose* as "impotent" is not to be confused with Hegel's term *Ohnmacht* used to describe Nature as "impotent" or "unconscious." Many of Hegel's ontological

insights are rooted in Aristotle's philosophy. The bifurcation of familial and political life that Hegel subscribes to here can be found in Aristotle's *Politics*. For a thought-provoking article on this problem as it is developed in Aristotle see Jean Bethke Elshtain, "Moral Woman and Immoral Man: A Consideration of the Public-Private Split and Its Political Ramifications," *Politics and Society* 4 (Fall 1974): 453–73.

23. Hegel, *Phenomenology of Spirit*, p. 268, paragraph 450.

24. J. N. Findlay, *Hegel: A Re-Examination* (London: Unwin Brothers, 1958), pp. 116–17; Kojève, *Reading Hegel*, pp. 60–61 and 296–98; Charles Taylor, *Hegel* (Cambridge: Cambridge University Press, 1975), pp. 172–77.

25. Kojève, *Reading Hegel* pp. 60–61 and 297–98.

26. Hegel, *Phenomenology of Spirit*, p. 280, paragraph 466.

27. Ibid., pp. 274–75, paragraph 457; see also G. W. F. Hegel, *The Phenomenology of Mind*, trans. J. B. Baillie (New York: Harper Torchbooks, 1967), p. 477. In both the Miller and Baillie translations of this passage the word *particular* is added in several places to reveal Hegel's meaning. Hegel sometimes underscores the word for "this" (*dieser*) instead of using the word *Einzelheit* to refer to the particular individual.

28. Hegel, *Phenomenology of Spirit*, p. 274, paragraph 457, and p. 273, paragraph 456.

29. Ibid., p. 274, paragraph 457.

30. Ibid., p. 275, paragraph 457.

31. G. W. F. Hegel, *The Philosophy of History*, trans. J. Sibree (New York: Dover Publications, 1965), pp. 245–46.

32. George Steiner, *Antigones* (New York: Oxford University Press, 1984), p. 1.

33. It is true that the brother-sister relationship had a special place in the lives of many nineteenth-century men, including Hegel, Nietzsche, and Wordsworth. The question that remains is what this relationship meant to the sisters. Hegel's sister, Christiane, for example, committed suicide. Nietzsche's sister, Elisabeth, spent many years taking care of her brother when he was bedridden and deranged, but the relationship between them was a tortured one of love and hate. Elisabeth, an ardent Nazi in her later years, extracted a form of revenge by creating and then manipulating and exploiting her brother's fame. In a more traditional way, Wordsworth's sister, Dorothy, seems to have sacrificed a life of autonomous creative work to live vicariously through her brother.

What is most compelling in Steiner's account is his statement concerning the paradigm shift inaugurated by Freud in which Oedipus came to replace Antigone: "Between the 1790s and the start of the twentieth century, the radical lines of kinship run horizontally, as between brothers and sisters. In the Freudian construct they run vertically, as between children and parents. The Oedipus complex is one of inescapable verticality. The shift is momentous; with it Oedipus replaces Antigone. As we saw, it can be dated c. 1905" (Steiner, p. 18). Interestingly, Freud referred to his *daughter* Anna as "My Antigone." Whatever one might make of Freud's relation to Anna based on this fact, the important point is that the paradigm shift from a horizontal relation to a vertical one, which Freud achieved, was indeed momentous, especially for women.

34. Adrienne Rich, "Natural Resources," in *The Dream of a Common Language: Poems 1974–77* (New York: W. W. Norton, 1978), pp. 62–63.

35. Hegel, *Phenomenology of Spirit*, p. 274, paragraph 457.

36. Hegel, *Phenomenology of Spirit*, p. 275, paragraph 458.

37. Sophocles, *Antigone*, in *Ten Greek Plays in Contemporary Translations*, trans. Shaemus O'Sheel and ed. L. R. Lind (Boston: Riverside Press, 1957), lines 901–20. Many modern translations omit Antigone's speech in which she defends her decision to bury her brother yet says she would not make the same sacrifice for a husband or son. (I use the Lind edition here because it includes this speech. However, I use the Reinert edition elsewhere because it is more accurate for my purposes.) For an interesting analysis of the speech from an Hegelian perspective within a psychoanalytic framework, i.e., from a perspective that focuses on the problem of recognition between man and woman, see Robert Seidenberg and Evangelos Papathomopoulos, "The Enigma of Antigone," *International Review of Psycho-Analysis* 1 (1974):197–205.

It is also worth noting that this paradigm of mutual recognition between sister and brother, which is supposed to be devoid of desire, is rooted in the incestuous house of Thebes. Antigone's father, Oedipus, is also her brother, which means that Polyneices is her uncle as well as her brother and she his aunt as well as his sister. In choosing this seemingly atypical family to represent the family as natural ethical life, Hegel gives significance to the Oedipus myth long before Freud. In *The Bull from the Sea* (New York: Penguin Books, 1980), Mary Renault provides an interesting interpretation of Antigone: she sees her as having resolved the incestuous dilemma by "keeping faith with her childhood." As Theseus observes Oedipus and Antigone he muses: "I had been going to say, 'This man and his daughter,' when I remembered she was his sister too, out of the one womb. She took her head-scarf and wiped his face where a stone had grazed it; I saw she was daughter in her heart, keeping faith with her childhood" (p. 63).

38. This shift and the emphasis on the uterine relationship in the Greek text are obscured in contemporary translations but are revealed in the Oxford translation of the *Antigone*, lines 465–511 and lines 512–13. See *Antigone* in *The Tragedies of Sophocles: In English Prose*, the Oxford translation, new edition, revised according to the text of Dindorf (New York: Harper & Brothers, 1880), pp. 178–79.

39. Hegel, *Phenomenology of Spirit*, pp. 285–87, paragraphs 473 and 474.

40. Ibid., p. 289, paragraph 475, and p. 286, paragraph 474.

41. Ibid., p. 288, paragraph 475.

42. Ibid. By claiming that woman shows man the power of his authority, especially that as son he is master over his mother, Hegel suggests that woman conspires to realize male domination.

43. Ibid., p. 289, paragraph 476.

44. Kojève, *Reading Hegel*, p. 62; Taylor, *Hegel*, p. 177.

45. Theodor W. Adorno, *Negative Dialectics*, trans. E. B. Ashton (New York: Seabury Press, 1973), p. 173.

46. Ibid. Michele LeDoeuff has written an important article in which she argues that a radical transformation of philosophy itself is required to eliminate the sexism that pervades it. She uses Hegel's treatment of woman to show that philosophical discourse, as a discipline that represents a closure, necessarily excludes parts of experience that woman has come to symbolize. Although LeDoeuff misses the distinction between a philosopher and an academic who teaches philosophy and although she slides over the difference between the sexual distinction of male/female and the cultural distinction of masculine/feminine, her article is a ground-breaking piece of work. See LeDoeuff, "Women in Philosophy," trans. Debbie Pope, in *Radical Philosophy* 17 (Summer 1977): 2–11.

47. Hegel, *Phenomenology of Spirit*, p. 276, paragraph 460.

48. Ibid.

49. Sophocles, *Antigone*, in *Drama: An Introductory Anthology*, alternate edition, edited by Otto R. Reinert (Boston: Little, Brown & Company, 1964), p. 22 (amended translation; the translators, Dudley Fitts and Robert Fitzgerald, translate "gods" as "God"). See also Hegel, *Phenomenology of Spirit*, p. 284, paragraph 470, and *The Phenomenology of Mind*, p. 491.

50. Sophocles, *Antigone*, Reinert edition, p. 31.

51. One might want to argue that these gods are the divine representatives of male authority to which Antigone bows. Nevertheless, she does not accept male domination in its more obvious human guise.

52. Sophocles, *Antigone*, Reinert edition, p. 21.

53. Later, in his *Lectures on Fine Art*, Hegel himself describes Antigone as choosing her course of action: insofar as she has "pathos," she has free will. Here Hegel describes Antigone's pathos as less than that of Creon because she worships the underworld gods of Hades while Creon worships the daylight gods of self-conscious political life. However, the argument concerning the deliberate choice involved in Antigone's actions undermines the claim in the *Phenomenology* that the sister's ethical life is not conscious or actualized. See G. W. F. Hegel, *Aesthetics: Lectures on Fine Art*, trans. T. M. Knox (Oxford: Clarendon Press, 1975), pp. 232 and 264.

54. Sophocles, *Antigone*, Reinert edition, p. 2.

55. Ibid., p. 14.

56. Joyce Nower, "A Feminist View of Antigone," *The Longest Revolution*, February/March 1983, p. 6. Antigone rejects Ismene's offer of sisterly solidarity. One could interpret this rejection as a response to Ismene's failure to understand the ethical issue involved. However, I believe that Antigone's rejection of Ismene is best understood in light of the fact that patriarchal society attempts to set women against each other so that we learn to see ourselves primarily in relation to men. With Antigone's death one presumes that Ismene continues the everyday life of woman in the patriarchal family. Ismene's actions and plight require a more comprehensive analysis than is possible here.

57. "The individual, so far as he is not a citizen but belongs to the Family, is only an unreal insubstantial shadow." Hegel, *Phenomenology of Spirit*, p. 270, paragraph 451 (amended translation).

58. G. W. F. Hegel, *Natural Law*, trans. T. M. Knox (Philadelphia: University of Pennsylvania Press, 1975), pp. 90–92. See also Kojève, *Reading Hegel*, pp. 247–48.

59. Seidenberg and Papathomopoulos, "The Enigma of Antigone," p. 198.

60. Hegel, *The Phenomenology of Mind*, p. 483.

61. Sophocles, *Antigone*, Reinert edition, pp. 17 and 18. Creon's reproach to Haemon underscores Hegel's contention that woman acts on the adolescent male in her effort to destroy the pagan world. The psychological basis of Creon's fear of womankind is explored in Eli

Sagan, *The Lust to Annihilate: A Psychoanalytic Study of Violence in Ancient Greek Culture* (New York: Psychohistory Press, 1979), pp. 95–101.

62. Sophocles, *Antigone*, Reinert edition, pp. 16 and 18.

63. In their play *The Island* Athol Fugard, John Kani, and Winston Ntshona present *Antigone* as a play within a play to reveal the ancient drama's relevance to the situation of South African political prisoners. In both plays moral laws are juxtaposed to state laws to demonstrate that justice and the law do not necessarily coincide. This point, as we have seen, is lost in Hegel's interpretation.

64. My intent is not to demean "feminine intuition" but rather to reveal the sexist implications in this context, which does demean it. Steiner's analysis of Hegel's interpretation of the *Antigone* is quite different from mine; nonetheless, Steiner introduces an interesting note concerning the Antigone-Socrates comparison. Steiner argues that Hegel sets Antigone above Socrates because she accepts the possibility that she may be wrong and trusts in the gods to reveal the truth. Socrates, on the other hand, maintains his innocence at all times and contests the legitimacy of his trial and his sentence. See Steiner, *Antigones*, pp. 37–42.

65. Sophocles, *Antigone*, Reinert edition, p. 20.

66. Antigone may also be seen as the precursor of the suffragists of the late nineteenth and early twentieth centuries and the women involved in the temperance movement insofar as those women were trying to achieve familial goals in the public realm. For an interesting analysis of this process see Elshtain, "Moral Woman and Immoral Man," pp. 453–73.

67. G. W. F. Hegel, *Philosophy of Right*, trans. T. M. Knox (London: Oxford University Press, 1967), p. 111, paragraph 161.

68. Alexandre Kojève claims that for Hegel the family is the sphere of particularity as opposed to the universality of the state, but he concerns himself only with the *Phenomenology* and does not consider the *Philosophy of Right*, where this problem is worked out in greater detail. As we have outlined above, it is (male) civil society—not the family—that is the sphere of particularity in Hegel's later system. Since woman never leaves the family she never becomes a consciously particular self, and the family represents, in the *Phenomenology*, only an unconscious sphere of particularity for man. Mary O'Brien claims that in Hegel's system woman represents particularity necessarily defeated by man as the agent of universality. But according to Hegel woman is the agent

of destruction that defeats the universal male community in the pagan state. More important, Hegel does not address and Kojève and O'Brien do not raise the question of exactly how woman can represent particularity while never knowing herself as a particular being. To focus on the dualism of familial and political spheres, as Kojève does, or the dualism of sex, as O'Brien does, is to elide the more developed tripartite structure of the *Philosophy of Right*, where the family represents the *universal* in its first moment of immediacy and male civil society, as the "universal family," is the sphere of conscious particularity. See Kojève, *Reading Hegel*, pp. 60–61; O'Brien, "The Politics of Impotence," pp. 147–62.

69. Art, religion, and philosophy also figure as ultimate expressions of humanity in the work of Marcuse, Horkheimer, and Adorno.

70. Hegel, *Philosophy of Right*, p. 155, paragraph 257.

71. It should be noted that Hegel shifts the principle of the family from "particularity" in the *Phenomenology* to "love" in the first part of the *Philosophy of Right* and to "blood" in the last analysis; this shift to blood as the principle of the family contradicts Hegel's claim that the "true" principle of the family, as the sphere of immediacy, is love.

72. See Hyppolite, *Marx and Hegel*, p. 27.

73. Hegel, *Philosophy of Right*, p. 263, addition to paragraph 164.

74. Ibid., p. 112, paragraph 163.

75. Ibid., p. 116, paragraph 171.

76. Ibid., p. 116, paragraphs 169 and 170.

77. Herbert Marcuse, *Studies in Critical Philosophy*, trans. Joris De Bres (Boston: Beacon Press, 1973), pp. 106–07. Hegel later tells us that while the bourgeois family principle calls for the equality of inheritance, "in the higher sphere of the state, a right of primogeniture arises together with estates rigidly entailed: it arises, however, not arbitrarily but as the inevitable outcome of the Idea of the state" (*Philosophy of Right*, p. 122, paragraph 180). Thus, the family of the landed aristocracy is overreached by the state in such a way that woman and all her children, except for the firstborn male, are denied the rights of inheritance. According to Hegel, any social group that maintains its property by inheritance through the family not only protects family members from the arbitrary developments of civil society but guarantees that they will conduct themselves according to high ethical standards because the family is the sphere of substantive ethical life. Therefore, the landed aristocracy, because they receive their property through the right of primogeniture, are unusually fitted to hold positions as civil servants

and political leaders. This argument, however, not only contradicts Hegel's view of property as something that can be freely disposed of by the owner but also makes nonsense of the idea of family solidarity since only one of the male children of this class inherits everything. Through the right of primogeniture, property concerns "infect" the family of the landed aristocracy with the antagonisms of particularity that are supposed to be confined to civil society.

78. Hegel, *Philosophy of Right*, pp. 264–65, addition to paragraph 173.

79. Ibid., p. 117, paragraph 173.

80. Hegel's philosophy is ideological in its lack of an analysis of the difference between the working-class and bourgeois family as well as in its patriarchal assumptions. It is difficult to know how the nineteenth-century working-class woman, who was *in* but not *of* civil society, who was restricted to a subsistence level of existence within her own family (which was *not* based on property and capital) or relegated to the bourgeois family as a domestic servant, fits Hegel's schema. The working-class woman produced and reproduced laborers, not heirs to the family property.

81. G. W. F. Hegel, *Philosophy of Nature*, trans. A. V. Miller (Oxford: Clarendon Press, 1970), p. 413.

82. Hegel, *Philosophy of Right*, p. 114, paragraphs 165 and 166.

83. Ibid., p. 114, paragraph 166.

84. Ibid., pp. 263–64, addition to paragraph 166.

85. Ibid., pp. 111–14, paragraphs 161–64. The question that emerges here, which Hegel does not address, is why this particular "ethical" relationship requires a public ceremony. Surely friendship is an ethical bond and yet it requires no public declaration or contract in the way that marriage does. In fact, as Hegel himself says, civil society and the state offer all sorts of opportunities for ethical behavior to the man, yet how many of these require a public ceremony to acknowledge their "ethicality"?

86. Ibid., p. 116, paragraph 172; Hegel also maintains this understanding of the relation between the family of origin and the family of procreation in the *Aesthetics*, pp. 463–64.

87. Ibid., pp. 114–15, paragraph 166.

88. For Hegel it is precisely the Aufhebung or reconciliation of the modern world that reveals the dualistic conflict of the ancient world. Given the inadequacy of Hegel's formulation of the modern reconciliation in the context of sexual difference, he must necessarily misrep-

resent this conflict in his interpretation of *Antigone* in the *Phenomenology.*

CHAPTER 2. MARX: THE DOUBLE DIALECTIC

1. In my analysis of Marx I shall not attempt to discuss Engels' understanding of the dialectic. Although this should not be construed as a simple dismissal of Engels, I do believe that he distorts Marx's understanding of the dialectic and contributes to the development of mechanical Marxism. A comprehensive account of the relation between Marx and Engels on the dialectic exceeds the scope of this book. For a more detailed analysis of this relation and its role in the development of Marxism see Alfred Schmidt, *The Concept of Nature in Marx,* trans. Ben Fowkes (London: New Left Books, 1971), pp. 51–61, and Jack Mendelson, "On Engels' Metaphysical Dialectics: A Foundation of Orthodox Marxism," *Dialectical Anthropology* 4 (March 1979): 65–73. For a comparative analysis of Marx and Engels on the dialectic in terms of woman's liberation see Raya Dunayevskaya, "Relationship of Philosophy and Revolution to Women's Liberation: Marx's and Engels' Studies Contrasted," *News & Letters* 24 (January/February 1979): 5–8.

2. In Karl Marx and Friedrich Engels, *Collected Works,* vol. 3., trans. Jack Cohen et al. (New York: International Publishers, 1975). See Shlomo Avineri, *The Social and Political Thought of Karl Marx* (New York: Cambridge University Press, 1975), pp. 5–47. Avineri's insightful analysis of Marx's critique of Hegel provides the foundation for my discussion of the *Critique.*

3. Avineri, pp. 27–29, 44. Marx also shows that Hegel's argument concerning the ethical role of the entailment of property through primogeniture is vitiated by his earlier claim that owners must be free to dispose of their property as they see fit.

4. Marx and Engels, *Collected Works* 3:7, 10.

5. See Marx and Engels, *Collected Works,* 3:11.

6. Karl Marx and Friedrich Engels, *Historisch-Kritische Gesamtausgabe,* as cited by Avineri, *Social and Political Thought of Marx,* p. 32.

7. Karl Marx, *Karl Marx: Early Writings,* trans. and ed. T. B. Bottomore (New York: McGraw Hill, 1963), p. 58. For an insightful discussion of Marx's concept of the proletariat see William Leiss, "Critical Theory and Its Future," *Political Theory* 2 (August 1974): 330–

49; and Erica Sherover, "The Virtue of Poverty: Marx's Transformation of Hegel's Concept of the Poor," *Canadian Journal of Political and Social Theory* 3 (Winter 1979): 53–66.

8. Johann Wolfgang Goethe, *Torquato Tasso: A Play*, trans. John Prudhoe (Manchester: Manchester University Press, 1979), p. 103. According to Adorno, "Iphegenie and Tasso are civilization dramas"; Adorno, "Zum Klassizimus von Goethe's Iphegenie," as cited in George Steiner, *Antigones* (New York: Oxford University Press, 1984), p. 46.

9. Marx and Engels, *Collected Works* 3:273.

10. Ibid., p. 332.

11. Ibid., p. 91.

12. In Karl Marx and Friedrich Engels, *Selected Works* (Moscow: Progress Publishers, 1968), pp. 182–83.

13. Marx and Engels, *Collected Works* 3:276.

14. My discussion of Marx's understanding of objectification is indebted to Marcuse's analysis. See especially Marcuse, *Critical Philosophy*, pp. 14, 22–23, 38, 44–45.

15. Marcuse, *Critical Philosophy*, p. 47.

16. See Bernstein, *Praxis and Action*, pp. 44–45; Karl Marx, *Writings of the Young Marx on Philosophy and Society*, trans. and ed. Loyd D. Easton and Kurt H. Guddat (New York: Anchor Books, 1967), pp. 287–301.

17. Marx and Engels, *Collected Works* 3:227–28.

18. Ibid., p. 301.

19. Ibid., p. 304; see Avineri, *The Social and Political Thought of Marx*, p. 88.

20. In *The Politics of Reproduction* Mary O'Brien claims that the redefinition of the proletariat from the original Latin meaning (the class that has no wealth but its children) to the meaning it has in Marx (the class that has no wealth but its labor) is significant. Capitalism, as a system that produces and reproduces itself, transforms the meaning of human *continuity* from that which occurs through human biological reproduction to that which occurs through economic relations.

21. Georg Lukács, *History and Class Consciousness: Studies in Marxist Dialectics*, trans. Rodney Livingstone (Cambridge, Mass.: M.I.T. Press, 1973), p. 91.

22. Marcuse, *Critical Philosophy*, pp. 34–35.

23. Karl Marx, *Capital*, vol. 1, trans. Samuel Moore and Edward Aveling (Moscow: Progress Publishers, n.d.), p. 604.

24. Marx and Engels, *Selected Works*, p. 77 (amended translation).

Gillian Rose corrects the mistranslation of *die phantasmagorische form* in her book *The Melancholy Science: An Introduction to the Thought of Theodor W. Adorno* (New York: Columbia University Press, 1978), pp. 30–31.

25. Marx, *Capital* 1:76.

26. Ibid., p. 46.

27. My account of Marx's critique of political economy is indebted to the work of Ian H. Angus. See Angus, "Aristotelian and Hegelian Aspects of Marx's Concept of Labour" (paper presented to the Canadian Political Science Association, Learned Societies, Halifax, June 1981).

28. Ibid., pp. 8–9.

29. Karl Marx and Friedrich Engels, *The Communist Manifesto*, ed. Samuel H. Beer (Northbrook: AHM Publishing, 1955), p. 32.

30. Karl Marx, *Capital*, vol. 3 (Moscow: Foreign Languages Publishing House, 1962), p. 800.

31. Schmidt, *The Concept of Nature in Marx*, p. 80.

32. Marx, *Writings of the Young Marx*, pp. 304, 306.

33. Ibid., pp. 294–95 (my emphasis).

34. Ibid., p. 308 (amended translation). See also Herbert Marcuse, *Counterrevolution and Revolt* (Boston: Beacon Press, 1972), pp. 63–64.

35. See Schmidt, *The Concept of Nature in Marx*, pp. 177–81.

36. Marcuse, *Counterrevolution and Revolt*, pp. 68–69.

37. Karl Marx, *Grundrisse: Foundations of the Critique of Political Economy*, trans. Martin Nicolaus (Harmondsworth: Penguin Books, 1973), pp. 409–10 (my emphasis on nature as an object).

38. Marx, *Grundrisse*, p. 705 (my emphasis). See also Schmidt, *The Concept of Nature in Marx*, p. 147; Angus, "Marx's Concept of Labour," pp. 18–20.

39. Schmidt, *The Concept of Nature in Marx*, pp. 147–55, 179.

40. The concept of a "dominant moment" in the dialectical process appears in Marx's consideration of the relation between production and consumption in capitalist society. After a brilliant analysis of the dialectical relation between production and consumption Marx makes production a "dominant moment" and consumption a "moment" of production (*Grundrisse*, pp. 90–95). Even if one concedes that the "moment" of production was *historically* dominant in the nineteenth century and/or that which theoretically *begins* the dialectical process, once it has begun there can be no "dominant moment." This formulation is

also an "abstract negation" wherein consumption, as the necessary opposite of production, no longer maintains an independent identity— consumption and production do not form a unity in which there is an "identity-in-difference."

41. Adorno, *Negative Dialectics*, p. 244.

42. Marx, *Capital* 1:173; see also Leiss, *The Domination of Nature*, p. 53.

43. Karl Marx, "Speech at the Anniversary of the *People's Paper*" (April 1856), as cited by Schmidt, *The Concept of Nature in Marx*, p. 7.

44. Angus, "Marx's Concept of Labour," p. 19; Schmidt, *The Concept of Nature in Marx*, p. 144. Angus shows these two conceptions of freedom rooted in Marx's appropriation of Hegel's philosophical model of freedom *in* labor and his appropriation of Aristotle's model of freedom *from* labor.

45. Karl Marx and Friedrich Engels, *The German Ideology*, in *Collected Works*, vol. 5 (New York: International Publishers, 1976), p. 47. See Angus, "Marx's Concept of Labour," pp. 18–20.

46. Marx, *Capital* 1:458.

47. Schmidt, *The Concept of Nature in Marx*, pp. 140–42; Angus, "Marx's Concept of Labour," p. 25.

48. Marx, *Grundrisse*, p. 706.

49. Angus, "Marx's Concept of Labour," p. 19.

50. Marx, *Grundrisse*, p. 708.

51. Stanley Aronowitz, *The Crisis in Historical Materialism: Class, Politics and Culture in Marxist Theory* (New York: Praeger, 1981), pp. 47–49, 116.

52. Nicole-Claude Mathieu, "Man-Culture and Woman-Nature?" trans. D. M. Leonard Barker, *Women's Studies International Quarterly* 1 (1978): 55; Susan Sontag, "The Third World of Women," *Partisan Review* 40 (1973): 180–206.

53. Marx, *Writings of the Young Marx*, pp. 302–03.

54. Karl Marx and Friedrich Engels, *The Holy Family, or Critique of Critical Criticism*, trans. Richard Dixon and Clemens Dutt (Moscow: Progress Publishers, 1975), p. 230.

55. Marx, *Writings of the Young Marx*, p. 303 (my emphasis at beginning and end of quote).

56. Avineri, *The Social and Political Thought of Marx*, p. 89; Mary O'Brien, "Reproducing Marxist Man," in *The Sexism of Social and*

Political Theory: Women and Reproduction from Plato to Nietzsche,
ed. Lorenne M. G. Clark and Lynda Lange (Toronto: University of
Toronto Press, 1979), pp. 108–09.
  57. Marx, *Writings of the Young Marx,* pp. 419–22.
  58. Ibid., p. 421. See Rosalind Pollack Petchesky, "Reproductive
Freedom: Beyond 'A Woman's Right to Choose,' " in *Women: Sex and
Sexuality,* ed. Catherine R. Stimpson and Ethel Spector Person (Chicago:
University of Chicago Press, 1980), pp. 102–04.
  59. Marx, *Writings of the Young Marx,* p. 420.
  60. Marcuse, *Critical Philosophy,* pp. 140–43.
  61. Marx and Engels, *Collected Works* 3:99.
  62. Marx and Engels, *The Communist Manifesto,* p. 29. Even here
woman is seen as passive, as the object of man's seduction. While it is
true that woman is often at the mercy of man's sexual advances, adulterous affairs require woman's active cooperation. Infidelity in the nineteenth century might be viewed more accurately as one of the few escapes
a bourgeois woman had from the confines of an unhappy marriage. The
seduction of female servants is another matter. A domestic servant was
always in a precarious position and was often victimized by her male
employer.
  Marx's relationship with his wife, Jenny, reflects ironically on his
critique of bourgeois marriage, male domination, and love as ideology.
In his marriage Marx conducted himself just like the bourgeois men he
so scathingly attacked.
  Late in their marriage (1856) Marx writes to Jenny: "Love—not of
Feuerbachian man, ... not of the proletariat, but love of one's darling,
namely you, makes a man into a man again ... where I can find another
face in which every trait, even every wrinkle brings back the greatest
and sweetest memories of my life. Even my infinite sorrows, my irreplaceable losses I can read on your sweet countenance, and I kiss my
sorrows away when I kiss your sweet face" (David McLellan, *Karl Marx:
His Life and Thought* [London: Macmillan, 1973], p. 274). Jenny,
however, discloses a love filled with fear at the very beginning of their
relationship (1839–40): "In ordinary circumstances ... the girl must find
her complete satisfaction in the man's love, she must forget everything
in love.... The more I were to surrender myself to happiness, the more
frightful would my fate be if your ardent love were to cease and you
became cold and withdrawn" (Marx and Engels, *Collected Works*
1:695–96). While Marx writes of realizing himself in this love relation,
finding himself in an Other, Jenny fears losing herself. She does not

focus on intersubjective mutuality as the true expression of selfhood; instead she dreads annihilation of the self through abandonment. Jenny believes that she must live only for and through love, but because she is socially and economically dependent on Marx she perceives love as a precarious bond and searches for a way to ensure that he will remain bound to her with a need equal to her own: "*I vividly imagined that you had lost your right hand, and,* Karl, *I was in a state of rapture,* of bliss, because of that. You see, sweetheart, *I thought that in that case I could really become quite indispensable to you,* you would then always keep me with you and love me. I also thought that then I could write down all your dear, heavenly ideas and be really useful to you" (Marx and Engels, *Collected Works* 1:696–97; my emphasis).

Marx's letter was written five years after he had fathered a child by the family servant, Helen Demuth, a woman "given" to Jenny by her mother when she and Marx married. Jenny gave birth to her fifth child that same year. Even though Marx had denounced the sexual exploitation of working-class and bourgeois women by bourgeois men in *The Communist Manifesto*, he too victimized both his wife and his domestic servant. (See McLellan, *Karl Marx*, p. 271; Marx and Engels, *The Communist Manifesto*, p. 29. Hegel also fathered a child out of wedlock. But this occurred in 1807, prior to his marriage to another woman. After his marriage in 1811 he brought the boy into his household with his wife's consent, according to his account.)

Many scholars believe that Jenny never knew that Marx was the father of the Demuth boy. In order to conceal the truth Engels claimed paternity and assumed financial responsibility for the child, who was sent to live in a foster home. Perhaps Jenny did not know. But if Marx behaved like a typical bourgeois husband Jenny may have played the part of a typical bourgeois wife, refusing to acknowledge out loud the "open secret" of her husband's infidelity. One has only to look at the pictures of Jenny taken in her later years to see that she was a woman traumatized by her life. And her life was her marriage—marriage of continuous pregnancies, poverty, and exile that left her physically ill, emotionally disturbed, and betrayed. (See McLellan, *Karl Marx*, pp. 271–73, 328–31, 460–61, and plate 26; Yvonne Kapp, *Eleanor Marx*, vol. 1 [New York: Pantheon Books, 1972], pp. 289–97.)

Jenny's life with Marx, in which the lie of the unacknowledged son sits center-stage, recalls Adrienne Rich's "Women and Honor: Some Notes on Lying": "When we discover that someone we trusted can be trusted no longer, it forces us to re-examine the universe, to question the whole instinct and concept of trust. For a while, we are thrust back onto some bleak, jutting ledge, in a dark pierced by sheets of fire, swept by sheets of rain, in a world before kinship, or naming, or tenderness exist; we are brought close to formlessness" (Rich, *On Lies, Secrets, and Silence: Selected Prose, 1966–1978* [New York: W. W. Norton, 1979], p. 192).

63. Ibid., p. 12; Marx and Engels, *The German Ideology,* in *Collected Works* 5:180.

64. Marx and Engels, *The German Ideology,* in *Collected Works* 5:180, 181.

65. Marx and Engels, *The Communist Manifesto,* p. 28.

66. Marx, *Capital* 1:460 (my emphasis).

67. Karl Marx, letter to Ludwig Kugelmann, 12 December 1868, as cited by Raya Dunayevskaya, "Relationship of Philosophy and Revolution to Women's Liberation," p. 6.

68. Shulamith Firestone, *The Dialectic of Sex: The Case for Feminist Revolution* (New York: Bantam Books, 1971), pp. 10 and 198–200; Petchesky, "Reproductive Freedom," p. 108*n.* For contemporary feminist critiques of reproductive technology see R. Arditti, R. Duelli Klein, and S. Minden, eds., *Test-Tube Women: What Future for Motherhood?* (London: Pandora Press, 1984); Somer Brodribb, "Off the Pedestal and onto the Block?: Motherhood, Reproductive Technologies and the Canadian State," *Canadian Journal of Women and the Law* 1 (1986); Gena Corea, *The Mother Machine: Reproductive Technologies from Artificial Insemination to Artificial Wombs* (New York: Harper & Row, 1985); Anne Donchin, "The Future of Mothering: Reproductive Technology and Feminist Theory," *Hypatia: A Journal of Feminist Philosophy* 1 (Fall 1986); Helen Roberts, ed., *Women, Health and Reproduction* (London: Routledge and Kegan Paul, 1981).

69. Virginia Held focuses on one paragraph concerning the man-woman relation in the 1844 *Manuscripts* in her analysis of Marx; Ann Foreman attempts to use the concept of alienation to explain woman's domination; and the "wages for housework" debate extrapolates Marx's labor theory of value to analyze woman's unwaged domestic labor. See Virginia Held, "Marx, Sex and the Transformation of Society," *Philosophical Forum* 5 (1973–74): 168–83; Ann Foreman, *Femininity as Alienation: Women and the Family in Marxism and Psychoanalysis* (London: Pluto Press, 1977); Ellen Malos, "Housework and the Politics of Women's Liberation," *Socialist Review,* no. 37 (Jan-

uary–February 1978), pp. 41–71; Ellen Malos, *The Politics of House-work* (London: Allison & Busby, 1980).

CHAPTER 3. PSYCHE AND SOCIETY

1. Herbert Marcuse, *Eros and Civilization: A Philosophical Inquiry into Freud* (New York: Vintage Books, 1962), p. 31. See *The Essential Frankfurt School Reader*, edited with introductions by Andrew Arato and Eike Gebhardt (New York: Urizen Books, 1978), p. 388; Martin Jay, *The Dialectical Imagination: A History of the Frankfurt School and the Institute of Social Research, 1923–1950* (Boston: Little, Brown & Co., 1973), pp. 97–108; and Schmidt, *The Concept of Nature in Marx*, pp. 137–38, 230.

2. Leiss, "Critical Theory and Its Future," p. 336.

3. Max Horkheimer, *Critical Theory*, trans. Matthew J. O'Connell and Others (New York: Herder and Herder, 1972), pp. 47–97.

4. William Leiss, "The Problem of Man and Nature in the Work of the Frankfurt School," *Philosophy of the Social Sciences* 5 (1975): 163–72.

5. Max Horkheimer and Theodor W. Adorno, *Dialectic of Enlightenment*, trans. John Cumming (New York: Herder and Herder, 1972), p. 186 (amended translation). See Horkheimer and Adorno, *Dialektik der Aufklärung: Philosophische Fragmente* (Frankfurt: S. Fischer, 1969), p. 195. The translation of *bloße Natur* as "mere" nature rather than "pure" nature is a more accurate interpretation.

6. Arato and Gebhardt, *Frankfurt School Reader*, pp. 17–18; David Held, *Introduction to Critical Theory: Horkheimer to Habermas* (Berkeley: University of California Press, 1980), pp. 134–37; Agnes Heller, "Individual and Community," *Social Praxis* 1 (1973): 20; Jay, *The Dialectical Imagination*, p. 141. Marcuse, Horkheimer, and Adorno fled the Nazi holocaust.

7. Benjamin, "Authority and the Family Revisited: or, A World without Fathers?" p. 48; Helmut Dubiel, "The Origins of Critical Theory: An Interview with Leo Lowenthal," *Telos* 49 (Fall 1981): 153–54; Jay, *The Dialectical Imagination*, pp. 121, 156–57.

8. Leiss, "The Problem of Man and Nature," p. 164.

9. Benjamin, "Authority and the Family Revisited," pp. 35–44.

10. Herbert Marcuse, *An Essay on Liberation* (Boston: Beacon Press, 1969), p. 19; Joel Whitebook, "The Problem of Nature in Habermas," *Telos* 40 (Summer 1979): 41–44.

11. Horkheimer, *Dawn & Decline*, p. 234; Horkheimer, *Critical Theory*, pp. 97–114, 127–28; Benjamin, "Authority and the Family Revisited," pp. 42–49; Arato and Gebhardt, *Frankfurt School Reader*, p. 207; Jay, *The Dialectical Imagination*, pp. 126–27.

12. Arato and Gebhardt, *Frankfurt School Reader*, pp. 196–97; Horkheimer and Adorno, *Dialectic of Enlightenment*, pp. 54–55; Leiss, *The Domination of Nature*, pp. 148–55; see also Lukács, *History and Class Consciousness*, pp. 83ff.

13. Horkheimer and Adorno, *Dialectic of Enlightenment*, p. 38.

14. Ibid.

15. Ibid., p. 38. See also Max Horkheimer, *Eclipse of Reason* (New York: Seabury Press, 1974), p. 54; Benjamin, "Authority and the Family Revisited," p. 36; Arato and Gebhardt, *Frankfurt School Reader*, p. 11; Leiss, "The Problem of Man and Nature," p. 165.

16. Horkheimer, *Eclipse of Reason*, p. 174; Horkheimer, *Critical Theory*, pp. 188–243; Jay, *The Dialectical Imagination*, p. 260; Leiss, "The Problem of Man and Nature," p. 166.

17. Jay, *The Dialectical Imagination*, pp. 47, 60–61, 73, 119. The rejection of identity theory differentiates critical theory from Marxist humanism. See Martin Jay, "The Frankfurt School's Critique of Marxist Humanism," *Social Research* 39 (Summer 1972): 285–305.

18. Adorno, "Kunst und die Künste," as cited in Arato and Gebhardt, *Frankfurt School Reader*, p. 222.

19. Horkheimer and Adorno, *Dialectic of Enlightenment*, p. 40.

20. Again it is interesting to note the parallelism with Hegel's philosophy, where art, religion, and philosophy are the ultimate expressions of humanity.

21. The study appeared in German in 1936 as *Studien über Autorität und Familie* (Paris: Felix Alcan) with English abstracts. Horkheimer's essay was published in English as "Authority and the Family" in *Critical Theory*; Marcuse's essay was published in English as "A Study on Authority" in *Studies in Critical Philosophy*.

22. Horkheimer, "Authority and the Family," in *Critical Theory*, pp. 108, 113, 122–24.

23. Ibid., pp. 123–28; Max Horkheimer, "Authoritarianism and the Family," in *The Family: Its Function and Destiny*, ed. Ruth Anshen (New York: Harper & Brothers, 1949), pp. 382 and 391; Gillian Rose, "How Is Critical Theory Possible? Theodor W. Adorno and Concept Formation in Sociology," *Political Studies* 27 (1976): 75–76.

24. Horkheimer, "Authoritarianism and the Family," pp. 381–98.

25. Theodor W. Adorno, Else Frenkel-Brunswik, Daniel J. Levinson, R. Nevitt Sanford, *The Authoritarian Personality* (1950; reprint, New York: John Wiley & Sons, 1964). For a discussion of *The Authoritarian Personality* see Susan Buck-Morss, *The Origin of Negative Dialectics: Theodor W. Adorno, Walter Benjamin, and the Frankfurt Institute* (New York: Free Press, 1977), pp. 177–84; Held, *Introduction to Critical Theory*, pp. 138–47; Rose, *The Melancholy Science*, pp. 103–04.

26. Horkheimer, "Authority and the Family," in *Critical Theory*, p. 54; see also Dubiel's interview with Lowenthal, "The Origins of Critical Theory," p. 151.

27. Horkheimer, "Authority and the Family," in *Critical Theory*, pp. 59 and 57.

28. Horkheimer, *Critical Theory*, p. v.

29. Ibid., p. 71.

30. In "Authoritarianism and the Family" (p. 397) some interesting findings throw the analysis of child development into a dilemma that is recorded but never theoretically resolved. In the empirical research done by the Institute of Social Research in conjunction with the Institute of Child Welfare in Berkeley, Horkheimer and Adorno had expected to find that "submissive" or "good" children would be the ones to disclose authoritarian personality traits while the more "rebellious and refractory" ones would reveal antiauthoritarian traits. This assumption was proven false. The nonaggressive or "good" children were the ones least inclined to authoritarian character traits, while the disobedient and difficult children were most likely to exalt strength and revile the weak. Thus they concluded: "The authoritarian character's conventionalism and his concern with correctness and the 'things to be done' seem to be acquired during adolescence, or even later, because then the effect of reality in endorsing conventional values is overpowering. The prospective fascists, then, seem to be those who in childhood were somehow crude and 'uncivilized.' " This entire passage about the role of adolescence seems to question the Freudian concept of child development quite radically, but the implications of these findings are not worked out in detail.

31. The terms "society without the father" and "fatherlessness" come from Alexander Mitscherlich, *Auf dem Weg zur vaterlosen Gesellschaft* (Munich: Piper, 1963) translated by Eric Mosbacher as *Society without the Father* (New York: Harcourt, Brace & World, 1969).

32. Benjamin, "Authority and the Family Revisited," pp. 35–42.

33. Horkheimer, "Authority and the Family," in *Critical Theory*, p. 107; see also pp. 100–01.

34. Ibid., pp. 108–09; Benjamin, "Authority and the Family Revisited," pp. 44–46.

35. Horkheimer, "Authority and the Family," in *Critical Theory*, p. 101.

36. Ibid., p. 128; Horkheimer, "Authoritarianism and the Family," pp. 386–87; Benjamin, "Authority and the Family Revisited," pp. 35–39. Horkheimer and Adorno do not make a clear and distinct separation between ego and superego but see both in terms of the son's relation to the father. Adorno writes in *Negative Dialectics* (p. 273): "The separation of ego and super-ego, which the analytical topology insists upon, is a dubious affair; genetically, both of them lead equally to the internalization of the father image. The analytical theories about the super-ego, however bold their beginnings, will therefore flag in short order, lest they be obliged to spread to the coddled ego."

37. Horkheimer, "The End of Reason," in Arato and Gebhardt, *Frankfurt School Reader*, p. 37.

38. Benjamin, "Authority and the Family Revisited," pp. 38–42.

39. Horkheimer, "Authoritarianism and the Family," pp. 388–93; Benjamin, "Authority and the Family Revisited," pp. 42–49. The work of Christopher Lasch with its critique of the family and its critique of culture is merely a reversionary elaboration of themes developed much earlier by critical theory. See Christopher Lasch, *Haven in a Heartless World* (New York: Basic Books, 1979), and *The Culture of Narcissism* (New York: Warner Books, 1979). See also Jessica Benjamin, "The Oedipal Riddle: Authority, Autonomy and the New Narcissism," in *The Problem of Authority in America*, ed. John P. Diggin and Mark E. Kann (Philadelphia: Temple University Press, 1981).

40. Horkheimer, in Arato and Gebhardt, *Frankfurt School Reader*, p. 48.

41. Benjamin, "Authority and the Family Revisited," pp. 36 and 41. Benjamin rejects Horkheimer's view that we are now directly manipulated into conformity and that internalization of the father image is necessary to the development of an autonomous ego and a superego or conscience.

42. Simone de Beauvoir, *The Second Sex* (New York: Bantam Books, 1968), p. 133.

43. Horkheimer, "Authority and the Family," in *Critical Theory*, pp. 114–15 (amended translation).

44. Ibid., p. 114.
45. Ibid., pp. 117–18.
46. Erich Fromm, M. Horkheimer, H. Mayer, H. Marcuse, u.a., *Studien über Autorität und Familie* (English abstracts; Paris: Felix Alcan, 1936), p. 906.
47. Horkheimer, "Authority and the Family," in *Critical Theory*, pp. 114–19; Benjamin, "Authority and the Family Revisited," p. 47.
48. Horkheimer, "Authoritarianism and the Family," p. 390 (my emphasis).
49. Horkheimer, "Authority and the Family," in *Critical Theory*, pp. 120 and 118. Horkheimer does not spell out exactly how and under what circumstances love for the mother foments rebellion.
50. Horkheimer, "Authority and the Family," in *Critical Theory*, pp. 115–16.
51. Ibid., p. 117.
52. Ibid.
53. Ibid., p. 118. This was never Marx's phrase. See Dunayev-skaya, "Relationship of Philosophy and Revolution to Women's Liberation." In "The Future of Marriage" (1966) Horkheimer acknowledges the debate concerning the relationship of matriarchy to patriarchy within a discussion of the family in several different countries. He gives an account of the retreat from the revolutionary attempt of Russian society in the early nineteenth century to free both men and women from the necessity to marry and remain married and to free women from unwanted pregnancies. He discusses the reestablishment of the traditional family as a reactionary move. However, he believes that because woman is a worker in the factory as well as in the home her role has changed. He quotes an official Soviet press, which claims the "stabilized" family is "matriarchically oriented"; Max Horkheimer, *Critique of Instrumental Reason*, trans. Matthew O'Connell (New York: Seabury Press, 1974), pp. 90–92, 85. This "official" line concerning woman's role in the family has been exposed as ideology in the recent *Feminist Samizdat* put out by women in Russia. They show that the cult of the mother does not mean that woman is the center of power and authority; rather, woman is a slave to the family, enduring degradation, not respect for her motherhood. See *Woman and Russia: First Feminist Samizdat*, translated by the Women and Eastern Europe Group (London: Sheba Feminist Publishers, 1980), especially "The Matriarchal Family" by N. Malakhovskaya, "Human Birth" by R. Batalova, and "The Other Side of the Medal" by V. Golubeva.

54. Horkheimer, "Authority and the Family," in *Critical Theory*, p. 119.
55. De Beauvoir, *The Second Sex*, pp. 159–60.
56. Ibid., pp. 156–59.
57. Isak Dinesen, *Seven Gothic Tales* (New York: Vintage Books, 1972), pp. 87–88.
58. Horkheimer, "Authority and the Family," in *Critical Theory*, p. 119.
59. See Barbara Ehrenreich and Deirdre English, *Witches, Midwives, and Nurses* (New York: Glass Mountain Pamphlets, n.d.) and Paul Boyer and Stephen Nissenbaum, *Salem Possessed: The Social Origins of Witchcraft* (Cambridge, Mass.: Harvard University Press, 1974).
60. Horkheimer, "Authority and the Family," in *Critical Theory*, p. 119.
61. Dorothy Dinnerstein claims that an important reason for woman's anomalous image, which combines or fluctuates between the "good" mother-goddess and the "evil" bitch, lies in the trouble we have in accepting the discovery that our mother has subjectivity, that she embodies an autonomous awareness corresponding to our own. What develops is a tendency to see in woman a mystic continuity with non-human processes. While the small boy can carry over into manhood a superstitious awe, often loathing, for the processes of menstruation and parturition, the girl's difficulty in coming to accept the "I"ness of woman is less serious since she comes to experience a physical identification with the mother and, of course, cannot help being an "I" to herself. Dorothy Dinnerstein, *The Mermaid and the Minotaur: Sexual Arrangements and Human Malaise* (New York: Harper & Row, 1976).
62. Horkheimer, "Authority and the Family," in *Critical Theory*, pp. 120–21.
63. Horkheimer, "Authoritarianism and the Family," pp. 391–94.
64. Horkheimer, "Authority and the Family," in *Critical Theory*, pp. 119–20; Fromm et al., *Studien über Autorität*, pp. 906–07.
65. Horkheimer, "Authoritarianism and the Family," pp. 385–86. See also Horkheimer, *Critical Theory*, pp. 122–23.
66. Horkheimer, "Authoritarianism and the Family," pp. 390–91. Horkheimer refers to the work of Philip Wylie as having described the American version of "momism." See Philip Wylie, *Generation of Vipers* (New York: Rinehart, 1942), especially chap. 11. A more contemporary

account of this phenomenon is found in the novels of Philip Roth, especially *Portnoy's Complaint*.

67. Horkheimer, "Authoritarianism and the Family," pp. 389–90 (my emphasis).

68. Ibid., p. 389. See also Horkheimer, "The Concept of Man," in *Critique of Instrumental Reason*, pp. 10–12; and Benjamin, "Authority and the Family Revisited," pp. 47–49.

69. Horkheimer, "The Concept of Man," in *Critique of Instrumental Reason*, pp. 8–11.

70. Horkheimer, *Critique of Instrumental Reason*, pp. 16–17.

71. Horkheimer, "The Concept of Man," in *Critique of Instrumental Reason*, pp. 17 and 24; Horkheimer, "The Future of Marriage," in *Critique of Instrumental Reason*, p. 97.

72. Horkheimer, "Authority and the Family," in *Critical Theory*, p. 126.

73. Horkheimer, "Authoritarianism and the Family," p. 387; see also Horkheimer, *Critique of Instrumental Reason*, p. 17, and Theodor W. Adorno, *Minima Moralia: Reflections from Damaged Life*, trans. E. F. N. Jephcott (London: New Left Books, 1974), pp. 31–32.

74. Horkheimer, in Arato and Gebhardt, *Frankfurt School Reader*, p. 38.

75. Sheila Rowbotham, *Hidden from History: 300 Years of Women's Oppression and the Fight against It* (London: Pluto Press, 1974), pp. 27–32.

76. Fromm et al., *Studien über Autorität*, p. 906; Horkheimer, *Critical Theory*, p. 124.

77. Horkheimer, "Authoritarianism and the Family," p. 383.

78. Witness the experiences of Anny and Minny Thackeray and Elizabeth Barrett Browning in the nineteenth century as well as the more recent statement by Virginia Woolf that it was only because her father died when she was young that she blossomed into a writer. For a fascinating account of this relationship see Robert Seidenberg and Evangelos Papathomopoulos, "Daughters Who Tend Their Fathers: A Literary Survey," *Psychoanalytic Study of Society* 2, ed. W. Muensterberger and S. Axelrad (New York: International University Press, 1962). Seidenberg and Papathomopoulos claim: "It is quite possible that Freud derived his fundamental concepts of hysteria from the enslavement of daughters to the terminal needs of the parents [read fathers]" (p. 139).

79. Horkheimer, "Authoritarianism and the Family," p. 383.

234 Notes to Pages 114–120

80. Horkheimer, "Authority and the Family," in *Critical Theory,* p. 117.

81. Ibid., p. 121.

82. Horkheimer, "Traditional and Critical Theory," in *Critical Theory,* pp. 227 and 210.

83. Horkheimer, *Eclipse of Reason,* pp. 33, 130–33; Horkheimer, "The End of Reason," in Arato and Gebhardt, *Frankfurt School Reader,* p. 33.

84. Robert Seidenberg and Evangelos Papathomopoulos, "The Enigma of Antigone," *International Review of Psychoanalysis* 1 (1974): 197–205. While I find this article illuminating, the real enigma as I see it is Antigone's rejection of Ismene.

85. Horkheimer, *Critique of Instrumental Reason,* pp. 16–17.

86. See Rudolf Siebert, "Horkheimer's Sociology of Religion," *Telos* 30 (Winter 1976–77): 135n.

87. For a more comprehensive account of the horrors suffered by women who lack control over their bodies see Barbara Ehrenreich and Deirdre English, *For Her Own Good: 150 Years of the Experts' Advice to Women* (New York: Anchor Books, 1979); Ellen Frankfort, *Vaginal Politics* (New York: Bantam Books, 1973); Linda Gordon, *Woman's Body, Woman's Right: A Social History of Birth Control in America* (Baltimore: Penguin Books, 1977); Shirley A. Heslip, "A Poor Respectable Girl," *The Peak,* 6 October 1981, p. 5. The Heslip article reveals the female tragedy of unwed motherhood, which stands in stark contrast to the social right of the father in ancient society to expose unwanted infants to death. Infanticide, once the prerogative of the father, became a crime punishable by death when committed in desperation by an unwed mother during the seventeenth and eighteenth centuries.

88. Ann Jones, *Women Who Kill* (New York: Fawcett Columbine, 1981), pp. 93–116.

89. See *Crimes against Women: Proceedings of the International Tribunal,* compiled and edited by Diana Russell and Nicole Van de Ven (Millbrae, Calif.: Les Femmes, 1976); *Report on Violence in the Family: Wifebattering* by the Standing Committee on Health, Welfare, and Social Affairs, Marcel Roy, M.P. Chairman, House of Commons, Canada, Issue No. 34, 6 May 1982; Betsy Warrior, *Wifebeating* (Somerville, Mass.: New England Free Press, 1976); Judith Herman with Lisa Hirschman, *Father-Daughter Incest,* (Cambridge: Harvard University Press, 1981).

90. Horkheimer, in Arato and Gebhardt, *Frankfurt School Reader,* p. 37.

91. See Nancy Chodorow, *The Reproduction of Mothering: Psychoanalysis and the Sociology of Gender* (Berkeley: University of California Press, 1978), pp. 40 and 154; Nancy Wood, "Mothering the Child," review of Chodorow's *Reproduction of Mothering,* in the *Canadian Journal of Political and Social Theory* 3 (Winter 1979): 144–53.

92. Juliet Mitchell, *Psychoanalysis and Feminism: Freud, Reich, Laing and Women* (New York: Vintage, 1974), pp. 50–51; Rosemary Radford Reuther, *New Woman/New Earth: Sexist Ideologies and Human Liberation* (New York: Seabury Press, 1975), p. 138; Nancy Wood, "Mothering the Child." Freud sometimes describes libido as bisexual, or identical in males and females, but ultimately he describes it as essentially male and claims that female development involves a masculine libido. In his final paper on 'Femininity" (1933) he writes: "There is only one libido, which serves both the masculine and the feminine sexual functions. To it itself we cannot assign any sex; if, following the convention of activity and masculinity, we are inclined to describe it as masculine, we must not forget that it also covers trends with a passive aim. Nevertheless the juxtaposition 'feminine libido' is without any justification" (cited in Elizabeth Janeway, "On 'Female Sexuality,' " in *Women and Analysis,* ed. Jean Strouse (New York: Dell, 1974), p. 110.

93. Janeway, "On 'Female Sexuality,' " p. 85.

94. Sigmund Freud, "The Dissolution of the Oedipus Complex," in *The Standard Edition of the Complete Psychological Works of Sigmund Freud,* 24 vols., translated under the general editorship of James Strachey (London: Hogarth Press and the Institute of Psycho-Analysis, 1953–74), 19:177–78.

95. Juliet Mitchell, "On Freud and the Distinction between the Sexes," in Strouse, *Women and Analysis,* p. 42; Reuther, *New Woman,* pp. 138 and 151.

96. My account of the difference in the Freudian model of the male and female psyche comes primarily from Freud's three essays on the female ("Some Psychical Consequences of the Anatomical Distinction between the Sexes," 1925; "Female Sexuality," 1931; and "Femininity," 1933, all reprinted in Strouse, *Women and Analysis)* and the work of Juliet Mitchell in *Psychoanalysis and Feminism.*

97. Reuther, *New Woman,* pp. 138–39; M. Mitscherlich-Nielsen, "Psychoanalysis and Female Sexuality," *Partisan Review* 46 (1979): 61.

According to Mitscherlich-Nielsen, Freud, in his early work, explained the male ambivalence to women, which leads men to divide women into saints and whores, as rooted in the son's Oedipal jealousy.

98. Sigmund Freud, "Femininity," p. 103.

99. This hypothesis of the father replacing woman as the castrator is developed by Freud in his famous study of Wolf-Man, "History of an Infantile Neurosis"; see Mitchell, *Psychoanalysis and Feminism*, p. 66.

100. Herbert Marcuse, "The Obsolescence of the Freudian Concept of Man," in *Five Lectures*, trans. Jeremy Shapiro and Shierry Weber (Boston: Beacon Press, 1970), p. 46.

101. Sigmund Freud, "On the Universal Tendency to Debasement in the Sphere of Love," *Complete Works* 11:182–83. The article is mistitled in that Freud says, indirectly, that women do not need to debase their sexual object; instead, women require an element of the forbidden for sensual fulfillment: "the condition of forbiddenness in the erotic life of women is...comparable to the need *on the part of men* to debase their sexual object" (*Complete Works* 11:186–87; my emphasis). Since women do not debase the object of their desire, the tendency to degradation in love is not universal but male.

102. Freud, "Femininity," p. 113.

103. Ibid., p. 108.

104. Reuther, *New Woman*, p. 140.

105. Freud, as cited by Reuther, *New Woman*, p. 141.

106. Freud, "Femininity," p. 112.

107. Reuther, *New Woman*, p. 141.

108. Paul Ricoeur, *Freud and Philosophy: An Essay on Interpretation*, trans. Denis Savage (New Haven: Yale University Press, 1977), p. 272.

109. Sigmund Freud, *Civilization and Its Discontents*, trans. Joan Riviere (London: Hogarth Press and the Institute of Psycho-Analysis, 1975), p. 17.

110. Freud, "Femininity," p. 111.

111. Freud, *Civilization and Its Discontents*, pp. 40–41.

112. Sigmund Freud, " 'Civilized' Sexual Morality and Modern Nervousness," as cited by Janeway, "On 'Female Sexuality,' " pp. 83–84.

113. Freud, "Femininity," pp. 113–14.

114. Freud in a letter to Marie Bonaparte, as cited by Kate Millett, *Sexual Politics* (New York: Doubleday, 1970), p. 178.

115. Deborah Melman, "Feminist Explorations: Life under Patriarchy," *Canadian Journal of Political and Social Theory* 4 (Spring–Summer 1980): 68.

116. Reuther, *New Woman*, p. 150.

117. Herbert Marcuse, *Five Lectures*, pp. 12–13. Robert Seidenberg, "The Trauma of Eventlessness," in *Psychoanalysis and Women*, ed. Jean Baker Miller (Harmondsworth: Penguin Books, 1974), p. 360.

118. For an analysis of the "disappearance" of hysteria see "Panel on 'Hysteria Today' " reported by J. Laplanche, "The Revolution of Hysteria" by René Major, and "A Discussion of the Paper by René Major on 'The Revolution of Hysteria' " by Christian David, all in *International Journal of Psycho-Analysis* 55 (1974): 459–69 and 385–95.

119. It is true that a small percentage of males suffered from hysteria in Freud's time just as a small percentage of males suffer from anorexia nervosa today. Freud says that male hysteria can be explained through the concept of bisexuality: hysteria is a "feminine" neurosis that males experience due to the fact that males, like females, have both "feminine" and "masculine" character traits. Thus, when males develop hysteria it is rooted in the "feminine" aspects of their psyches. When males develop anorexia nervosa they do so before the onset of puberty, whereas females develop it at or following the onset of puberty. It may be that the concept of bisexuality explains this difference in that prior to puberty the "feminine" aspects of the male are not yet overwhelmed by the "masculine" biological changes that accompany adolescence.

Freud used the term *anorexia* (a condition) when confronted with anorexia nervosa (a syndrome) and made no attempt to analyze the various cases of anorexia as a unique form of neurosis. *Anorexia nervosa*, as a term used to describe the syndrome as we now know it, was first used by Sir William Gull in 1874, but Freud does not seem to be aware of Gull's work. See Frank Conroy, "Freud into Fiction," *Partisan Review* 49 (1982): 144. For an interesting account of the parallel between contemporary female anorexics and medieval female ascetics who became saints see Rudolph M. Bell, *Holy Anorexia* (Chicago: University of Chicago Press, 1985).

120. C. Hilde Bruch, *The Golden Cage: The Enigma of Anorexia Nervosa* (New York: Vintage Books, 1979), p. 58 (my emphasis).

121. Seidenberg, "The Trauma of Eventlessness," pp. 350–51. The fear of the streets based on the reality of male violence is eloquently

expressed by June Jordan in "Against the Wall" (*Seven Days*, May 1978) and revealed in Ruth Orkin's famous 1951 photograph "Sex Rays" in her *Photo Journal* (New York: Viking Press, 1981), pp. 90–91.

122. Robert Seidenberg and Karen DeCrow, *Women Who Marry Houses: Panic and Protest in Agoraphobia* (New York: McGraw-Hill, 1983), pp. 34–35. For an interesting analysis of television in the lives of house-bound women see Carol Lopate, "Daytime Television: You'll Never Want to Leave Home," *Feminist Studies* 3 (Spring-Summer 1976): 69–82. Lopate discusses game shows and soaps to show how the tone and format of daytime television fits the rhythm of the housewife's routine. The game shows with their commodity prizes recreate and transform woman's economic powerlessness as well as her role as consumer, while soaps eroticize the family and make it seem as if all one's needs and fantasies can be fulfilled within the family circle.

123. Seidenberg, "The Trauma of Eventlessness," pp. 356 and 362.

124. Luce Irigaray, *Speculum of the Other Woman*, trans. Gillian C. Gill (Ithaca: Cornell University Press, 1985); Luce Irigaray, *This Sex Which Is Not One*, trans. Catherine Porter (Ithaca: Cornell University Press, 1985).

125. Gayatri Spivak, "Feminism and Critical Theory," *Woman's Studies International Quarterly* 1 (1978): 241–46. Adorno claims that because woman experiences sexual intercourse in a situation of domination there is no possibility of pleasure available to her, not even a masochistic one: women "undergo love in unfreedom, as objects of violence. . . . The experience of pleasure presupposes a limitless readiness to throw oneself away, which is . . . beyond women in their fear." (*Minima Moralia: Reflections from Damaged Life*, trans. E. F. N. Jephcott [London: New Left Books, 1974], pp. 90–91).

126. Erich Neumann, *Amor and Psyche: The Psychic Development of the Feminine*, trans. Ralph Manheim (Princeton: Princeton University Press, 1956), pp. 112–13.

127. Robert J. Stoller, *Perversion—The Erotic Form of Hatred*, as cited by Max Allen, *The Birth Symbol in Traditional Women's Art from Eurasia and the Western Pacific* (Toronto: Museum for Textiles, 1981), p. 13.

128. Allen, *The Birth Symbol*, p. 13.

129. Monique Plaza, " 'Phallomorphic' Power and the Psychology of 'Woman,' " *Feminist Issues* 1 (Summer 1980): 90–95. Plaza's critique

focuses on the fact that Irigaray appeals to a "real" and "eternal" feminine essence rooted in female biology as a "new" starting point. This merely leads back to "old" ideological constructs of woman in terms of her "nature." In addition, Plaza claims that Irigaray's focus on the "a priori of the Same" in Western logic misses the fact that Western philosophy has integrated the concept of difference such that woman *is* differentiated from man but simultaneously evaluated as inferior.

130. Mitchell, *Psychoanalysis and Feminism*, pp. 350–54.

CHAPTER 4. THE DOMINATION OF NATURE

1. Herbert Marcuse, "The Obsolescence of the Freudian Concept of Man," in *Five Lectures*, pp. 60–61.
2. Herbert Marcuse, "Marxism and Feminism," *Women's Studies* 2 (1974): 279.
3. Herbert Marcuse, *Eros and Civilization*, pp. 15–18 and 220.
4. Ibid., pp. 11 and 7.
5. Sigmund Freud, *Moses and Monotheism*, trans. Katherine Jones (New York: Vintage Books, 1958), pp. 163–64.
6. Marcuse, *Eros and Civilization*, pp. 181, 185.
7. Marcuse, "Marxism and Feminism," p. 280.
8. Marcuse, *Eros and Civilization*, p. 142.
9. Ibid., pp. 196–97. This argument concerning the necessity for freedom in labor reappears in "The End of Utopia" where Marcuse argues against Marx, whom he sees as an unambiguous proponent of freedom from labor (Marcuse, *Five Lectures*, pp. 62–63). Although Marx did not conceive of work ever becoming play he did maintain a concept of freedom in labor (as shown in chapter 2's account of the two unreconciled forms of freedom in Marx's work). Marcuse's interpretation here is an oversimplification that contradicts his interpretation of the early Marx in other works.
10. Marcuse, *Eros and Civilization*, p. 63.
11. Ibid., pp. 209–10.
12. Ibid., pp. 213 and 18.
13. Ibid., p. 54.
14. Ibid., pp. 55–68. See Sigmund Freud, *Totem and Taboo*, trans. James Strachey (New York: W. W. Norton, 1950), pp. 141–43; and Freud, *Moses and Monotheism*, pp. 102–06.
15. Marcuse, *Eros and Civilization*, p. 69.

16. Ibid., pp. 210–11.
17. Ibid., p. 69.
18. Ibid., pp. 210, 246–47.
19. Ibid., p. 214.
20. Charles Odier, "Von Ueber-Ich," as cited by Marcuse in *Eros and Civilization*, p. 209.
21. Herbert Marcuse, *Counterrevolution and Revolt* (Boston: Beacon Press, 1972), p. 75.
22. Ibid., pp. 75, 74, and 77.
23. Horkheimer and Adorno, *Dialectic of Enlightenment*, p. 7.
24. Marcuse, "Marxism and Feminism," pp. 280 and 287.
25. Marcuse, *Counterrevolution and Revolt*, p. 77.
26. Kathryn Pauly Morgan, "Androgyny: A Conceptual Analysis," *Social Theory and Practice* 8 (1982): 256.
27. Herbert Marcuse, *One-Dimensional Man: Studies in the Ideology of Advanced Industrial Society* (Boston: Beacon Press, 1964), p. 76.
28. Ibid., p. 75.
29. Ibid., p. 72.
30. Ibid., pp. 72–73; see also Gad Horowitz, *Repression. Basic and Surplus Repression in Psychoanalytic Theory: Freud, Reich and Marcuse* (Toronto: University of Toronto Press, 1977), p. 79.
31. Marcuse, *Five Lectures*, p. 47.
32. Marcuse, *One-Dimensional Man*, pp. 56–83; Marcuse, *Five Lectures*, p. 47.
33. Horkheimer, *Eclipse of Reason*, pp. 109 and 121–22. Horkheimer, like Marcuse, uses repression in a broad, nontechnical sense but differs from Marcuse insofar as he sees distortion as a necessary part of repression.
34. Ibid., p. 94.
35. Theodor Adorno, *Minima Moralia*, pp. 95–96, and see pp. 92–93, 111, and 173. See also Adorno, "Veblen's Attack on Culture," in *Prisms*, trans. Samuel and Shierry Weber (London: Spearman, 1967), pp. 81–82; and Horkheimer and Adorno, *Dialectic of Enlightenment*, pp. 247–52.
36. Much of the feminist literature on matriarchy seems motivated by the belief that it is necessary to prove that woman was once free and powerful in order to justify the current movement for woman's future liberation.
37. Marcuse, *Eros and Civilization*, p. 106.

38. Marcuse, *Counterrevolution and Revolt*, p. 70.

39. This is the basis for Marcuse's seeming vacillation—that remembrance redeems the past but that, "in reality," it does not; *Eros and Civilization*, 106–07; on the end of history, see pp. 176 and 211.

40. Horkheimer and Adorno, *Dialectic of Enlightenment*, p. 225.

41. Adorno, *Negative Dialectics*, pp. 17–18. Horkheimer, *Eclipse of Reason*, p. 126; on nature's suffering see also p. 101. Horkheimer and Adorno's view of the relation of suffering to critique reveals the influence of Walter Benjamin and echoes through critical theory in the many references to Benjamin's statement that "it is only for the sake of those without hope that hope is given to us." Benjamin put this view into a concretely political context in his "Theses on the Philosophy of History": "Social Democracy thought fit to assign to the working class the role of the redeemer of future generations, in this way cutting the sinews of its greatest strength. This training made the working class forget both its hatred and its spirit of sacrifice, for both are nourished by the image of enslaved ancestors rather than that of liberated grandchildren." Benjamin, *Illuminations*, trans. Harry Zohn (New York: Schocken Books, 1973), p. 260.

42. Adorno, *Negative Dialectics*, pp. 179–80.

43. Unfortunately the contemporary critique of the domination of nature often has an abstract understanding of nature "itself" as benign and omniscient and, consequently, it takes an abstract, pronature stance. See, for example, Isaac D. Balbus, *Marxism and Domination* (Princeton: Princeton University Press, 1982) and my critique of this book, "Man-Made Motherhood and Other Sleights of Hand," *Phenomenology + Pedagogy* 3 (1985): 207–17.

44. Horkheimer, *Eclipse of Reason*, p. 127.

45. Adorno, *Negative Dialectics*, p. 163.

46. This concept of history is derived from the work of Walter Benjamin. In Benjamin's "Theses on the Philosophy of History" liberation is not the end product of a long march through "homogeneous, empty time" but an explosion that causes time to stand still; see *Illuminations*, pp.261-64.

47. William Leiss's *Domination of Nature* is the best example of an attempt to discuss ecological concerns within critical theory's critique of the domination of external nature. However, this book does not address the domination of internal nature or the link between the domination of nature and the domination of woman.

CHAPTER 5. WOMAN'S EXPERIENCE: RENAMING THE DIALECTIC OF DESIRE AND RECOGNITION

1. See Paul Ricoeur, *Freud and Philosophy: An Essay on Interpretation.*

2. Paul Ricoeur, "Fatherhood: From Phantasm to Symbol," trans. Robert Sweeney, in *The Conflict of Interpretations: Essays in Hermeneutics*, ed. Don Ihde (Evanston: Northwestern University Press, 1974).

3. Horkheimer and Adorno, *Dialectic of Enlightenment*, pp. 59–60.

4. Ibid., pp. 75–76.

5. Ibid., p. 73.

6. Ibid., p. 73.

7. Interestingly, the other female figure who aids Odysseus in his journey is Athena, who also found a place in the patriarchal world through a denial of the power of the mother: her birth from the head of Zeus proclaimed her man's daughter, not woman's.

8. Ibid., p. 74.

9. Ibid., p. 71.

10. Horkheimer and Adorno do not discuss the fact that the only human being to immediately recognize Odysseus is Eurycleia, his old nurse; she recognizes him by the scar above his knee where he was wounded by a boar when he was an adolescent. This recognition results in a death threat: Odysseus threatens to kill Eurycleia if she tells anyone, including Penelope, who he is. She sides with male power and betrays womankind. Not only does she keep Penelope in the dark but she informs on the women who are hanged: it is she who volunteers to name names. The first *creature* to recognize Odysseus is his dog. The dog, Argus, is too old and sick from abandonment to do anything more than acknowledge Odysseus as a prelude to its death.

11. Homer, *The Odyssey* (Harmondsworth: Penguin Books, 1961), p. 343.

12. Ibid., p. 176.

13. Edna St. Vincent Millay, "An Ancient Gesture," as cited in *Shakespeare's Sisters: Feminist Essays on Women Poets*, ed. Sandra M. Gilbert and Susan Gubar (Bloomington: Indiana University Press, 1979), p. 199. Millay compares Penelope's tears to Odysseus' to show that Odysseus learned to cry from Penelope and then used what he had learned as a rhetorical device.

14. Alkis Kontos, "Memories of Ithaca," in *Ethnicity in a Technological Age,* ed. Ian H. Angus (Edmonton: Canadian Institute of Ukrainian Studies, 1987). Kontos gives a moving analysis of Odysseus' journey as the journey of an exile; however, his reading ignores Penelope's plight.

15. Karl Kerényi, *Goddesses of Sun and Moon,* trans. Murray Stein (Irving, Texas: University of Dallas, 1979), pp. 13–17.

16. Euripides, *Medea,* in *Women in Drama,* ed. Harriet Kriegel (New York: Mentor Books, 1975), pp. 8–9.

17. Ibid., p. 9.

18. Ibid., pp. 22–23.

19. Ibid., p. 36.

20. Ibid., p. 37. The power of this tragic tension is revealed in the painting of Medea by Delacroix.

21. Marcuse, *Eros and Civilization,* p. 60.

22. Freud, *Moses and Monotheism,* pp. 103–04.

23. Freud, *Group Psychology and the Analysis of the Ego,* as cited by Marcuse, *Eros and Civilization,* p. 70.

24. Sigmund Freud, *Group Psychology and the Analysis of the Ego,* trans. James Strachey (New York: Bantam Books, 1965), p. 72.

25. Freud, *Civilization and Its Discontents,* as cited by Marcuse, *Eros and Civilization,* p. 38.

26. Freud, *Beyond the Pleasure Principle,* as cited by Marcuse, *Eros and Civilization,* p. 38.

27. Marcuse, *Eros and Civilization,* p. 39.

28. If Marcuse had integrated into his reinterpretation the more well-known version of the Orpheus legend (in which Orpheus defies death for the love of a woman, Eurydice) and had observed that the Echo of nature in the Narcissus legend is represented by a female nymph, he might have provided the aesthetic representation of a fuller Eros that he is seeking.

29. The actual incidents of rape and incest in the lives of girls and women are devastating experiences that must not be ignored; my argument here, however, does not respond to the symbolic with statistical evidence but calls for an immanent critique of the symbolic. For accounts of the prevalence of rape and incest in women's lives see Susan Brownmiller, *Against Our Will: Men, Women and Rape* (New York: Simon and Schuster, 1975); Lorenne Clark and Debra Lewis, *Rape: The Price of Coercive Sexuality* (Toronto: Women's Press, 1977); Judith Lewis

Herman, *Father-Daughter Incest* (Cambridge, Mass.: Harvard University Press, 1981); Diana Russell, *The Secret Trauma: Incest in the Lives of Girls and Women* (New York: Basic Books, 1986.)

30. Irigaray, *Speculum of the Other Woman*; see also Heather Jon Maroney, "Language, Persephone and Sacrifice: An Interview with Luce Irigaray," *Borderlines*, Winter 1985–86, pp. 30–32.

31. Susan Cavin, *Lesbian Origins* (San Francisco: ism press, 1985).

32. Wendy Hollway, "Heterosexual Sex: Power and Desire for the Other," in *Sex and Love: New Thoughts on Old Contradictions*, ed. Sue Cartledge and Joanna Ryan (London: Women's Press, 1983), pp. 124–40; Jack Litewka, "The Socialized Penis," in *For Men against Sexism*, ed. Jon Snodgrass (Albion: Times Change Press, 1977), pp. 16–35. The analogy of the burning witches was suggested to me in conversation by Somer Brodribb.

33. Here I include the theories of Lacan and Irigaray as giving no new account of heterosexual desire as a female-male relation.

34. It is important to note that the shift from the focus on sisterhood to a focus on motherhood has entailed a shift away from the politics of *non*motherhood, the politics of abortion. But the liberatory attempt to reclaim and reconstruct motherhood *began* with women who found themselves suffering from the alienation of enforced motherhood— women who found themselves pregnant when they did not want to be and were forced either to have an unwanted child or to risk death with an illegal abortion. The contemporary concern with motherhood, as a politics of reproduction, cannot forget its origin: it must remain first and foremost woman's right to choose *not* to reproduce, the right to *not* mother. Within contemporary progressive social movements an abstract understanding of the domination of nature has led to support for the antiabortion movement. For a critique of this position see my review essay, "Man-Made Motherhood and Other Sleights of Hand."

35. This concept of sisterhood was clarified in a conversation with Frieda Forman.

36. Woman as Other became the starting point for an understanding of what all women share, the starting point for a universal understanding of the experience of male domination and for a new political practice. However, this has led to an exploration of differences among women and to the present allegiances of women to smaller and more "particular" or exclusive groups. From thinking and acting on the belief that all women are sisters, women have regrouped into specific forms of separatism based on race, sexual preference, religion, and ethnic identity.

This multiplicity of Otherness challenges the solidarity that once made the woman's movement powerful even as it discloses the importance of understanding the non-identity of women. The question of the shared ground of sisterhood raised by this multiplicity is intensified by the fact that, as the politics of the woman's liberation movement is institutionalized as feminism, sisterhood is sometimes invoked by women only to do intimate violence to other women.

37. The reclaiming of motherhood is a contentious issue within feminist theory. Dinnerstein and Chodorow see only negative features in human development due to the absence of the father from early childcare: male domination of woman and the domination of nature are reactions to the overwhelming and unbearable power of the mother experienced by the preverbal, prerational infant. In contrast, feminists like Rich, Ruddick, Ryan, and Whitbeck see positive features in mother-raised children; mothering may provide the basis for the transformation of society through a model of the nondominating relation between self and Other. See Adrienne Rich, *Of Woman Born: Motherhood as Experience and Institution* (New York: W. W. Norton, 1976); Sara Ruddick, "Maternal Thinking," in *Mothering: Essays in Feminist Theory*, ed. Joyce Trebilcot (Totowa, N.J.: Rowman & Allanheld, 1984); Joanna Ryan, "Psychoanalysis and Women Loving Women," in *Sex and Love: New Thoughts on Old Contradictions*, ed. Sue Cartledge and Joanna Ryan (London: Women's Press, 1984); Caroline Whitbeck, "Maternal Instinct" and "Afterword," in Trebilcot, *Mothering*; Iris Young, "Is Male Gender Identity the Cause of Male Domination?", in Trebilcot, *Mothering*.

My account of the relation between motherhood and sisterhood within feminism is not meant to be exhaustive but to allow for a reconsideration of the relation. For an interesting discussion of sisterhood as friendship, as a relationship of recognition between two women (S-S), see Janice G. Raymond, *A Passion for Friends: Toward a Philosophy of Female Affection* (Boston: Beacon Press, 1986); and Carroll Smith-Rosenberg, "The Female World of Love and Ritual: Relations between Women in Nineteenth-Century America," in *The Signs Reader: Women, Gender and Scholarship*, ed. Elizabeth Abel and Emily K. Abel (Chicago: University of Chicago Press, 1983), pp. 27–55.

38. Marcuse, *Counterrevolution and Revolt*, p. 78. Marcuse keeps searching for the revolutionary subject all through the 1960s and 1970s but then writes against this search and returns to an expanded working class as the revolutionary subject within a focus on the concept of

"surplus-consciousness." See Marcuse, "The Reification of the Proletariat," *Canadian Journal of Political and Social Theory* 3 (Winter 1979): 20–23.

39. Judith Butler, Response to "Women: The One and the Many" by Elizabeth Spelman. Paper presented to the American Philosophical Association, Washington, D.C., 29 December 1985.

40. Adorno, *Negative Dialectics*, p. 191.

41. Ibid., pp. 309 and 12.

42. Adorno, *Minima Moralia*, p. 87. A wonderful poem in *Ceremony* by Leslie Marmon Silko (Harmondsworth: Penguin Books, 1986) echoes this relation between naming and the creative activity of the spider:

> Ts'its'tsi'nako, Thought-Woman,
> is sitting in her room
> and whatever she thinks about
> appears.

> She thought of her sisters,
> Naut'ts'ity'i and I'tcts'ity'i,
> and together they created the Universe
> this world
> and the four worlds below.

> Thought-woman, the spider,
> named things and
> as she named them
> they appeared.

43. Theodor W. Adorno, "Commitment," *New Left Review*, September–December 1974, p. 85.

44. Horkheimer, *Eclipse of Reason*, p. 179.

45. Betty Friedan, *The Feminine Mystique* (New York: Dell, 1963).

Bibliography

Adorno, Theodor W. "Commitment." *New Left Review*, September–December, 1974, pp. 75–89.

———. *Minima Moralia: Reflections from Damaged Life*. Translated from the German by E. F. N. Jephcott. London: New Left Books, 1974.

———. *Negative Dialectics*. Translated by E. B. Ashton. New York: Seabury Press, 1973.

———. *Prisms*. Translated by Samuel and Shierry Weber. London: Neville Spearman, 1967.

Adorno, Theodor W., Else Frenkel-Brunswik, Daniel J. Levinson, and R. Nevitt Sanford, in collaboration with Betty Aron, Maria Hertz-Levinson, and William Morrow. *The Authoritarian Personality*. Reprint. New York: John Wiley & Sons, Science Editions, 1964.

Allen, Max. *The Birth Symbol in Traditional Women's Art from Eurasia and the Western Pacific*. Photographs by Brian Knoll. Toronto: Museum for Textiles, 1981.

Angus, Ian. "Aristotelian and Hegelian Aspects of Marx's Concept of Labour." Paper presented to the Canadian Political Science Association, Learned Societies, Halifax, June 1981.

———. "Instrumental Rationality and the New Left." Unpublished paper. Toronto, 1975.

Arato, Andrew, and Eike Gebhardt, eds. *The Essential Frankfurt School Reader*. New York: Urizen Books, 1978.

Arditti, R., R. Duelli Klein, and S. Minden, eds. *Test-Tube Women: What Future for Motherhood?* London: Pandora Press, 1984.

Aronowitz, Stanley. *The Crisis in Historical Materialism: Class, Politics and Culture in Marxist Theory.* New York: Praeger, 1981.

Avineri, Shlomo. *Hegel's Theory of the Modern State.* Cambridge: Cambridge University Press, 1974.

———. *The Social and Political Thought of Karl Marx.* New York: Cambridge University Press, 1975.

Balbus, Isaac D. *Marxism and Domination: A Neo-Hegelian, Feminist, Psychoanalytic Theory of Sexual, Political and Technological Liberation.* Princeton: Princeton University Press, 1982.

Bell, Rudolph M. *Holy Anorexia.* Chicago: University of Chicago Press, 1985.

Benjamin, Jessica. "Authority and the Family Revisited: or, a World without Fathers?" *New German Critique* 13 (Winter 1978): 35–57.

———. "The End of Internalization: Adorno's Social Psychology." *Telos* 32 (Summer 1977): 42–64.

———. "The Oedipal Riddle: Authority, Autonomy and the New Narcissism." In *The Problem of Authority in America,* edited by John P. Diggin and Mark E. Kann, pp. 195–224. Philadelphia: Temple University Press, 1981.

Benjamin, Walter. *Illuminations.* Translated from the German by Harry Zohn. New York: Schocken Books, 1973.

Bernstein, Richard. *Praxis and Action.* Philadelphia: University of Pennsylvania Press, 1971.

Boyer, Paul, and Stephen Nissenbaum. *Salem Possessed: The Social Origins of Witchcraft.* Cambridge, Mass.: Harvard University Press, 1974.

Brodribb, Somer. "Off the Pedestal and onto the Block?: Motherhood, Reproductive Technologies and the Canadian State." *Canadian Journal of Women and the Law* 1 (1986): 407–23.

Brownmiller, Susan. *Against Our Will: Men, Women and Rape.* New York: Simon and Schuster, 1975.

Bruch, C. Hilde, *The Golden Cage: The Enigma of Anorexia Nervosa.* New York: Vintage Books, 1979.

Buck-Morss, Susan. *The Origin of Negative Dialectics: Theodor W. Adorno, Walter Benjamin, and the Frankfurt Institute.* New York: Free Press, 1977.

Butler, Judith. Response to "Women: The One and the Many" by

Elizabeth Spelman. Paper presented to the American Philosophical Association, Washington, D.C., 29 December 1985.

Cavin, Susan. *Lesbian Origins.* San Francisco: ism press, 1985.

Chodorow, Nancy. *The Reproduction of Mothering: Psychoanalysis and the Sociology of Gender.* Berkeley: University of California Press, 1978.

Clark, Lorenne M. G., and Debra Lewis. *Rape: The Price of Coercive Sexuality.* Toronto: Women's Press, 1977.

Clark, Lorenne M. G., and Lynda Lange, eds. *The Sexism of Social and Political Theory: Women and Reproduction from Plato to Nietzsche.* Toronto: University of Toronto Press, 1977.

Conroy, Frank. "Freud into Fiction." Book review of *The White Hotel* by D. M. Thomas. *Partisan Review* 49 (1982): 142–47.

Copleston, Frederick, S. J. *A History of Philosophy,* vol. 7. Garden City: Image Books, 1963.

Corea, Gena. *The Mother Machine: Reproductive Technologies from Artificial Insemination to Artificial Wombs.* New York: Harper & Row, 1985.

David, Christian. "A Discussion of the Paper by René Major on 'The Revolution of Hysteria.' " *International Journal of Psycho- Analysis* 55 (1974): 393–95.

De Beauvoir, Simone. *The Second Sex.* New York: Bantam Books, 1968.

Dinesen, Isak. *Seven Gothic Tales.* New York: Vintage Books, 1972.

Dinnerstein, Dorothy. *The Mermaid and the Minotaur: Sexual Arrangements and Human Malaise.* New York: Harper & Row, 1976.

Donchin, Anne. "The Future of Mothering: Reproductive Technology and Feminist Theory." *Hypatia: A Journal of Feminist Philosophy* 1 (Fall 1986).

Dubiel, Helmut. "The Origins of Critical Theory: An Interview with Leo Lowenthal." *Telos* 49 (Fall 1981): 141–54.

Dunayevskaya, Raya. "Relationship of Philosophy and Revolution to Women's Liberation: Marx's and Engels' Studies Contrasted." *News & Letters* 24 (January–February 1979): 5–8.

Ehrenreich, Barbara, and Deirdre English. *For Her Own Good: 150 Years of the Experts' Advice to Women.* New York: Anchor Books, 1979.

———. *Witches, Midwives and Nurses.* New York: Glass Mountain Pamphlets, n.d.

Elshtain, Jean Bethke. "Moral Woman and Immoral Man: A Consid-

eration of the Public-Private Split and Its Political Ramifications."
Politics and Society 4 (Fall 1974): 453–73.

Euripides. *Medea*. In *Women in Drama*, edited by Harriet Kriegel. New
York: Mentor Books, 1975.

Fackenheim, Emil. *The Religious Dimension in Hegel's Thought*. Boston: Beacon Press, 1970.

Findlay, J. N. *Hegel: A Re-Examination*. London: Unwin Brothers,
1958.

Firestone, Shulamith. *The Dialectic of Sex: The Case for Feminist Revolution*. New York: Bantam Books, 1971.

Foreman, Ann. *Femininity as Alienation: Women and the Family in
Marxism and Psychoanalysis*. London: Pluto Press, 1977.

Frankfort, Ellen. *Vaginal Politics*. New York: Bantam Books, 1973.

Freud, Sigmund. *Civilization and Its Discontents*. Translated from the
German by Joan Riviere. London: Hogarth Press and the Institute
of Psycho-Analysis, 1975.

———. "The Dissolution of the Oedipus Complex." Translated by
James Strachey. In *The Complete Psychological Works of Sigmund
Freud*, vol. 19. London: Hogarth Press and the Institute of Psycho-
Analysis, 1961.

———. "Female Sexuality." In *Women and Analysis: Dialogues on
Psychoanalytic Views of Femininity*, edited by Jean Strouse, pp. 53–
72. New York: Dell, 1974.

———. "Femininity." In *Women and Analysis: Dialogues on Psychoanalytic Views of Femininity*, edited by Jean Strouse, pp. 91–115. New
York: Dell, 1974.

———. *Group Psychology and the Analysis of the Ego*. Translated by
James Strachey. New York: Bantam Books, 1965.

———. *Moses and Monotheism*. Translated by Katherine Jones. New
York: Vintage Books, 1958.

———. *New Introductory Lectures in Psychoanalysis*. Translated by
James Strachey. New York: Penguin Books, 1979.

———. "Some Psychical Consequences of the Anatomical Differences
between the Sexes." In *Women and Analysis: Dialogues on Psychoanalytic Views of Femininity*, edited by Jean Strouse, pp. 27–38.
New York: Dell, 1974.

———. *The Standard Edition of the Complete Works of Sigmund Freud*,
24 vols. Translated under the general editorship of James Strachey.
London: Hogarth Press and the Institute of Psycho-Analysis, 1953–
74.

————. *Three Contributions to the Theory of Sex.* Translated by A. A. Brill. New York: E. P. Dutton, 1962.

————. *Totem and Taboo.* Translated by James Strachey. New York: W. W. Norton, 1950.

————. "On the Universal Tendency to Debasement in the Sphere of Love." In *The Complete Psychological Works of Sigmund Freud,* vol. 11. Translated by James Strachey. London: Hogarth Press and the Institute for Psycho-Analysis, 1957.

Friedan, Betty. *The Feminine Mystique.* New York: Dell, 1963.

Fromm, Erich, M. Horkheimer, H. Mayer, H. Marcuse, u.a. *Studien über Autorität und Familie.* Paris: Felix Alcan, 1936.

Fugard, Athol, John Kani, and Winston Ntshona. *The Island.* In *Statements.* Oxford: Oxford University Press, 1974. *The Island* was first performed 2 July 1973 in Cape Town, South Africa.

Gearhart, Suzanne. Book review of *Speculum de l'autre femme* by Luce Irigaray. *Telos* 26 (Winter 1975–76): 230–35.

Gilbert, Sandra M., and Susan Gubar. *Shakespeare's Sisters: Feminist Essays on Women Poets.* Bloomington: Indiana University Press, 1979.

Goethe, Johann Wolfgang. *Torquato Tasso: A Play.* Translated from the German by John Prudhoe. Manchester: Manchester University Press, 1979.

Gordon, Linda. *Woman's Body, Woman's Right: A Social History of Birth Control in America.* Baltimore: Penguin Books, 1977.

Gould, Carol, ed. *Beyond Domination: New Perspectives on Women and Philosophy.* Totowa, N.J.: Rowman & Allanheld, 1984.

Graves, Robert. *The White Goddess.* New York: Farrar, Straus and Giroux, 1976.

Hegel, G. W. F. *Aesthetics: Lectures on Fine Art.* Translated from the German by T. M. Knox. Oxford: Clarendon Press, 1975.

————. *Hegel's Logic.* Translated by William Wallace. Oxford: Clarendon Press, 1975.

————. *Hegel's Phenomenology of Spirit.* Translated by A. V. Miller. Oxford: Oxford University Press, 1979.

————. *Hegel's Philosophy of Mind.* Translated by A. V. Miller and J. N. Findlay. Oxford: Clarendon Press, 1971.

————. *Hegel's Philosophy of Right.* Translated by T. M. Knox. London: Oxford University Press, 1967.

————. *Natural Law.* Translated by T. M. Knox. Philadelphia: University of Pennsylvania Press, 1975.

————. *The Phenomenology of Mind.* Translated by J. B. Baillie. New York: Harper Torchbooks, 1967.

————. *The Philosophy of History.* Translated by J. Sibree. New York: Dover Publications, 1965.

————. *Philosophy of Nature.* Translated by A. V. Miller. Oxford: Clarendon Press, 1970.

Held, David. *Introduction to Critical Theory: Horkheimer to Habermas.* Berkeley: University of California Press, 1980.

Held, Virginia. "Marx, Sex and the Transformation of Society." *The Philosophical Forum* 5 (Fall–Winter 1973–74): 168–83.

Heller, Agnes. "Individual and Community." *Social Praxis* 1 (1973): 11–22.

Herman, Judith Lewis, and Lisa Hirschman. "Father-Daughter Incest." *Signs: Journal of Women in Culture and Society* 2 (1977): 735–56.

Herman, Judith Lewis, with Lisa Hirschman. *Father-Daughter Incest.* Cambridge, Mass.: Harvard University Press, 1981.

Heslip, Shirley A. "A Poor Respectable Girl." *The Peak* (student newspaper, Simon Fraser University), 6 October 1981, p. 5.

Hollway, Wendy. "Heterosexual Sex: Power and Desire for the Other." In *Sex and Love: New Thoughts on Old Contradictions,* edited by Sue Cartledge and Joanna Ryan, pp. 124–40. London: Women's Press, 1983.

Homer. *The Odyssey.* Harmondsworth: Penguin Books, 1961.

Horkheimer, Max. "Authoritarianism and the Family." In *The Family: Its Function and Destiny,* edited by Ruth Nanda Ashen, pp. 381–98. New York: Harper & Brothers, 1949.

————. *Critical Theory.* Translated from the German by Matthew O'Connell and Others. New York: Herder and Herder, 1972.

————. *Critique of Instrumental Reason.* Translated by Matthew O'Connell and Others. New York: Seabury Press, 1974.

————. *Dawn & Decline.* Translated by Michael Shaw. New York: Seabury Press, 1978.

————. *Eclipse of Reason.* New York: Seabury Press, 1974.

Horkheimer, Max, and Theodor W. Adorno. *Dialectic of Enlightenment.* Translated by John Cumming. New York: Herder and Herder, 1972. Originally published as *Dialektik der Aufklärung: Philosophische Fragmente.* Frankfurt: Fischer, 1971.

Horowitz, Gad. *Repression. Basic and Surplus Repression in Psychoanalytic Theory: Freud, Reich and Marcuse.* Toronto: University of Toronto Press, 1977.

Hyppolite, Jean. *Studies on Marx and Hegel.* Translated from the French by John O'Neill. New York: Harper Torchbooks, 1973.

Irigaray, Luce. *Speculum of the Other Woman.* Translated from the French by Gillian C. Gill. Ithaca: Cornell University Press, 1985.

———. *This Sex Which Is Not One.* Translated by Catherine Porter. Ithaca: Cornell University Press, 1985.

Jameson, Fredric. "Herbert Marcuse: Toward a Marxist Hermeneutic." *Salmagundi* 20 (Summer–Fall 1972): 126–33.

Janeway, Elizabeth. "On 'Female Sexuality.'" In *Women and Analysis: Dialogues on Psychoanalytic Views of Femininity,* edited by Jean Strouse, pp. 73–88. New York: Dell, 1974.

Jay Martin. *The Dialectical Imagination: A History of the Frankfurt School and the Institute of Social Research, 1923–1950.* Boston: Little, Brown & Co., 1973.

———. "The Frankfurt School's Critique of Marxist Humanism." *Social Research* 39 (Summer 1972): 285–305.

Jones, Ann. *Women Who Kill.* New York: Fawcett Columbine, 1981.

Jordan, June. "Against the Wall." *Seven Days,* May 1978, p. 23.

Kapp, Yvonne. *Eleanor Marx,* vol. 1. New York: Pantheon Books, 1972.

Kelly, George Armstrong. *Idealism, Politics and History.* Cambridge: Cambridge University Press, 1969.

Kerényi, Karl. *Goddesses of Sun and Moon.* Translated from the German by Murray Stein. Irving, Texas: University of Dallas, 1979.

Kojève, Alexandre. *Introduction to the Reading of Hegel.* Translated from the French by James H. Nichols, Jr. New York: Basic Books, 1969.

Kontos, Alkis. "Memories of Ithaca." In *Ethnicity in a Technological Age,* edited by Ian H. Angus. Edmonton: Canadian Institute for Ukrainian Studies, 1987.

Laplanche, J. Report on "Panel on 'Hysteria Today.'" *International Journal of Psycho-Analysis* 55 (1974): 459–69.

Lasch, Christopher. *The Culture of Narcissism.* New York: Warner Books, 1979.

———. *Haven in a Heartless World.* New York: Basic Books, 1979.

LeDoeuff, Michele. "Women in Philosophy." Translated from the French by Debbie Pope. *Radical Philosophy* 17 (Summer 1977): 2–11.

Leiss, William. "Critical Theory and Its Future." *Political Theory* 2 (August 1974): 330–49.

————. *The Domination of Nature.* Boston: Beacon Press, 1974.

————. "The Problem of Man and Nature in the Work of the Frankfurt School." *Philosophy of Social Science* 5 (1975): 163–72.

Levine, Stephen. "Civilization and Its Contents." Book review of *Repression. Basic and Surplus Repression in Psychoanalytic Theory: Freud, Reich and Marcuse* by Gad Horowitz. *Canadian Forum* 59 (October 1979): 24–27.

Lewis, C. S. *Till We Have Faces: A Myth Retold.* New York: Harcourt Brace Jovanovich, 1956.

Litewka, Jack. "The Socialized Penis." In *For Men against Sexism*, edited by Jon Snodgrass, pp. 16–35. Albion: Times Change Press, 1977.

Lopate, Carol. "Daytime Television: You'll Never Want to Leave Home." *Feminist Studies* 3 (Spring–Summer 1976): 69–82.

Lukács, Georg. *History and Class Consciousness: Studies in Marxist Dialectics.* Translated from the German by Rodney Livingstone. Cambridge, Mass.: M.I.T. Press, 1973.

————. *The Young Hegel.* Translated from the German by Rodney Livingstone. London: Merlin Press, 1975.

McLellan, David. *Karl Marx: His Life and Thought.* London: Macmillan, 1973.

Major, René. "The Revolution of Hysteria." *International Journal of Psycho-Analysis* 55 (1974): 385–92.

Malos, Ellen. "Housework and the Politics of Women's Liberation." *Socialist Review*, no. 37 (January–February 1978), pp. 41–71.

————. *The Politics of Housework.* London: Allison & Busby, 1980.

Marcuse, Herbert. *Counterrevolution and Revolt.* Boston: Beacon Press, 1972.

————. *Eros and Civilization: A Philosophical Inquiry into Freud.* New York: Vintage Books, 1962.

————. *An Essay on Liberation.* Boston: Beacon Press, 1969.

————. *Five Lectures.* Translated from the German by Jeremy Shapiro and Shierry Weber. Boston: Beacon Press, 1970.

————. "Marxism and Feminism." *Women's Studies* 2 (1974): 279–88.

————. *One-Dimensional Man: Studies in the Ideology of Advanced Industrial Society.* Boston: Beacon Press, 1964.

————. *Reason and Revolution: Hegel and the Rise of Social Theory.* Boston: Beacon Press, 1960.

————. "The Reification of the Proletariat." *Canadian Journal of Political and Social Theory* 3 (Winter 1979): 20–23.

————. *Studies in Critical Philosophy.* Translated by Joris De Bres. Boston: Beacon Press, 1973.

Maroney, Heather Jon. "Language, Persephone and Sacrifice: An Interview with Luce Irigaray." *Borderlines*, Winter 1985–86, pp. 30–32.

Marx, Karl. *Capital*, vol. 1. Translated from the German by Samuel Moore and Edward Aveling. Moscow: Progress Publishers, n.d.

————. *Capital*, vol. 3. Moscow: Foreign Languages Publishing House, 1962.

————. *Grundrisse: Foundations of the Critique of Political Economy (Rough Draft).* Translated with a foreword by Martin Nicolaus. Harmondsworth: Penguin Books, 1973.

————. *Karl Marx, Early Writings.* Translated and edited by T. B. Bottomore. New York: McGraw Hill, 1963.

————. *Writings of the Young Marx on Philosophy and Society.* Translated and edited by Loyd D. Easton and Kurt H. Guddat. New York: Anchor Books, 1967.

Marx, Karl, and Friedrich Engels. *Collected Works*, vols. 1, 3, and 5. Translated by Richard Dixon, Clemens Dutt, Jack Cohen, et al. New York: International Publishers, 1975–76.

————. *The Communist Manifesto.* Edited by Samuel H. Beer. Northbrook: AHM Publishing, 1955.

————. *The Holy Family, or Critique of Critical Criticism.* Translated by Richard Dixon and Clemens Dutt. Moscow: Progress Publishers, 1975.

————. *The Marx-Engels Reader*, 2d ed. Edited by Robert C. Tucker. New York: W. W. Norton, 1978.

————. *Selected Works.* Moscow: Progress Publishers, 1968.

Mathieu, Nicole-Claude. "Man-Culture and Woman-Nature?" Translated from the French by D. M. Leonard Barker. *Women's Studies International Quarterly* 1 (1978): 55–65.

Melman, Deborah. "Feminist Explorations: Life under Patriarchy." *Canadian Journal of Political and Social Theory* 4 (Spring–Summer 1980): 64–68.

Mendelson, Jack. "On Engels' Metaphysical Dialectics: A Foundation of Orthodox 'Marxism.'" *Dialectical Anthropology* 4 (March 1979): 65–73.

Millay, Edna St. Vincent. *Collected Poems.* Edited by Norma Millay. New York: Harper & Row, 1956.

Millett, Kate. *Sexual Politics.* New York: Doubleday, 1970.

Mills, Patricia Jagentowicz. "Hegel and 'The Woman Question': Recognition and Intersubjectivity." In *The Sexism of Social and Political Theory: Women and Reproduction from Plato to Nietzsche*, edited by Lorenne M. G. Clark and Lynda Lange, pp. 74–98. Toronto: University of Toronto Press, 1979.

———. "Hegel's *Antigone*." *The Owl of Minerva: Journal of the Hegel Society of America* 17 (Spring 1986): 131–52.

———. "Man-Made Motherhood and Other Sleights of Hand." Review of *Marxism and Domination* by Isaac D. Balbus. *Phenomenology + Pedagogy* 3 (1986): 207–17.

Mitchell, Juliet. "On Freud and the Distinction between the Sexes." In *Women and Analysis: Dialogues on Psychoanalytic Views of Femininity*, edited by Jean Strouse, pp. 39–50. New York: Dell, 1974.

———. *Psychoanalysis and Feminism: Freud, Reich, Laing and Women*. New York: Vintage, 1974.

———. *Woman's Estate*. Baltimore: Penguin Books, 1971.

Mitscherlich, Alexander. *Society without the Father: A Contribution to Social Psychology*. Translated from the German by Eric Mosbacher. New York: Harcourt, Brace & World, 1969.

Mitscherlich-Nielsen, M. "Psychoanalysis and Female Sexuality." *Partisan Review* 46 (1979): 61–74.

Morgan, Kathryn Pauly. "Androgyny: A Conceptual Analysis." *Social Theory and Practice* 8 (Fall 1982): 245–83.

Neumann, Erich. *Amor and Psyche: The Psychic Development of the Feminine*. Translated from the German by Ralph Manheim. New York: Princeton University Press, Bollingen Series, 1956.

Nower, Joyce. "A Feminist View of Antigone." *The Longest Revolution*, February/March 1983, p. 6.

O'Brien, Mary. "The Politics of Impotence." In *Contemporary Issues in Political Philosophy*, edited by William Shea and John King-Farlow, pp. 147–62. New York: Science History Publications, 1976.

———. *The Politics of Reproduction*. Boston: Routledge & Kegan Paul, 1981.

———. "Reproducing Marxist Man." In *The Sexism of Social and Political Theory: Women and Reproduction from Plato to Nietzsche*, edited by Lorenne M. G. Clark and Lynda Lange, pp. 99–116. Toronto: University of Toronto Press, 1979.

Orkin, Ruth. *A Photo Journal*. New York: Viking Press, 1981.

Petchesky, Rosalind Pollack. *Abortion and Woman's Choice: The State, Sexuality, and Reproductive Freedom*. Boston: Northeastern University Press, 1985.

————. "Reproductive Freedom: Beyond 'A Woman's Right to Choose.' " In *Women: Sex and Sexuality*, edited by Catherine R. Stimpson and Ethel Spector Person, pp. 92–116. Chicago: University of Chicago Press, 1980.

Plaza, Monique. " 'Phallomorphic' Power and the Psychology of 'Woman.' " *Feminist Issues* 1 (Summer 1980): 70–102.

Randall, John Herman, Jr. *The Career of Philosophy*, vol. 2. New York: Columbia University Press, 1965.

Raymond, Janice G. *A Passion for Friends: Toward a Philosophy of Female Affection*. Boston: Beacon Press, 1986.

Renault, Mary. *The Bull from the Sea*. New York: Penguin Books, 1980.

Report on Violence in the Family: Wifebattering. The Standing Committee on Health, Welfare, and Social Affairs, Marcel Roy, M.P., Chairman, House of Commons, Canada. Issue No. 34, 6 May 1982.

Reuther, Rosemary Radford. *New Woman/New Earth: Sexist Ideologies and Human Liberation*. New York: Seabury Press, 1975.

Rich, Adrienne. *The Dream of a Common Language: Poems, 1974–77*. New York: W. W. Norton, 1978.

————. *On Lies, Secrets and Silence: Selected Prose, 1966–1978*. New York: W. W. Norton, 1979.

————. *Of Woman Born: Motherhood as Experience and Institution*. New York: W. W. Norton, 1976.

Ricoeur, Paul. "Fatherhood: From Phantasm to Symbol." Translated from the French by Robert Sweeney. In *The Conflict of Interpretations: Essays in Hermeneutics*, edited by Don Ihde, pp. 468–97. Evanston: Northwestern University Press, 1974.

————. *Freud and Philosophy: An Essay on Interpretation*. Translated by Denis Savage. New Haven: Yale University Press, 1977.

Roazen, Paul. *Freud: Political and Social Thought*. New York: Vintage Books, 1968.

Roberts, Helen, ed. *Women, Health and Reproduction*. London: Routledge and Kegan Paul, 1981.

Rose, Gillian. "How Is Critical Theory Possible? Theodor W. Adorno and Concept Formation in Sociology." *Political Studies* 24 (1976): 69–85.

————. *The Melancholy Science: An Introduction to the Thought of Theodor W. Adorno*. New York: Columbia University Press, 1978.

————. Review of *Negative Dialectics* by Theodor W. Adorno. *American Political Science Review* 70 (1976): 598–99.

Rowbotham, Sheila. *Hidden from History: 300 Years of Women's Oppression and the Fight against It*. London: Pluto Press, 1974.

————. *Woman's Consciousness, Man's World.* Baltimore: Penguin Books, 1973.

Ruddick, Sara. "Material Thinking." In *Mothering: Essays in Feminist Theory*, edited by Joyce Trebilcot, pp. 213–30. Totowa, N.J.: Rowman & Allanheld, 1984.

Russell, Diana. *The Secret Trauma: Incest in the Lives of Girls and Women.* New York: Basic Books, 1986.

Russell, Diana, and Nicole Van de Ven, eds. *Crimes against Women: Proceedings of the International Tribunal.* Millbrae, California: Les Femmes, 1976.

Ryan, Joanna. "Psychoanalysis and Women Loving Women." In *Sex and Love: New Thoughts on Old Contradictions*, edited by Sue Cartledge and Joanna Ryan, pp. 196–209. London: Women's Press, 1984.

Sagan, Eli. *The Lust to Annihilate: A Psychoanalytic Study of Violence in Ancient Greek Culture.* New York: Psychohistory Press, 1979.

Schmidt, Alfred. *The Concept of Nature in Marx.* Translated from the German by Ben Fowkes. London: New Left Books, 1971.

Seidenberg, Robert, "The Trauma of Eventlessness." In *Psychoanalysis and Women*, edited by Jean Baker Miller, pp. 350–62. Harmondsworth: Penguin Books, 1974.

Seidenberg, Robert, and Evangelos Papathomopoulos. "Daughters Who Tend Their Fathers: A Literary Survey." In *The Psychoanalytic Study of Society*, vol. 2, edited by W. Muensterberger and S. Axelrad, pp. 135–60. New York: International University Press, 1962.

————. "The Enigma of Antigone." *International Review of Psycho-Analysis* 1 (1974): 197–205.

Seidenberg, Robert, and Karen DeCrow. *Women Who Marry Houses: Panic and Protest in Agoraphobia.* New York: McGraw-Hill, 1983.

Sherover, Erica. "The Virtue of Poverty: Marx's Transformation of Hegel's Concept of the Poor." *Canadian Journal of Political and Social Theory* 3 (Winter 1979): 53–66.

Siebert, Rudolf. "Horkheimer's Sociology of Religion." *Telos* 30 (Winter 1976–77): 127–44.

Silko, Leslie Marmon. *Ceremony.* Harmondsworth: Penguin Books, 1986.

Smith-Rosenberg, Carroll. "The Female World of Love and Ritual: Relations between Women in Nineteenth-Century America." In *The Signs Reader: Women, Gender and Scholarship*, edited by Elizabeth

Abel and Emily K. Abel, pp. 27–55. Chicago: University of Chicago Press, 1983.

Sontag, Susan. "The Third World of Women." *Partisan Review* 40 (1973): 180–206.

Sophocles. *Antigone.* In *Drama: An Introductory Anthology.* Translated by Dudley Fitts and Robert Fitzgerald and edited by Otto R. Reinert. Boston: Little, Brown & Co, 1964.

———. *Antigone.* In *Ten Greek Plays in Contemporary Translations.* Translated by Shaemus O'Sheel and edited by L. R. Lind. Boston: Riverside Press, 1957.

———. *Antigone.* In *The Tragedies of Sophocles: In English Prose,* new edition, revised according to the text of Dindorf. New York: Harper & Brothers, 1880.

Spivak, Gayatri. "Feminism and Critical Theory." *Women's Studies International Quarterly* 1 (1978): 241–46.

Steiner, George. *Antigones.* New York: Oxford University Press, 1984.

Strouse, Jean, ed. *Women and Analysis: Dialogues on Psychoanalytic Views of Femininity.* New York: Dell, 1974.

Taylor, Charles. *Hegel.* Cambridge: Cambridge University Press, 1975.

Trebilcot, Joyce, ed. *Mothering: Essays in Feminist Theory.* Totowa, N.J.: Rowman & Allanheld, 1984.

Warrior, Betsy. *Wifebeating.* Somerville, Mass.: New England Free Press, 1976.

Whitbeck, Caroline. "A Different Reality: Feminist Ontology." In *Beyond Domination: New Perspectives on Women and Philosophy,* edited by Carol C. Gould, pp. 64–88. Totowa, N.J.: Rowman & Allanheld, 1984.

———. "Maternal Instinct" and "Afterword." In *Mothering: Essays in Feminist Theory,* edited by Joyce Trebilcot, pp. 185–98. Totowa, N.J.: Rowman & Allanheld, 1984.

Whitebook, Joel. "The Problem of Nature in Habermas." *Telos* 40 (Summer 1979): 41–69.

Woman and Russia: First Feminist Samizdat. Translated by the Women and Eastern Europe Group. London: Sheba Feminist Publishers, 1980.

Wood, Nancy. "Mothering the Child." Review of *The Reproduction of Mothering* by Nancy Chodorow. *Canadian Journal of Political and Social Theory* 3 (Winter 1979): 144–53.

Wylie, Philip. *Generation of Vipers.* New York: Rinehart, 1942.

Wyschogrod, Edith. *Spirit in Ashes: Hegel, Heidegger, and Man-Made Mass Death*. New Haven: Yale University Press, 1985.

Young, Iris. "Is Male Gender Identity the Cause of Male Domination?" In *Mothering: Essays in Feminist Theory*, edited by Joyce Trebilcot, pp. 129–46. Totowa, N.J.: Rowman & Allanheld, 1984.

Index

Abortion, 117–18, 234n, 244n
Adolescence, 22, 34, 96, 106, 136–37, 180, 216n, 229n
Adorno, Theodor W.: critique of Hegel, 26–27; critique of Marx, 67; and Horkheimer and Marcuse, 85–88 passim, 148, 150; *Dialectic of Enlightenment*, 89–93, 149, 162, 172, 178, 195; critique of identity theory, 92, 142, 205; on art, 92–93; on philosophy, 93; authority and the family studies, 95; on woman, 108, 169–70, 181–91, 206–07; *Negative Dialectics*, 143, 149, 174, 175, 205–07; and Freud, 168–70; on memory, 171–75 passim, 241n; on truth, 172; on the domination of nature, 172–74
Aesthetic theory: in Marx, 64; in critical theory, 92–93, 171–72; in Marcuse, 155, 162, 204–05; in Adorno, 206–07
Agoraphobia, 137–39, 237n, 238n
Alienation: in Hegel, 5, 55; in Marx, 56–60 passim, 81; in critical theory, 91, 178, 190; and motherhood, 117, 141; and woman, 187–88
Androgyny, 162–63, 165
Anorexia nervosa, 136–37, 139, 237n

Antigone: in Hegel, 3, 14, 16, 17–36, 43–49, 59, 213n, 214n, 215n, 216n, 217n; in Horkheimer, 113–16; and suicide, 31–32, 33, 35–36, 114, 115, 192
Aristotle, 11, 212n
Art: in Hegel, 37; in critical theory, 228n. *See also* Aesthetic theory
Authority: and woman, 40; and the family in critical theory, 85–122 passim, 142, 148; and eros, 110; and antiauthoritarian moment, 98, 103, 106, 121

Benjamin, Jessica, 12–13, 99
Benjamin, Walter, 241n
Brother-sister relation: in Hegel, 19–24, 26, 31, 35, 44–46, 112–16, 213n, 214n, 215n, 216n; and the primal horde, 155–57, 195–99

Capitalism: analysis of in Hegel, 10, 36–38, 40–41, 48; Marx's critique of, 10–11, 50–71 passim; and commodity structure, 60–62, 79–80; and commodity fetishism, 60, 80, 88; and woman's liberation, 76–81; critique of in critical theory, 85–95 passim, 98. *See also* Alienation, Domination of nature, Family, Objectification

261